D0861630

Getting Real

Getting Real

Pneumatological Realism and the Spiritual, Moral,
and Ministry Formation of Contemporary Christians

GARY TYRA

Foreword by
Frank D. Macchia

 CASCADE *Books* · Eugene, Oregon

GETTING REAL
Pneumatological Realism and the Spiritual, Moral, and Ministry Formation of Contemporary Christians

Cascade Books
An Imprint of Wipf and Stock Publishers
199 W. 8th Ave., Suite 3
Eugene, OR 97401

www.wipfandstock.com

PAPERBACK ISBN: 978-1-4982-9231-3
HARDCOVER ISBN: 978-1-4982-9233-7
EBOOK ISBN: 978-1-4982-9232-0

Cataloguing-in-Publication data:

Names: Tyra, Gary, 1955–, author. | Macchia, Frank D., 1952–, foreword.

Title: Getting real : pneumatological realism and the spiritual, moral, and ministry formation of contemporary Christians / Gary Tyra ; foreword by Frank D. Macchia.

Description: Eugene, OR : Cascade Books, 2018 | Includes bibliographical references and index.

Identifiers: ISBN 978-1-4982-9231-3 (paperback) | ISBN 978-1-4982-9233-7 (hardcover) | ISBN 978-1-4982-9232-0 (ebook)

Subjects: LCSH: Holy Spirit. | Theology, Doctrinal.

Classification: BT121.3 .T97 2018 (print) | BT121.3 .T97 (ebook)

Manufactured in the U.S.A.   FEBRUARY 5, 2018

This book is dedicated to my wife, Patti, whose patience, support, and proofreading skills have blessed each of my publishing endeavors. An enduringly beautiful bride, wise mother of two wonderful adult children, soon-to-be grandmother, talented coauthor with me of one volume and partner in several others, it's time she had a book dedicated solely to her. Here it is at last. With all my heart: *Thank you, my love.*

Contents

Foreword by Frank D. Macchia ix

Introduction 1

PART ONE: THEOLOGICAL AND MINISTRY FOUNDATIONS

1. Pneumatological Realism: Theological Corrective/Ministry Cure 15

2. Functional Deism: A Surprisingly
Pervasive Theological/Ministry Malady 36

PART TWO: THE SPIRIT AND THE THREEFOLD
FAITHFULNESS GOD DESIRES AND DESERVES

3. Pneumatological Realism and a Spiritual Faithfulness 61

4. Pneumatological Realism and a Moral Faithfulness 81

5. Pneumatological Realism and a Missional Faithfulness 100

PART THREE: GETTING REAL ABOUT GETTING REAL

6. Encouraging a Pneumatological Realism in the Local Church 121

Conclusion 137

*Appendix : From Sola Scriptura to the Sacramental Sermon:
Karl Barth and the Phenomenon of Prophetic Preaching* 141

Bibliography 183

Author Index 191

Subject Index 195

Scripture Index 203

Foreword

EVERY NOW AND THEN a term is introduced that catches on as significant because it speaks to us in a timely way of something that we need to hear but have not heard very well. So it is with Gary Tyra's use of the term *pneumatological realism*. Professor Tyra writes from the conviction that the basic challenges facing ministry today are partly rooted in a lack of scriptural and theological awareness. He rightly laments the fact that so many in the church today get their basic theological ideas from common sense notions of religion or morality that pervade a culture at a given time or place. As Tyra shows us, many of our young today are under the sway of a moralistic therapeutic deism that features God as relatively uninvolved in the world, except to rubber-stamp our feeble efforts to be religious or good. Tyra meets this challenge head on with a biblical version of reality, a theological realism that centers on God as revealed in Christ and as encountered concretely by the Spirit. As Tyra points out, a Spirit-empowered witness to Christ in the world is the core reality to which we are called. A confession of God as Creator or the Son as Redeemer without the concrete reality of a Spirit-embodied witness to Christ in the world will not effectively overturn the false realisms that influence the churches. Thus, a theological realism must involve a strong pneumatological realism in order to produce the kind of faithful witness needed to overturn moralistic therapeutic deism.

Professor Tyra shows us that theological realism requires pneumatological realism to be fully Trinitarian in scope. This pneumatological dimension is also needed to fill the spiritual, moral, and vocational vacuum left behind by the devastating effects of cultural influence on our thinking. Of course, we must affirm God as Creator and the Son as Redeemer on our way towards rebuilding theological clarity of vision in the church. That God creates all things and that the divine Son has taken on flesh, died for us, and rose again to redeem us are all needed to combat the self-justifying delusions of moralistic therapeutic deism. Yet, Tyra has seen clearly that the rubber hits the road precisely in the realm of human experience. If false realisms are to be exposed effectively, it must be done by a witness to Christ that is lived and embodied in the world. This principle of faithful embodiment is the reality of the indwelling presence and work of the Holy Spirit. A theological realism will be recognized as an authentically compelling project today, if it involves a strong pneumatological realism as well. This is the great insight of this important book.

Professor Tyra is in an ideal position to awaken us to this important insight. I have had the privilege of knowing him personally during the years of our work together on the faculty of Vanguard University. I have come to know him as a thoughtful theologian and professor who is constantly working through theological problems for the sake of enlightening his many students and readers. This book is itself the culmination of ideas that came together while writing a number of important works on theology in relation to spirituality, ethics, and mission. One gets the sense while reading this book of tasting the ripe fruit of years of thinking and writing. This book, however, is not just the product of academic thinking and teaching, as important as these are. Tyra has also been involved in the pastorate, so his ideas have been hammered out at the front lines of local church ministry. He has listened carefully to both the theological academy and the voices of those within the churches. One senses in the pages of this book both the mind of a theologian and the heart of a pastor. Readers in both areas of the church's life will find that this book speaks to them. I know that it will inspire a broad and diverse audience for many years to come.

Frank D. Macchia

Associate Director, Centre for Pentecostal and Charismatic Studies, Bangor University, Wales (UK), and Professor of Christian Theology, Vanguard University of Southern California

Introduction

HAVE YOU EVER BEEN told that you needed to *get real* with respect to some issue or dynamic in your life? Have you ever felt the need to lovingly encourage someone else, perhaps a friend or family member, to *get real*, to press through the fog and gain a more accurate understanding and experience of some crucial component of reality? The fundamental premise of this book is that there's a need for significant numbers of Christ's followers to *get real* with respect to the Spirit of Christ.[1]

To be more precise, the branch of Christian theology that focuses on matters relating to the Holy Spirit is known as *pneumatology*. The aim of this work is to encourage evangelical Christians of all stripes to become more fully aware of the tremendous difference it makes when the Holy Spirit is experienced in ways that are real and existentially-impactful rather than *merely* theoretical, conceptual, and/or ritualistic. Intended to be read by church leaders, thoughtful church members, and students studying in Christian colleges and seminaries, the message of *Getting Real* is that there's such a thing as a *pneumatological realism,* and that this spiritual dynamic is a game-changer when it comes to just about everything having to do with the Christian life.

Why *Getting Real* Is Needed

Perhaps the best way to explain what I mean by the term "pneumatological realism" is to elaborate a bit on two big reasons why getting real with respect to Christ's Spirit is so important to one's walk with Christ. One reason has to do with the phenomenon of *faithfulness* before God and the world—a faithfulness which God desires and the world desperately needs to witness if it's to be impacted by the Christian gospel. The other reason has to do

1. For the various ways in which the Holy Spirit is referred to in the New Testament as the Spirit of Jesus, see Acts 16:7; Rom 8:9; Gal 4:6; Phil 1:19; 1 Pet 1:11.

with the defeat of a faux version of the Christian faith that's causing the lives of Christians (and the churches to which they belong) to be more redolent of the values of the surrounding culture than the teachings of sacred Scripture. How can such Christians (and churches) hope to function as spiritual salt and light in the surrounding culture if there's no contrast at all vis-à-vis that culture? An incarnational contextualization of the gospel is one thing; a complete accommodation or enculturation of the gospel is another.[2] In other words, it's not just the *faithfulness* of Christians and churches that require an ecclesial environment earmarked by a pneumatological realism, but their ministry *fruitfulness* as well!

Pneumatological Realism and the Phenomenon of Faithfulness

All of the fruits of the Spirit listed in Galatians 5:22–23 are, of course, important. However, I'd like to draw attention here to one fruit in particular—*faithfulness*. There are many biblical texts that describe God as "faithful" (e.g., Deut 7:9), while others refer to "faithfulness" as one of his chief characteristics (e.g., Ps 89:8). Also, the Bible tells us time and again that faithfulness is a quality God is looking for in the lives of those who've entered into a covenant relationship with him (e.g., Josh 24:14; Hos 4:1; Rev 13:10).

Many years of service in both the church and academy have caused me to conclude that there are three forms of faithfulness that lie at the heart of Christian discipleship: a *spiritual* faithfulness, a *moral* faithfulness, and a *missional* faithfulness. I'll have much more to say about the nature of each of these types of faithfulness later in this work. For now, it must suffice for me to say that, because this threefold faithfulness is so very crucial to a Christian life well-lived, very high on the job description of every evangelical pastor should be the enabling of congregants to embody it before God and the world.

The good news is that a careful study of the Scriptures and Christian history will reveal that the Holy Spirit wants to help Christ's followers experience this multifaceted faithfulness and the ministry fruitfulness that's

---

2. For more on the concept of an incarnational approach to ministry contextualization which seeks to do justice to *both* the apostle Jude's exhortation to contend for the faith once for all entrusted to the church (Jude 1:3) *and* Paul's implicit exhortation for the church to keep contextualizing the faith for new people groups (1 Cor 9:20–22), see Tyra, *Missional Orthodoxy*, 64–123.

produced by it.[3] The not-so-good news is that the Bible and Christian history also clearly indicate that it's possible for the enabling work of the Spirit to be *resisted* (Acts 7:51), *grieved* (Eph 4:30), *rejected* (1 Thess 4:8), and *quenched* (1 Thess 5:19). Thus, a fundamental first step toward enabling congregants to embody a spiritual, moral, and missional faithfulness is to help them adopt a posture of *expectancy* (rather than presumption or indifference) with respect to the Holy Spirit. Again, I'll have more to say about the importance of what I refer to as a sense of *pneumatological expectancy* later in the work. For now, the crucial point to be made is that, because of the connection that seems to exist between expectancy and experience, those of us in pastoral leadership simply must become advocates of what I refer to as a *pneumatological realism*. If we want our formational ministries to result in fully devoted Christ followers whose threefold faithfulness to God produces a fruitfulness for him, we must help them understand just how important the Holy Spirit is to just about every aspect of the Christian life, and what's actually involved in obeying the call of the Apostle Paul to "keep in step" with him (Gal 5:25). In other words, we must seek to cultivate ecclesial communities earmarked by a realist rather than non-realist understanding and experience of Christ's Spirit.

Pneumatological Realism and the Defeat of Functional Deism

Another reason why it's imperative that Christians get real with respect to the Spirit has to do with the "nature abhors a vacuum" phenomenon we learned about in high school physics. As it relates to the topic at hand, I'm suggesting that when a pneumatological realism is lacking in a person's walk with Christ, some other understanding of how the church member is to relate to God will rush in to fill the void. To be more precise, according to some reputable sociological research elaborated upon in chapter 2 of this work, it's very often a false, inauthentic version of the Christian faith— a functional deism with Christian trappings—that emerges in the lives of church members when a *realist* understanding and experience of Christ's Spirit is absent from their ecclesial environment. It's a *functional deism* that's at work when church members, who profess a belief in the Trinitarian God

---

3. This connection between faithfulness and fruitfulness is apparent in New Testament passages such as Matt 7:15–20; 21:43; 25:21; John 15:5; Rom 7:4; Eph 5:8–10; Col 1:3–7, 9–10; cf. Jude 1:12.

of the Bible, don't genuinely *expect* the Spirit of God to work in their lives in ways that are personal, transformational, and ministry-engendering.

Once again, I'm only previewing here, but if there's even the possibility that what I'm proposing is true, it's enormously important for both church leaders and members to take this lamentable reality seriously. I'm convinced that one of the reasons why many evangelical church-goers seem to be living out a version of the Christian life that's more informed by the values of the surrounding culture than the discipleship teachings of Jesus and his apostles is because of the "pneumatological deficit" that's at work in their church.[4] But, it doesn't have to be this way. This all-too-prevalent theological impoverishment, and the functional deism it tends to produce, can be addressed. This is a big part of what *Getting Real* is about.

How *Getting Real* Is Structured

What I've presented thus far is a quite cursory introduction to the main message of the book. What follows is an equally concise summary of how the work is structured.

In addition to this introduction and a formal conclusion, the book is composed of six chapters and an appended essay, all of which aims at the recovery of a robust, fully Trinitarian doctrine of the Holy Spirit. Though I've attempted to make the body of the work accessible to readers who haven't studied theology in an academic setting, a plethora of footnotes will provide some additional resources for those eager to think a bit more deeply about the issues addressed. (In particular, a recurring theme of several of these footnotes is the manner in which the theology of the famous Swiss theologian Karl Barth seems to provide some significant support for the main thesis of this work: the vital importance of a pneumatological realism to the life of individual Christians and the churches they belong to. While Barth's commitment to the authority of Scripture and the importance of the

---

4. This observation presumes that the church members in question have been made aware of the discipleship teachings of Jesus, but not the empowerment the Holy Spirit longs to provide toward their actual embodiment. Thus, the problem here is what I'm referring to as a "pneumatological deficit." There are, of course, evangelical and Pentevangelical churches in which a "discipleship deficit" also exists—where church members are not fully aware of how important the threefold faithfulness is to a biblically-informed understanding of Christian discipleship. In chapter 2 I'll have more to say about how both deficits create the ground from which a functional deism is allowed to flourish.

person of Christ to Christian theology is well-known, some of my readers may be surprised to find that Barth was a theologian of the Spirit as well.)[5]

Part One of *Getting Real* is titled "Theological and Ministry Foundations." The aim of the two chapters that make up this section of the work is to provide readers with a more thorough understanding of the nature of and need for a pneumatological realism. In chapter 1, I explain how my understanding of pneumatological realism compares with two other representative takes. In the process, I indicate why I believe the dynamic of getting real with respect to Christ's Spirit should be viewed as both a *theological corrective* and *ministry cure*. Chapter 2 then drills down a bit more deeply, carefully explaining why the *functional deism* briefly alluded to in this introduction should be considered a serious and surprisingly pervasive ministry malady for which a pneumatological realism is the ultimate remedy. Combined, these two chapters are intended to enable a crystal-clear understanding of why any sort of a "pneumatological deficit" in contemporary evangelical (and Pentevangelical) churches should be considered super serious. Such a theological lapse ends up producing ecclesial environments which frustrate rather than facilitate the making of authentic Christian disciples!

---

5. To be more specific, it's my suggestion that behind the theologizing of Barth is a "metaphysics of divine reality," of which the Holy Spirit plays a vital, indispensable role. Barth himself once stated: "It was the Spirit whose existence and action make possible and *real* (and possible and *real* up to this very day) the existence of Christianity in the world." Then, on the basis of this observation, he asserted: "It is clear that evangelical theology itself can only be pneumatic, spiritual theology. Only in the realm of the power of the Spirit can theology be realized as a humble, free, critical, and happy science of the God of the Gospel" (Barth, *Evangelical Theology*, 55, emphasis added). While Barth doesn't seem to call for the same degree of "pneumatological expectation" on the part of rank-and-file church members that my version of pneumatological realism entails (see chapter 2), I'm convinced that a familiarity with his theological realism and understanding of how very important the Holy Spirit is to just about every aspect of Christian existence will serve to point the reader toward, rather than away from, an embrace of many of the arguments presented in this book. As for my methodology, included within these several footnotes are not only more citations from Barth himself, but also from a cadre of Barth scholars including: Nigel Biggar, Eberhard Busch, John Franke, Colin Gunton, George Hunsinger, Frank Macchia, Joseph Mangina, Bruce McCormack, Kurt Anders Richardson, Philip Rosato, Aaron Smith, Sandra Sonderegger, John Thompson, Alan Torrance, and Graham Ward. I'm hopeful that the "subterranean discussion" embedded in the footnotes will make at least a small contribution to the scholarly conversation concerning the degree to which Barth's work, its Christocentrism notwithstanding, should be considered a "Spirit theology."

Part Two of *Getting Real* is titled "The Spirit and the Threefold Faithfulness God Desires and Deserves." The three chapters which comprise this section of the book elaborate upon the importance of the Holy Spirit to the cultivation of the spiritual, moral, and missional faithfulness before God that's so very necessary for a fruitful ministry engagement in an increasingly post-Christian cultural context.

To clarify, the term "post-Christian dynamic" refers to the fact that more and more people with some previous Christian experience are indicating that they are *over* Christianity and *done* with the church. While this dynamic affects our current culture at large, it's especially prevalent among the members of the emerging generations, as the following excerpt makes clear:

> In American culture, the trend of "losing the next generation" has become a crisis of equally epic proportions. According to Robert Wuthnow's research, there is both a decline in the number of young adults who attend religious services regularly and an increase in the number who seldom or never attend. This growing exodus of young people from churches, especially after they leave home and live on their own, is echoed in a 2007 study by Lifeway Research which reported that 70 percent of young Protestant adults between eighteen and twenty-two stop attending church regularly. The Barna Group's research reveals an equally startling statistic: "Perhaps the most striking reality of twentysomething's faith is their relative absence from Christian churches. Only 3 out of 10 twentysomethings (31%) attend church in a typical week, compared to 4 out of 10 of those in their 30s (42%) and nearly half of all adults age 40 and older (49%).[6]

Unfortunately, the post-Christian dynamic I keep referring to in this book is quite real. However, my ministry experience in both the church and academy has convinced me that many of our post-Christian peers can be successfully encouraged to take another look at Christ and his church. But, for this to happen, a Christian discipleship that's genuinely Spirit-empowered must be engaged in. This, in turn, requires that we as Christian disciples must move beyond simply talking about the importance of keeping in step with the Spirit (Gal 5:25), to actually doing it, bearing much

---

6. This excerpt is from Dunn and Sundene, *Shaping the Journey*, 20. The stats cited in it are from: Wuthnow, *After the Baby Boomers*, 52–53; Grossman, "Young Adults Aren't Sticking with Church," §1; Barna Group, "Twentysomethings Struggle," §3.

ministry fruit for God in the process.[7] With all this in mind, it's my hope that the three essays included in this section of the book will prove to be not only informational with respect to this tremendously important ministry possibility but inspirational as well.

Then, Part Three of the work—titled "Getting Real about Getting Real"—provides a succinct-yet-substantial discussion of what the leaders of evangelical congregations can do to cultivate an ecclesial ethos (church culture or environment) that's earmarked by an eager-yet-thoughtful embrace of a realist, rather than non-realist understanding of the Holy Spirit. A single essay aptly titled "Encouraging a Pneumatological Realism in the Local Church" is my attempt at suggesting some first steps toward this important pastoral objective. Indeed, always keen on doing theology that's of practical benefit to those leading the local church, I'd like to think that this chapter will prove useful to pastors of both evangelical and Pentevangelical churches—spiritual leaders committed to the recovery of a doctrine of the Holy Spirit that, because it's biblically grounded and Christ-honoring,[8] is also genuinely transformational.

Finally, late in the production process of this volume, the decision was made to append to it a paper I presented at an academic conference conducted at the Tyndale House in Cambridge, England in the summer of 2017. The conference was in celebration of the five hundredth anniversary of the Protestant Reformation. The paper I presented was titled "From Sola Scriptura to the Sacramental Sermon: Karl Barth and the Phenomenon

---

7. A passage in Eberhard Busch's chapter on Barth's pneumatology provides some support for the challenging tone of this exhortation. Commenting on how Barth saw the Spirit putting a "challenging claim" on those who belong to Christ, Eberhard Busch writes: "In the Holy Spirit a claim is put upon us because the 'Word that God directs to man' reaches us in him: 'the Word which concerns man, which claims man, and which completely absorbs his attention' (I/2 886 = 792 rev.). Barth likes to speak of direction here. 'To receive and have the Holy Spirit has nothing whatever to do with an obscure and romanticized being. It is simply to receive and have direction. To be or to walk in Him is to be under direction and to stand or walk as determined by it. . . . The Christian community exists as the people which is built up under this direction. Whether a man is a Christian . . . . is continually decided by whether his existence . . . is determined by this direction' (IV/2 404f. = 362)" (Busch, *The Great Passion*, 232).

8. For a brief but potent discussion of the critical relationship between pneumatology and Christology in the theology of Karl Barth, see Smith, *Theology of the Third Article*, 19n. In this footnote, Smith argues that in Barth: "There is no Christology that is not also Pneumatology. One simply cannot understand the Word, particularly as the center of dogmatic reflection in the light of which Christian thought takes defining shape and substance, apart from the living action and distinct identity of the Spirit" (ibid., 19n).

of Prophetic Preaching." Deriving from some of the research behind the writing of *Getting Real*, this essay draws attention to the dramatic manner a pneumatological realism can impact the preaching ministry of the local church. Therefore, this appended essay, even though it appears after the book's formal conclusion, essentially functions as an additional chapter which not only elucidates the book's message, but also provides some significant encouragement to put it into practice. I'm pleased it has been included in this work, and heartily recommend a careful perusal of it.

Why Some Discussions within *Getting Real* May Seem Familiar

Though the main message of *Getting Real* is constructive in nature, it's also the culmination of an emphasis I've placed throughout my teaching and writing career on the crucial importance of a theological and pneumatological realism to the spiritual, moral, and ministry formation of Christ's followers. Thus, those readers familiar with some of my previously published books will find a *synergistic synthesizing* here of some themes included in them. I wish to express here my deep gratitude to InterVarsity Press (IVP) for its willingness to allow me to cite and adapt material included in the following works: *Defeating Pharisaism: Recovering Jesus' Disciple-Making Method* (IVP Books, 2009), *Christ's Empowering Presence: The Pursuit of God through the Ages* (IVP Books, 2011), *The Holy Spirit in Mission: Prophetic Speech and Action in Christian Witness* (IVP Academic, 2011), *A Missional Orthodoxy: Theology and Ministry in a Post-Christian Context* (IVP Academic, 2013), and *Pursuing Moral Faithfulness: Ethics and Christian Discipleship* (IVP Academic, 2015).

Why *Getting Real* Is Worth the Effort

It's my assumption that the ultimate ambition of most sincere Christians, whether spoken or not, is to someday hear Jesus say to them:

> "Well done, good and *faithful* servant! You have been *faithful* with a few things; I will put you in charge of many things. Come and share your master's happiness!" (Matt 25:21, emphasis added)

This being the case, it only makes sense that those responsible for the spiritual, moral, and ministry formation of Christ's followers should do everything possible to steer their congregants away from a functional deism toward a Spirit-empowered embodiment of a spiritual, moral, and missional faithfulness.

Perhaps a personal ministry anecdote will serve to indicate what I have in mind here and why. As it happens, I've just completed (at the time of this writing) a nine-month stint as the interim preaching minister for a nearby church engaged in a careful search for their next full-time pastor. Indeed, the truth is that this church has, of late, experienced a spate of pastoral transitions. Not surprisingly, this frequent pastoral turnover had precipitated a corporate sense of spiritual discouragement and a fear among many congregants that their church wouldn't survive the current vacancy. When I met with the leadership of the church to discuss their invitation, the aura of despair was palpable. At one point in the conversation an elder looked across the boardroom table and, with pain in his eyes, asked: "What's wrong with us? Why can't we hold on to a pastor?" I was deeply impacted by this exchange. Frankly, it was this interaction that compelled me to accept the assignment. I sensed, deep down inside, that God was up to something with this hurting congregation and that he wanted my wife Patti and me to be part of it.

Over the course of nine months, I focused, in turn, on two main portions of scripture—the early chapters of both the Gospel of John and book of Acts. Sunday after Sunday I kept reminding these spiritually-confused-yet-curious church members of two principal themes: (1) the possibility of a theologically and pneumatologically real relationship with God,[9] and (2) the need for a missional rather than consumeristic, spectator-oriented approach to the Christian life. I'm pleased to be able to report that the response to this prayer-bathed biblical instruction was nothing short of amazing. Not only did this congregation hold together during this pastoral vacancy, the folks eventually selected a new pastor in a manner which demonstrated a remarkably strong consensus forged, it appears, by a renewed sense of hope for their future.

Patti and I are gratified by the fact that upon our departure, many members and leaders of this church expressed appreciation for the "new" understanding of Christian discipleship and missional ministry that had been presented to them. But I suspect it wasn't simply some ministry vision

9. For more on the notion that our Trinitarian God is not only personal, but hyper-personal and ultrarelational in his being, see Tyra, *Pursuing Moral Faithfulness*, 270. I'll elaborate upon what's involved in a theologically and pneumatologically real relationship with God throughout the remainder of this work.

casting supported by expositional teaching that provided this church with a new lease on life; it was a fervent, sustained reminder that Jesus himself embodied a dynamic, full-orbed faithfulness before God, and that a central part of a biblically-informed Christian discipleship is our learning how, with the help of the Spirit, to do the same.

The bottom line is that even Pentevangelical churches can experience a pneumatological deficit. Sometimes this deficiency is exacerbated by a *discipleship deficit* as well—a tragic lack of emphasis on the multifaceted faithfulness God desires and deserves. Whenever and wherever these two deficits occur, especially in tandem, a functional deism (and the Christian nominalism it produces) is likely to take the place of a vibrant, fruit-bearing, world-changing walk with the risen Jesus. However, what's also true is that it doesn't have to be this way. A realist, rather than non-realist, understanding and experience of Christ's Spirit, combined with an understanding of just how important the threefold faithfulness is to a genuine Christian discipleship, can revitalize the lives of individual Christians and churches, making it possible for them to reach their post-Christian peers for Christ. It's true that the post-Christian dynamic reported on by many is a real problem we evangelicals simply must take seriously.[10] But it's also true that many of our non- and post-Christian contemporaries, especially those from the emerging generations, are eager to experience God as a life-transforming power.[11] While a functional deism won't enable such an experience, a church impacted by a biblically-informed, Christ-honoring pneumatological realism will![12]

10. For example, see Barna Group, "Six Reasons Young Christians Leave Church"; Barna Group, "Twentysomethings Struggle"; Dyck, "The Leavers: Young Doubters Exit the Church"; Grossman, "Young Adults Aren't Sticking with Church." For book-length treatments of this topic, see Kinnaman, *You Lost Me*; Dean, *Almost Christian*; Powell and Clark, *Sticky Faith*; Powell et al., *Growing Young*; Wuthnow, *After the Baby Boomers*; Kimball, *They Like Jesus but Not the Church*.

11. Adler, "In Search of the Spiritual."

12. My contention that a biblically-informed pneumatological realism will necessarily be Christ-honoring finds support in George Hunsinger's essay titled "The Mediator of Communion: Karl Barth's Doctrine of the Holy Spirit." According to Hunsinger, "Barth argues that the operation of the Holy Spirit and the presence of Christ coincide. . . . The Holy Spirit is the power whereby Jesus as such attests and imparts himself as crucified and risen. . . . In short, the saving activity of the Holy Spirit as understood by Barth, is always Christ-centered in focus. In various Christocentric ways the Spirit functions as the mediator of communion. . . . In no sense that would be independent, supplemental, or superior does the Spirit's activity ever focus on itself, for in the one economy of salvation the Spirit serves the reconciliation accomplished by Christ from beginning to end"

Fully convinced of this, I've written a book which aims at the recovery of a robust doctrine of (and life in) the Holy Spirit. I consider it a huge privilege to be a part of such an important recovery endeavor.[13] If *Getting*

(Hunsinger, "Mediator of Communion," 181-82). Additional support is provided by Eberhard Busch who, citing Barth himself in the process, observes: "Where the Holy Spirit is sundered from Christ, sooner or later He is always transmuted into quite a different spirit, the spirit of the religious man, and finally the human spirit in general," or indeed, a universal creaturely spirit (I/2 271, 273 = 248, 251)" (Busch, *The Great Passion,* 222). On the other hand, my Vanguard University colleague, Frank Macchia, himself a Barth scholar, offers this important clarification: "Barth's approach to pneumatology is indeed Christocentric but in *CD* IV/4 (the fragment) (page 19) he qualifies this by saying that any 'true christocentricity' would also resist the idea that 'all anthropology and soteriology are thus swallowed up in Christology.' This would reduce humanity to total passivity (and I would say by implication leaves little room for the objectivity of the Spirit's work among humans as a counterbalance to Christology). This is Barth's resistance to the charge of 'Christomonism.' Barth applies this to the incarnation. He notes in his *Dogmatics in Outline* that in God's meeting with humanity in the incarnation, humanity 'does not turn into a marionette.' The humanity taken on in the incarnation is genuine humanity who is free. Why? The reason is in the fact that Christ is conceived by the Spirit in Mary's womb. Barth notes that because of the Spirit in the incarnation, God takes on 'this human existence in the freedom of God Himself, in the freedom in which the Father and Son are one in the bond of love, in the Holy Spirit' (see pages 97-99). So, for Barth, the Spirit is the great counterbalance to Christology because in the Spirit Christ as the Word of the Father binds himself to flesh in freedom, the freedom of the Spirit, and in the incarnation meets in this encounter 'free' humanity, and eventually a free creation that receives him in faith. To collapse anthropology into Christology is to reduce humanity to passivity and insignificance. Only the freedom of the Spirit opens up space for humanity to freely commune with Christ in a way that is conformed in his image but as a genuine partner created by God for this purpose, having their own free and distinct identity as covenant partners but without any myth of radical autonomy. So Christocentrism is not for Barth Christomonism. Pneumatological realism is Christocentric, refuses to detach anthropology from Christology, but this realism also refuses to collapse anthropology into Christology (Christomonism) so that humanity loses its distinct freedom in the Spirit as covenant partner to Christ. A true christocentricity would recognize the unique role of the Spirit in opening up all of creation to the love of the Father and to the work of the Son. The principle of the radical eschatological freedom of God is the principle of the Spirit" (Frank Macchia, email message to author, February 26, 2017).

13. I believe there's a sense in which this "recovery project" was not only anticipated by Karl Barth, but was also proleptically engaged in by him. Barth's comment near the end of his career regarding "the possibility of a theology of the third article" might be understood to mean that Barth was suggesting that a pneumatocentric, rather than Christocentric, approach to theology would lead to radically different ways of thinking and speaking of God (see Smith, *Theology of the Third Article,* 50–51). But, as Aaron Smith, points out, "Barth's christocentrism is at once pneumato-logical. His thought trades on the agency of the Spirit at every turn; apart from the event of faith, which is Spirit-inspired and maintained, there is no christocentric point of departure for pastoral

Real serves only to contribute in some small way to the promotion of a pneumatological realism among evangelicals in the West, I will view it as a huge success.

---

or theological thought and speech. And at the same time, apart from the exegetical work and Person of Christ, there is no pneumatocentric content upon which one could think and speak of God. . . . Thus, Barth has to be directing us to a pnematocentrisim materially and methodologically consistent with the content and shape of his christocentrism" (ibid., 52–53). In other words, Barth's theology is actually suggestive of what a theology of the third article might look like, his Christocentrism notwithstanding! Again, Smith says of Barth: "there is a substantive pneumatological undercurrent flowing with and even guiding his christological conclusions. One can draw out and build on Barth's own 'pneumatocentric dialectic'" (ibid., 18–19).

Part One: Theological and Ministry Foundations

Pneumatological Realism: Theological Corrective/Ministry Cure

No, we have not even heard that there is a Holy Spirit.

—ACTS 19:2

BLANK STARES, QUIZZICAL LOOKS, even indications of frustration: these are some of the ways people have tended to respond when made aware of what this new book is about. "Pneumatological realism," they'd say. "What's that? Is that even a thing?"

Well, yes, it is a thing—a very important thing. Indeed, I'm convinced that the cultivation of an ecclesial environment that's earmarked by a realist rather than non-realist understanding and experience of Christ's Spirit is one of the most significant endeavors the leaders of local churches can undertake.

The goal of this chapter is to help the reader better understand what I mean when I refer to pneumatological realism and why I've become such an outspoken advocate for it. Though I've endeavored to make the discussion as accessible as possible, and provide several illustrative figures toward that end, some of the ideas presented here may strike some readers as a bit obscure. Given the academic nature of the chapter's subject matter, this is to be expected. Still, I want to encourage those without formal theological training to hang in there. There is some important foundation-laying going on here, and I'd like to think that once completed, everyone reading this chapter will find that some important theological and ministry dots have been connected.

Pneumatological Realism: The Nature of the Notion

At the risk of oversimplifying things, I'll begin by indicating that, in theology, *pneumatology* is the area of study relating to the Holy Spirit. In philosophy, *realism* is the position which holds that "objects of sense perception or cognition exist independently of the mind."[1] In other words, philosophical realism contends that there is a "there" there; reality exists independently of our awareness or perception of it. So, the realist answer to the proverbial question about a tree falling in the uninhabited forest is: yes, such an event does indeed create the vibrations necessary for a sound to be heard, regardless of whether there's an ear nearby to perceive it.[2] Put all this together and a very rudimentary, initial definition for *pneumatological realism* might go like this: Speaking theologically, pneumatological realism contends that the Holy Spirit is *not* simply an idea, concept, or abstract theoretical notion. Rather, he is a very real, personal, divine entity—the third person of the Trinity—who can be interacted with in a real, interpersonal, phenomenal,[3] existentially-impactful (life-story shaping) manner.

Once again, this is an oversimplification, but it's a beginning that I'll build on as we go. And, lest you conclude that pneumatological realism is a fanciful notion that only I'm concerned about, I'll point out straightaway that, while one could probably count on one hand the number of theologians who've referred to the concept in an explicit manner, others have done so.[4] Indeed, before I elaborate any further on my understanding of

1. See *Merriam-Webster*, s.v. "Realism," http://www.merriam-webster.com/dictionary/realism.

2. For more on this, see Bhaskar, *Realist Theory of Science*, 21.

3. In this context, a phenomenal experience is one that is apparent to the senses. Biblical support for the contention that God's Spirit can be experienced in a phenomenal manner can be found not only the Old Testament (e.g., Ezek 2:2) but the New Testament as well (e.g., Acts 2:1–4, 32–33; 8:17–19; 19:6; Rom 8:15; Gal 4:6). In addition, some tacit theological support might be adduced from Aaron Smith's use of the concept of *inverberation*—the Holy Spirit meeting us through our senses—which he derives from Karl Barth's doctrines of revelation and the word of God (Smith, *Theology of the Third Article*, 7, 109-10).

4. While this is true, it should be noted that, even though my Vanguard University colleague, Frank Macchia, has yet to utilize the term "pneumatological realism" in print, his major publications are highly evocative of the concept. (See Macchia, *Baptized in the Spirit*; Macchia, *Justified in the Spirit*.) Likewise, though his theological agenda differs significantly from mine, the pneumatologically grounded metaphysics, epistemology, and hermeneutics of my friend Amos Yong resonate in some important respects with the pneumatological realism I'm promoting. See Yong, *Beyond the Impasse*; Yong, *Discerning*

what a pneumatological realism is and why it's so important to the life of the church, I'll briefly survey here two other representative versions of the notion: one put forward by a German systematic theologian named Wolfhart Pannenberg, and the other proffered by an American spiritual theologian named John Coe. Along with me, both Pannenberg and Coe conceive of pneumatological realism as a necessary corrective to a problem plaguing contemporary Western theology and practice. We differ some, however, in what we consider that problem to be. Thus, my survey of our respective takes will pay special attention to the theological/ministry malady each of us considers pneumatological realism to be an indispensable solution for.

Pneumatological Realism vs. Christian Gnosticism

Though he didn't use the term extensively, Pannenberg did refer in his systematic theology to a "pneumatological realism"—one that had been previously alluded to by fellow German theologian Otto Weber.[5] Admittedly, the practical ministry implications of pneumatological realism weren't at the forefront of Pannenberg's treatment of it. Nevertheless, his somewhat controversial take on the notion has proved to be an important development in the history of modern theology.

According to Pannenberg, Weber's concern had been to overcome the "common inclination" of theologians to refer to the Spirit in an overly ethereal/theoretical manner. Weber took issue with the tendency of theologians to "speak *docetically* of the Holy Spirit, making him a stopgap that always comes in where questions that are posed remain open."[6]

A little background is in order here, even if it is, once again, an oversimplification. *Gnosticism* refers to a teaching that posed a serious threat to the Christian faith during a critical era of its emergence—the second and third centuries AD. A central theme in gnosticism is the notion of saving *gnosis* or "knowledge." Thus, the gnostics viewed Christ as a divine messenger—an angelic bearer of an esoteric knowledge—rather than as an incarnate God-man whose suffering and death on the cross possessed an atoning significance. Coinciding with this take, "[o]ne of the key doctrines

---

the Spirit(s); Yong, *The Spirit Poured Out*; Yong, *Spirit-Word-Community*; and Yong, "On Divine Presence," 167–88.

5. See Pannenberg, *Systematic Theology*, 3–4. Pannenberg was referring here to Weber, *Foundations of Dogmatics*, 238.

6. Pannenberg, *Systematic Theology*, 3, emphasis added.

at the heart of Gnosticism was that Jesus only appeared to be human, but really was not. The name for this teaching is *Docetism* from the Greek words: *dokesis*–"semblance" or "appearance," and *dokein*–"to seem."[7] It's because a *docetic* view of Jesus, denying as it does Jesus' full humanity, creates huge problems for a biblically-informed and theologically coherent understanding of his twin ministries of revelation and redemption, that the early church fathers felt the need to label it a heresy and to argue against it in a very vociferous manner.[8] What Weber seems to have been concerned about is the tendency of some contemporary theologians to speak *docetically* of the Holy Spirit—that is, to refer to the Spirit as if he's simply a useful theoretical concept rather than an ontologically real, personal, divine entity who, himself, plays a critical role in redemption drama.[9]

For his part, Pannenberg too was concerned about an insufficient, reductionist treatment of the Spirit which limited his role in the Christian drama to helping believers arrive at a saving knowledge of Jesus. According to Pannenberg,

> Theology has often neglected the relation between the soteriological operations of the Spirit in believers and his activity as both the Creator of all life and also in its eschatological new creation and consummation. This is particularly true of the theology of the Christian West, whose views of the work of the Spirit have concentrated on his function as the source of grace or faith.[10]

Pannenberg was convinced that to speak of the Holy Spirit as "just an emanation of Jesus Christ,"[11] and to limit his activity to simply providing "cognitive divine help" in understanding the Christ-event,[12] was not only much too reminiscent of the Gnostic focus on an esoteric saving knowledge, but was also marginalizing and reductionist. It was in response to this concern that Pannenberg argued for "a much broader and more biblical doctrine that emphasizes the Spirit's all-pervasive, creative presence in

---

7. Braaten and Jenson, *Christian Dogmatics*, 1:499.

8. Olson, *Mosaic of Christian Belief*, 225–26, 232–33.

9. Ontology is the branch of metaphysics which focuses on the nature of being or existence. See *Merriam-Webster Dictionary*, s.v. "Ontology," http://www.merriam-webster.com/dictionary/ontology.

10. Pannenberg, *Systematic Theology*, 2.

11. Ibid., 6. Pannenberg seems especially concerned with avoiding a conflation of Jesus and the Spirit (see ibid., 4–7).

12. Ibid., 2.

creation and human life, climaxing in the new life of the believer."[13] Thus, I will offer that Pannenberg was concerned with providing the church with a more *comprehensive* doctrine of the Spirit—one that was genuinely Trinitarian and that fully appreciated the life-giving role the Spirit plays not only in the drama of redemption, but creation and consummation as well.[14] For Pannenberg, the Spirit is crucial to the entirety of the Christian life precisely because the Spirit is not only the source of all life—physical and spiritual, temporal and eternal—but to the very structure of reality (of being) itself.[15] Per the pneumatological realism of Pannenberg, it's hard to overstate the importance of the Holy Spirit to our very existence; much less our walk with Christ![16]

13. Grenz, "Wolfhart Pannenberg's Quest for Ultimate Truth," para. 16.

14. To be more specific, Pannenberg considered the general tendency of post-reformation theology to limit the role of the Spirit to the appropriation of salvation by imparting a special knowledge (of faith) inaccessible to human reason to be a gnosticizing move (Pannenberg, *Systematic Theology*, 3). He was also critical of the way in which some of his contemporaries failed to recognize the Spirit's role in both creation and consummation. On the one hand, Pannenberg accused Weber and Karl Barth of overemphasizing the connection between the Spirit and eschatology, almost dualistically setting "the Spirit as an eschatological gift in contrast to existing world reality" (ibid). On the other hand, he opined that while Paul Tillich was right to emphasize the Spirit's crucial import to "the phenomenon of life in all its breadth," he erred by not "noting the eschatological reference" (ibid., 3–4). Over against both forms of pneumatological imbalance, Pannenberg insisted: "In understanding the Spirit's activity it is only by linking eschatology and creation that we achieve the full *pneumatological realism* that Weber had in view, and that the theology and piety of the Orthodox churches have best preserved" (ibid. 4, emphasis added).

15. I will add here that the manner in which Pannenberg referred to the Spirit as a divine "force field" has prompted a debate as to whether his cosmological pneumatology is implicitly panentheistic despite his contention otherwise (see Cooper, *Panentheism*, 259–60; see also Sexton, *Trinitarian Theology*, 53–54). Acknowledging that not all theologians identify Pannenberg as a panentheist (Cooper, *Panentheism*, 260n4), Cooper nevertheless attributes to the German theologian a "trinitarian panentheism," arguing, "The unifying concept of Pannenberg's entire theology is the idea that the divine essence, which he identifies with the Spirit, is an infinite, all-inclusive 'force field' in which the ontological Trinity exists necessarily and the cosmos exists contingently. Constituting this force field, the ontological Trinity actualizes itself as the economic Trinity in the cosmos until the cosmos is fully included within the Trinity as the kingdom of God. All aspects of Pannenberg's theology—his doctrine of God and God's activity in creation, redemption, and consummation, radiate from the central notion that God is an infinite, triune force field of creative love" (ibid., 266–67). My point in raising this issue is not to weigh in on this debate, but to point out that an embrace of the pneumatological realism I have in mind doesn't require a panentheism—trinitarian or otherwise.

16. Another issue to keep in mind is the manner in which Pannenberg's more

Pneumatological Realism vs. Christian Moralism

For his part, John Coe has advocated for a slightly different version of pneumatological realism. In an article designed to discourage moralism (salvation/sanctification by self-improvement) and encourage instead an engagement in spiritual formation (the goal of which is a transformation toward Christlikeness that's effected by the Holy Spirit), Coe feels the need to push back against the critics of the spiritual formation movement. The critics Coe is responding to are theologians and church leaders concerned that a preoccupation with one's spirituality can lead to an engagement in practices that not only possess little or no biblical warrant, but may actually derive from non-Christian sources. There's also an apprehension that such a preoccupation often functions as an alternative to a fervent engagement in Christian mission.[17] Aware of these anxieties, and having conceded that the movement could do a better job of theologically grounding spiritual formation in a robust theology of the Cross and Spirit, Coe goes on to say:

> However, I also agree with some of the advocates of spiritual formation who criticize theologians and evangelicals who may have a robust theology of the cross but a non-realist pneumatology or theology of the Indwelling Spirit of Christ and His role in transformation. That is, they fail to make explicit the Bible's claim that it is not theology but rather the *reality* of

comprehensive doctrine of the Spirit can be viewed as providing some foundational support for what has come to be known as the "turn to pneumatology" (see Kärkkäinen, "How to Speak of the Spirit," 126n19). Desiring to forge an inclusive (perhaps even pluralistic) theology of religions, this "turn" has been advocated by many theologians, both Catholic and Protestant, liberal and evangelical, Pentecostal-charismatic and non-Pentecostal-charismatic. Put simply, the idea here is that if the work of the Spirit in the world at large (as the "Spirit of creation" or "Spirit of life") can be untethered or bracketed from the work of Christ (and the church), it may be possible to see the Holy Spirit working in other cultures and religions in a manner that's essentially salvific rather than merely preparatory to a saving embrace of the Christian gospel. For more on the pneumatological turn, see Pinnock, *A Wideness in God's Mercy*, and Yong, *Discerning the Spirit(s)*. (See also Yong, "Christological Constraints in Shifting Contexts," 19–33.) For a critique of this pneumatological turn from a Pentecostal perspective, see Chan, *Grassroots Asian Theology*, 129–42. For an evangelical critique, see Miles, *God of Many Understandings*, 150–61, 212–39. Once again, my point in raising this issue is not to weigh in on the debate, but simply to point out that an embrace of the pneumatological realism proffered in this work doesn't necessarily entail support for the pneumatological turn just described.

17. For a critique of the spiritual formation movement which aims at not being overly reactive and alarmist, see Patton, "Why I Don't Think Much of the Spiritual Formation Movement."

theology-being-applied-to-the-heart-by-the Spirit, a "pneumatological realism," that truly transforms.[18]

As this quote indicates, "pneumatological realism" is the term Coe
uses to describe what's going on when theology stops functioning as mere
theory and is actually applied to the hearts of believers by the indwelling
Spirit in a transformational manner. Coe seems to be convinced that it's
possible for believers to interact with the Spirit of Christ in biblically-informed yet existentially-impactful (i.e., life-shaping) ways.

In other words, Coe seems to be promoting a realist (rather than non-
realist) pneumatology as the remedy for moralism—the attempt of believers to achieve moral perfection in their own strength. With this thought in
mind, Coe calls for the Christian disciple to stop trying his or her best to be
good before God, and to open his or her "heart and mind deeply to (1) the
reality of Christ's work on the cross in justification and (2) the ministry of
the Holy Spirit in regeneration and in-filling."[19]

In sum, this version of pneumatological realism holds that the Holy
Spirit is much more than a theological construct. He is a personal, divine
agent of change who, having indwelt the follower of Christ, seeks to effect a
spiritual transformation from the inside out. According to Coe, this desperately needed transformation occurs only when the Christian disciple, with
the help of the Spirit, fully recognizes the implications of Jesus' work on
the cross on his or her behalf, and then cooperates in a disciplined manner
with the Spirit's ongoing work of applying this life-giving and life-shaping
truth to his or her heart.

Pneumatological Realism vs.
a Functional Deism/Christian Nominalism

It's important to note that my own understanding of "pneumatological realism," arrived at independently of both Pannenberg and Coe, shares points
of agreement with both. At the heart of my take on the term is the conviction that, given the radical importance of the Holy Spirit to every aspect
of the economy of God (from creation to redemption to consummation),
Christ's followers should expect to experience Christ's Spirit in ways that
are real—i.e., personal, interactive, and phenomenal—rather than merely

18. See Coe, "Resisting the Temptation of *Moral* Formation," 57n2, emphasis original.
19. Ibid., 73.

theoretical, conceptual, or ritualistic. Moreover, the sincere Christian disciple should expect that these interactions with the Spirit can and will prove to be both *epistemologically helpful*—i.e., revelatory in terms of God's love, will, and purposes (Eph 1:17; 3:16–19; Col 1:9; 1 Cor 2:6–16)—and *existentially impactful*—i.e., transformative, life-shaping, and ministry-engendering (Gal 5:22-23; Col 1:10–12)—in their effect.[20]

All three of the versions of a pneumatological realism surveyed here view it as a theological corrective to a pneumatological deficit at work in too many Western theologies and churches. My contention is that in many evangelical theologies, the role of the Holy Spirit has been both truncated and overly conceptualized with the result that in many evangelical churches the Spirit functions merely as an article in the creed or as a sanctifying force *presumed* to be at work in the lives of church members because of their having engaged in this or that religious ritual (e.g., water baptism, confirmation, the laying on of hands, etc.). What's missing in an ecclesial environment influenced by an overly scholastic/ritualistic—essentially non-realist—pneumatology is (1) a sufficient awareness of how important the Holy Spirit is to absolutely *every* aspect of the Christian life; (2) any sense that Christ's followers can and should *expect* to experience the Spirit in ways that are *phenomenal* in nature (i.e., immediate and evident to the senses); and (3) the notion that through the Spirit the disciple can interact with the risen Christ in an existentially-impactful manner resulting in a fully functional spiritual, moral, and ministry formation.[21]

---

20. Essentially affirming this understanding of pneumatological realism, Pentecostal theologian Frank Macchia has offered the following elucidation: "Pneumatological 'realism' takes for granted a biblically-informed vision of life, and of the Christ life in particular, as substantively and necessarily pneumatological. . . . We are made for the Spirit and for the Christ life that the Spirit inspires. . . . There is no life without the Spirit, and . . . there is no salvific or missional promise or challenge that does not have the presence of God through the Spirit at its very core. . . . A pneumatological realism entails the idea that the New Testament descriptions of life in the Spirit are not merely symbolic portrayals of life that can be translated into modern psychological, moral, or sociological categories. Though such categories can help us better understand how the life of the Spirit impacts us throughout various contexts of human experience, the presence and work of the Holy Spirit as described in the New Testament are to be taken at face value at the root of it all as realities that can be known and felt in analogous ways today." Frank Macchia, email message to author, August 10, 2014. For more on this, see Dunn, *Baptism in the Holy Spirit*, 225–26.

21. Barth scholar Colin Gunton reminds us that at the heart of Barth's soteriology is the theme: "Jesus *is* victor." Understanding that this statement makes no sense unless Jesus *is* risen and real rather than dead and gone, he goes on to observe: "Barth's theology,

As indicated in this book's introduction, I believe that a crucial, if complicated, connection exists between a non-realist pneumatology and the phenomenon of *functional deism*—rank-and-file church members professing an orthodox theology but living day-to-day in a de facto deistic manner. I'm referring here to a nominal Christianity where prayer, worship, and service, if engaged in at all, are directed toward the idea of God rather than God himself. I'm convinced that a very dangerous reciprocal relationship exists between the pneumatological realism I have in mind and the phenomenon of functional deism. On the one hand, the lack of the former contributes to the emergence of the latter in the lives of Christians and churches. On the other hand, once a functional deism has been allowed to take root in the lives of God's people, it does anything but elicit an expectation of intimate, interactive, ministry-engendering encounters, through the Holy Spirit, with the risen Christ. In the next chapter, I'll have more to say about just how hugely problematic this lack of expectation is. For now, allow me to simply state that what I'm advocating for in this work is a functional-deism-defeating pneumatological realism that is crucial to the spiritual, moral, and missional faithfulness the Scriptures enjoin upon the followers of Christ.

The Story Behind My Version of the Notion

It's because of the practical importance of a pneumatological realism to the lives of Christians and congregations that I've become an ardent proponent of it. Indeed, the crucial role a realist understanding of the Holy Spirit plays in both a Christian orthodoxy (right believing) and orthopraxy (right behaving) has functioned as a meta-theme in my most recent preaching, teaching, and writing endeavors. Perhaps a brief recounting of the process

---

with its insistence on a living Christ, is infinitely preferable to Schleiermacher's [i.e., liberal Protestantism's] conception of salvation as influence mediated from a historical past and his accompanying assertion that the resurrection and ascension have no determinative place in Christian dogmatics" (Gunton, "Salvation," 154). Likewise, George Hunsinger, in an essay focusing on Barth's Christology, argues that, while Barth accepted the "full 'historicity' of Christ's resurrection," he "does not allow the question of historicity (a peculiarly modern obsession) to obscure the resurrection's chief theological significance. Christ's resurrection means, above all, that the reconciliation Christ accomplished enjoys eternal *reality* and significance" (Hunsinger, "Karl Barth's Christology," 138, emphasis added). A crucial implication of this, says Hunsinger is that, for Barth, "[t]he resurrection means Christ's 'real presence' to us now, and 'our contemporaneity to him' in what he so perfectly accomplished then in our stead (*CD* IV/1, p. 348)" (ibid., 138–39).

by which I've come to this understanding of a pneumatological realism will further elucidate what I have in mind when I refer to it and why I'm so thoroughly convinced of its importance.

I was working on the manuscript for a book titled *The Holy Spirit in Mission* when my editor at the time, Gary Deddo, suggested that I might want to make use of the concept of a "theological realism" as I laid out for the book's evangelical readership the case for a prophetic (Spirit-prompted and Spirit-empowered) engagement in evangelism, edification, and equipping. Thus, it was at Gary's suggestion that I acquired a copy of *Worship and the Reality of God*, by John Jefferson Davis.[22]

As the name of this book suggests, its primary focus is the renewal of worship in evangelical churches. It was with this goal in mind that Davis issued a strong call for evangelical churches located in post-Christian North America to embrace an ontology (or theory regarding the nature of existence) he refers to as *"trinitarian supernaturalism."*[23] Instead of assuming that the universe is eternal or owes its existence to random, natural causes, this model argues that the eternal triune God is the fundamental reality from which all other realities (entities) derive. Furthermore, trinitarian supernaturalism holds that our universe is an open (rather than closed) system in which encounters with the divine are possible. In other words, there is no lid on the box, so to speak. God is free to reach into the "box" and interact with the universe he's created. Because of this, Davis insists, Christians are justified in taking seriously the possibility of interacting with a *real presence* of God during their times of corporate worship. Believing that this theological realism has huge implications for the renewal of worship occurring in contemporary evangelical churches, Davis boldly calls for the evangelical church in the West to unsaddle itself from theological views

22. Davis, *Worship and the Reality of God.*

23. Though Davis does not explicitly acknowledge the influence of either T. F. Torrance or his brother James on the "supernatural trinitarianism" ontology he proffers in this work, ancillary references to the Torrance brothers suggest it. Furthermore, while *Worship and the Reality of God* also contains a footnote in which volume 3 of Pannenberg's *Systematic Theology* is cited, it is a glancing reference, having to do with ecclesiology rather than cosmology (see Davis, *Worship and the Reality of God*, 62n59). That said, one might wonder about the degree of influence (either direct or indirect) Pannenberg had upon Davis's notion of a trinitarian supernaturalism, especially since Davis refers to the "inexorable reality-field of God" which lies at the center of "this world" (*Worship and the Reality of God*, 24). For an interesting discussion of how the points of agreement and disagreement in the scientific theology of both Pannenberg and Torrance can be viewed over against the influence of Karl Barth, see Peterson, *"Scientia Dei."*

that "can handcuff the Holy Spirit in the life of the church and blind it to where the Spirit may be working dramatically in the world today."[24]

This was my first exposure to theological realism as a formal, analytical concept, and I was struck by the manner in which Davis had been led by his embrace of it to call for what is essentially a more *realist* approach to the work of the Spirit in evangelical churches. Indeed, implying that the prolific growth of Pentecostal and charismatic churches worldwide is due mainly to the manner in which Pentecostal-charismatic doctrine and practice resonates with the supernaturalistic worldview prevalent in the Global South, Davis cites this growth as a reason why evangelicals in America need to "become more reflective about their basic assumptions about what is real."[25] As a Pentevangelical scholar desiring to encourage Christians living in the industrial West to become more open to the possibility of a Spirit-empowered engagement in missional ministry, I immediately saw value in what Davis was up to. Though I did not refer to a "pneumatological realism," per se, in *The Holy Spirit in Mission*, throughout the book there are indications of the strong connection I believed could and should be made between a theological realism and one specifically related to pneumatology.[26]

It was in a subsequent book—*A Missional Orthodoxy*—that my advocacy for a pneumatological (as well as theological) realism became explicit. Given to understand that behind the proposal presented in *Worship and the Reality of God* was the influence of T. F. Torrance, I began my own research into the work of that renowned Scottish theologian, especially with respect to what's known as his scientific theology and Christian realist epistemology (theory regarding how we come to know things).

In chapter 2 of *A Missional Orthodoxy,* I endeavored to provide my readers with an alternative to the two main epistemological theories that currently occupy the extreme positions on the proverbial pendulum's swing: foundationalism and non-foundationalism. One extreme perspective (foundationalism) holds that an *objective certainty* regarding reality can be achieved on the basis of logic and deduction. In other words, the edifice of certain, objective knowledge is thought to be built upon the foundation of a few rationally provable, indubitable truths. Once these first-order truths have been "proved," the theory goes, other second- and third-order truths can be derived from them through logic and deduction. The result,

24. Davis, *Worship and the Reality of God*, 121–25, 197–98.

25. Ibid., 18.

26. For example, see Tyra, *Holy Spirit in Mission*, 112–17.

it's held, is a body of knowledge that can be considered impeccable to any honest, fair-minded, intelligent thinker.

The other extreme view (non-foundationalism) insists that there are no foundational truths that can be observed objectively and held with certainty. Everything we think we know has been historically and culturally conditioned. All knowledge is so thoroughly *subjective* and *socially constructed* that we might as well not speak of "Truth" or "Reality" at all.[27]

So, the two extreme positions in this discussion hold that we can either know reality with objective certainty, or we can't know it at all.

FIGURE 1

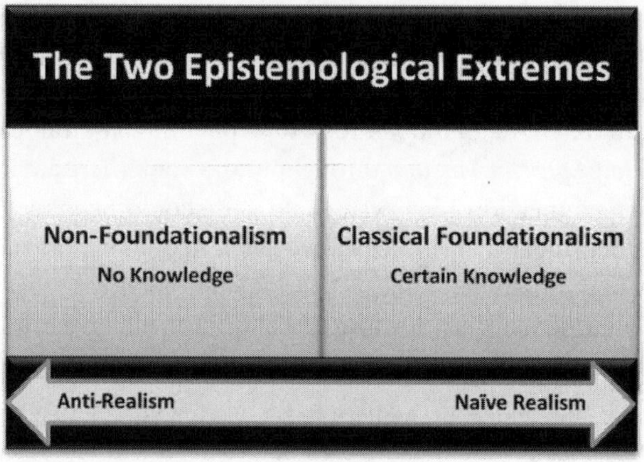

But in truth these aren't our only options. Doing my best not to over-simplify things, I drew my readers' attention to Torrance's interaction with the work of scientist/philosopher Michael Polanyi, who spoke of a *tacit knowledge* of reality that's accrued as human beings from childhood on indwell, "bump around" within, and adapt to the physical and social worlds around them.[28] In sum, according to Torrance and Polanyi, it's through a holistic indwelling of the world (physical and social) that people are able to acquire the cognitive framework necessary to assimilate real, trustworthy (even if not perfect) knowledge of the way the world works and how to best

27. For more on this, see Tyra, *Missional Orthodoxy*, 118–23.

28. We might think of tacit knowledge as an implicit, inherent, reflexive, "below-the-radar" kind of knowledge—a capacity to know things we don't know we know. For more on this, see Torrance, "Place of Michael Polanyi," 60, as cited in Colyer, *How to Read T. F. Torrance*, 335. See also ibid., 337.

navigate their way in and through it. [29] Thus, as an alternative to the two extreme epistemological perspectives mentioned above—foundationalism on the one hand and non-foundationalism on the other—what we find in Torrance (following Polanyi) is a cogent argument for the possibility of a *post-foundationalism*—the ability of humans to acquire a personal, experience-based, *good enough* knowledge of reality.[30]

FIGURE 2

An Alternative to the Epistemological Extremes

Non-Foundationalism	Post-Foundationalism	Classical Foundationalism
No Knowledge	Good Enough Knowledge	Certain Knowledge
Anti-Realism	Critical Realism	Naïve Realism

Moreover, Torrance went on to suggest that this same dynamic holds true with respect to the acquisition of spiritual knowledge. In his *Reality & Evangelical Theology: The Realism of Christian Revelation*, Torrance articulated the following theological/christological tenet: "what God is antecedently and eternally in himself he really is toward us in the concrete embodiment of his Truth in Jesus Christ the word made flesh."[31] The point

---

29 To be more specific, Torrance described the dynamic of "indwelling" as a "holistic, significantly informal, integrative and heuristic process of investigating a field of inquiry." Torrance went on to assert that "[a]s this inquiry develops, our minds begin to assimilate the internal constitutive relations embodied in what we seek to know." See Torrance, *Transformation and Convergence*, 114, as cited in Colyer, *How to Read T. F. Torrance*, 336.

30. For more on how Torrance's concept of a "personal knowledge" avoids being merely subjective, see Colyer, *How to Read T. F. Torrance*, 342–44, 357. For more on the notion of a post-foundationalism, see Vanhoozer, *Drama of Doctrine*, 286–91, 293–305; Vanhoozer, "Pilgrim's Digress," 88–89; and Shults, *Postfoundationalist Task*, 11–12, 17–19, 25–81.

31. Torrance, *Reality & Evangelical Theology*, 141. See also see Barth, *Church Dogmatics*, I/1, 466.

Torrance was emphasizing is the dramatic importance of Christ's incarnation to God's self-revelation, and precisely why nothing less than a real knowledge of God is possible because of it. This was and is a bold advocacy for a *theological realism*.[32] But that's not all. Supportive of the notion of a

32. As previously indicated in the footnotes, it's my contention that a "metaphysics of divine reality" undergirds the pneumatological realism I believe is evident in the work of Karl Barth. In support of this contention, I'll point out that in his book, *How to Read Karl Barth: The Shape of His Theology*, George Hunsinger argues that six motifs "run throughout the *Church Dogmatics*" and "shape the doctrinal content of the Barth's mature theology as a whole": "actualism," "particularism," "objectivism," "personalism," "*realism*," and "rationalism" (Hunsinger, *How to Read Karl Barth*, 4–5, emphasis added). Even though "realism" is the label Hunsinger attaches to one of these six motifs, I will offer that the theological/pneumatological realism I have in mind, and see in Barth's work, comprises elements of all six of the motifs to which Hunsinger refers (see Hunsinger's survey of the motifs in ibid., 27–64). Furthermore, some additional support for my thesis is provided by Barth scholar, Sandra Sonderegger, who speaks of Karl Barth's "taste for realism in theology, both in knowledge and in the nature of things" (Sonderegger, "Barth and Feminism," 264). As well, in an essay focusing on "the role of God's gracious election in Karl Barth's theological ontology, Bruce McCormack makes the assertion: "What Barth accomplished with his doctrine of election was to establish a hermeneutical rule which would allow the church to speak authoritatively about what God was/is—'before the foundation of the world,' *without engaging in speculation*" (McCormack, "Grace and Being," 92, emphasis original). Moreover, while in an essay titled "Barth, Modernity, and Postmodernity," Graham Ward refers to Barth's "nonfoundationalism" and "nonrealism" (281). I will aver that Barth's position can also be described as a post-foundationalism/ critical realism that was influenced greatly by his antagonism to any philosophical ground for a natural revelation. As Ward himself explains: "Barth's nonfoundationalism is a form of philosophical skepticism made possible by a *theological realism*. . . . It is important to distinguish this form of nonfoundationalism from the nonfoundationalism of those convinced there is nothing outside the words we employ to bring something into existence" (see ibid., emphasis added). Indeed, in a subsequent passage, the way Ward describes Barth's "non-realism" actually connotes a firm commitment to the type of theological realism Torrance would later champion. According to Ward: "The basis of Barth's non-realism lies in his refusal to accept anything as true or *real* outside of the knowledge given to human creatures through Christ. Jesus Christ is the ontic and noetic possibility for any true and objective understanding of what we, other people, and the things of our world are as created" (ibid., 284, emphasis added). Finally, some support for the epistemological payoff that results when the pneumatological realism I'm advocating for is combined with the theological realism of Torrance, is evidenced when Ward clarifies that for Barth: "Only the noetic operation of the Spirit of Christ, establishing *analogia fidei* or *analogia Christi* [as opposed to *analogia entis*], can enable us to have some understanding of the world as it is. Only God sees things as they are. This theological position, as I pointed out, critiques notions of 'presence' and 'identity,' for the world (and God's unveiling of himself within the world) is always and only mediated to us. This position is reiterated and developed in *CD* III/1 with respect to countering naturalism and emphasizing the *unreality* of human constructions of creation (which are, after Kant,

pneumatological realism is the fact that Torrance also spoke of the dramatic importance of the *indwelling of the Holy Spirit* to the process of divine self-revelation. In a passage underscoring the need for orthodox understandings of both Christ and the Spirit, Torrance wrote:

> Everything hinges on the *reality* of God's *self-*communication to us in Jesus Christ, in whom there has become incarnate, not some created intermediary between God and the world, but the very Word who eternally inheres in the Being of God and is God, so that for us to know God in Jesus Christ is really to know him as he is in himself. It is with the same force that attention is directed upon the Holy Spirit, whom the Father sends through the Son to dwell with us, and who, like the Son, is no mere cosmic power intermediate between God and the world, but is the Spirit of God who eternally dwells in him and in whom God knows himself, so that for us to know God in his Spirit is to know him in the hidden depths of his divine Being.[33]

According to this passage, it's both the *incarnation of Christ* and the *indwelling of his Spirit* that makes a theological realism—a real, trustworthy knowledge of our Trinitarian God—possible.[34]

'worldviews,' *Weltanschauungen*)" (ibid., 285, emphasis added). (For a succinct, helpful summary of the relationship between Barth's critical realism and theological realism, see Bruce McCormack's *Karl Barth's Critically Realistic Dialectical Theology: Its Genesis and Development 1909–1936*, 67.)

33. Torrance, *Reality & Evangelical Theology*, 23, emphasis added. Furthermore, in support of his uncle's contention that both the incarnate Christ and the Holy Spirit are crucial to God's self-communication, and that this self-communication is phenomenal rather than ethereal in nature, Alan Torrance asserts: "As the recognition story of Matthew 16 makes clear, the perception and acknowledgement of God's being and purposes with and for humanity is invariably 'from above'—flesh and bone simply do not provide the relevant epistemic access. At the same time, this 'from above' element is *for the sake of* our perceiving the One who is *concretely* 'with us.' God's Self-revelation does not direct us 'above' or to some spiritual beyond, it directs us to the 'Thou' who comes to us as the suffering servant, the Son in the far country. The *concrete presence of the Holy Spirit* with humanity occurs in order that God might be recognized precisely there and in that context" (Torrance, "The Trinity," 74, emphasis added).

34. Some additional support for this thesis is provided in Philip Rosato's discussion of the manner in which Karl Barth viewed the work of the Spirit as crucial to man's knowledge of the trinitarian nature of God. Says Rosato: "Barth grounds his insistence on a single source of man's knowledge about the Trinity on nothing less than the Holy Spirit. Biblical faith itself, as the work of the Holy Spirit, is the one source of man's knowledge about God's triune being which man can rely on with certainty. God the Spirit has formed such a relationship with man that man's own language and experience, his very

FIGURE 3

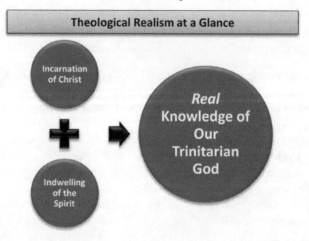

To be more specific, Torrance's theological realism contends that as the members of a Christian community "bump around" within the "world" presented to us in the pages of the Spirit-inspired Scriptures,[35] this spiritually disciplined, communal, Spirit-illuminated *indwelling* of the biblical narratives facilitates an existentially-impactful enculturation experience. Not only do we begin more and more to see the world the way the biblical characters did; but the Holy Spirit gradually enables the acquisition of a "cognitive framework"[36] which, I will suggest, we might associate with

lips and heart, may become capable of reflecting the inner-trinitarian being of God in the midst of the world. For, to comprehend all the implications of hearing the word of God is not traceable to data lying within man's experience, but only to faith, to the Holy Spirit. Since the doctrine of the Trinity lies at the core of the revealed Word, and since the Word can only be known through the power of the Spirit, Barth links the knowledge of the Trinity to the mystery of the Spirit at work in Christian experience" (Rosato, *The Spirit as Lord,* 55.) Rosato continues, saying: "The Holy Spirit, God's own historical self-impartation to man, guarantees a correspondence between God in himself and God as He is known by man. Clearly the solution to the problem concerning knowledge of the immanent Trinity must be for Barth a pneumatological solution. Only the Spirit, as the spiritual power of God's own eternal Word, can create through faith a human knowledge which substantially corresponds to the truth of God himself. That man can know the immanent nature of God as the mystery which coincides with the economic activity of God on man's behalf is the work of the Holy Spirit" (ibid., 57).

35. Torrance, *Reality and Scientific Theology,* 83–84, as cited in Colyer, *How to Read T. F. Torrance,* 351. See also Colyer, *How to Read T. F. Torrance,* 352–53, 356–57; Torrance, *Reality & Evangelical Theology,* xv, 48–49.

36. For his part, Barth scholar Aaron Smith refers to Christ restructuring our

the Apostle Paul's reference to the "mind of Christ" (1 Cor 2:16)—a Spirit-enabled capacity to know the deep things of God (1 Cor 2:10–11).[37] All that's required, then, for a *real* knowledge of God and what he is up to in the world is the grace-enabled acquisition on our part of the tacit knowledge produced by this intentional, Spirit-illuminated indwelling of the Spirit-inspired Scriptures.[38] It's through this God-commissioned, Christ-centered, Spirit-enabled cognitive framework that we find access to spiritual wisdom—that is, real, trustworthy (even if not perfect) knowledge (see 1 Cor 13:12) of the way the spiritual world works and how to best navigate our way in and through it. [39]

Now, keeping the focus of this book in mind, I want to underscore how crucial the revelatory, illuminating work of the Holy Spirit is to Torrance's epistemological proposal. Indeed, as a biblical and practical theologian committed to exploring and articulating how theology can and should

---

"cognitive processes," and the Spirit creating within us a "perceptual apparatus." Smith, *Theology of the Third Article*, 60.

37. Commenting on Barth's conviction regarding the "pneumatic ground of man's understanding of God" and the manner in which he developed "within his pneumatology a unique metaphysics by which the believer is given a share in God's ontic truth through the noetic activity of the Holy Spirit," Philip Rosato states: "Just as God the Father knows Himself in His Son through the Spirit, the man of faith can come to know his Father in Jesus Christ though the Spirit. Only a metaphysics rooted in *divine reality* guarantees that man can mediately know God as God immediately knows Himself" (Rosato, *The Spirit as Lord*, 72, emphasis added). This reference to a "metaphysics rooted in divine reality" and the role of the Holy Spirit within it would certainly seem to lend some support for the notions of both a theological and pneumatological realism.

38. Kurt Anders Richardson describes Torrance's version of this indwelling of Scripture when he writes, "We do not pretend to be the original readers of the Bible, nor do we ignore the distance between the times and spaces of the original writings and our own. Instead, through continual practice of reading and rereading and meditating on the words of Scripture, *with the guidance of the Holy Spirit* and the witness of the foundational doctrines of Christianity, believers acquire living and relational knowledge of God in each generation of the church" (Richardson, "Foreword: Introducing Torrance," xv, emphasis added). See also Lesslie Newbigin's crucial discussion of what it means to indwell the biblical text and the implications of this for missional ministry in Newbigin, *Gospel in a Pluralist Society*, 97–102.

39. Put differently, fundamental to Torrance's critical/theological realism is an insistence that our present epistemological condition is not subject/object but object/object accountable to God the one true Subject (see Torrance, *Reality & Evangelical Theology*, 27–30). Since the one true Subject has, via the incarnation and outpouring of the Spirit, entered into our epistemological environment and spoken revelatory words to the creatures he desires to be in relationship with, this has implications for our ability to know God as he really is.

influence the everyday lives of Christian disciples, I want to take the discussion a step further, arguing here that, given the role the Holy Spirit plays in Torrance's theological realism, it not only possesses huge epistemological implications; it also entails the possibility that, *through the Spirit of Christ,* Jesus' followers can have *existentially-impactful* (life-shaping, ministry-engendering, faithfulness-producing) encounters with him. In other words, a pneumatological realism is nothing less than a logical, biblically-mandated, life-altering entailment of a theological realism![40]

40. Some rather impressive support for this contention can be found in Philip Rosato's discussion titled "The Father and the Son Meeting Man from Within" in which we find several allusions to the realism implicit in the pneumatology of Karl Barth—a realism which possesses an existential as well as epistemological significance. Scattered throughout this discussion are repeated references to God's reality and his very real working in human history toward the goal of a real, transformational "relationship" or "communion" with humanity through the Holy Spirit (see Rosato, *The Spirit as Lord,* 60–65). For example, Rosato explains that "it is the God the Holy Spirit, God in His third mode of existence, who according to Barth makes the actions of the Father and of the Son become historical *realities. . . .* The Holy Spirit is God personally manifest to and in men . . . 'men who become what by themselves and of themselves they can neither be nor become, men who belong to God, who are in *real communion* with God, who live before God and with God.' Man's being-related to God, being present before him and with him is the distinct work of the Holy Spirit" (Rosato, *The Spirit as Lord,* 60, emphasis added. The citation is from Barth, *Church Dogmatics,* I/1, 450). And again, says Rosato: "When Barth first turns his attention to an explicit chapter on the Holy Spirit in the *Church Dogmatics,* he speaks of God coming to man, binding himself to man, claiming man for Himself, becoming man's, making man His own. When this does happen, it can only be God's own *reality* at work; such a close *union* of God and man can lie only in God's power: 'It is God's *reality,* by God being subjectively present to men not only from without, not only from above, but also from within, from beneath. It is *reality,* therefore, by God not only coming to man, but meeting Himself from man's end. God's freedom to be thus present to man and hence to introduce this meeting—that is the Spirit of God, the Holy Spirit in God's revelation'" (Rosato, *The Spirit as Lord,* 60, emphasis added. The citation is from Barth, *Church Dogmatics,* I/1, 451). Moreover, it's worth noting that a detail included in the middle of this discussion that is quite relevant to the thesis I'm proffering in this work is provided by Rosato when he explains that "Barth reiterates here that his presentation of the Spirit as the sole source of *communion* not only between the Father and the Son from eternity but also between man and God in revelation is intended to be a clear answer to the ambiguities of either an *overly philosophical, overly-institutional* or *overly-personal* understanding of the Holy Spirit (Rosato, *The Spirit as Lord,* 63, emphasis added). Apparently, Barth himself felt the need to argue for a pneumatological realism against understandings of the Spirit he considered deficient.

FIGURE 4

This is why, throughout both *A Missional Orthodoxy* and my latest work, *Pursuing Moral Faithfulness*, I make numerous references to the idea that by means of the incarnation of Christ and outpouring of the Holy Spirit, our Trinitarian God has made it possible for those "in Christ"[41] to know and interact with him in a real, rather than merely conceptual, abstract, or ideal, manner.[42] While to my knowledge neither Torrance nor Davis refer to a "pneumatological realism" per se, both of their versions of a theological realism are highly evocative of it and support the notion that something akin to it is critical to the cultivation of ecclesial environments that actually succeed in the spiritual, moral, and ministry formation of church members, mitigating a functional deism/Christian nominalism in the process.[43]

41. See Eph 1:3–4; cf. Acts 26:18; Rom 15:14–16; 1 Cor 1:2; 6:9–11.

42. I would like to think that, because of my emphasis on the possibility of phenomenal, transformational, history-shaping encounters with the Spirit, my version of a pneumatological realism avoids the gnosticizing of the Spirit Pannenberg complained about.

43. Since writing *A Missional Orthodoxy* and *Pursuing Moral Faithfulness*, I have become aware of the manner in which Amos Yong likewise emphasizes the role of the Holy Spirit in his version of a critical realism. In addition to the other works included in this book's bibliography, I'd like to draw the reader's attention to Christopher Stephenson's helpful treatment of Yong's concepts of "foundational pneumatology," "pneumatological imagination," and "communal interpretation" in Stephenson, *Types of Pentecostal Theology*, 86–92.

Apologia: Paul and the "Disciples" in Ephesus

The ultimate goal of this foundational essay was to explain what I have in mind when I refer to a pneumatological realism, and why I've become such a persistent advocate for it. I'd like to think that I accomplished this task even if some sections of the chapter may have been especially challenging for my non-academic readers. I want to conclude the essay by underscoring here why it's very important that our journey together continues.

In Acts 19:1–2 we read that after spending an unspecified amount of time with some "disciples" he'd come across in the city of Ephesus, the Apostle Paul felt impressed to inquire about their experience with the Holy Spirit. Apparently, there was something about these folks that, at first, suggested they were followers of Jesus. And yet, something didn't add up; Paul was expecting to see more. When he didn't, he boldly posed the question, "Did you receive the Holy Spirit when you believed?" To which their answer was, "No, we have not even heard that there is a Holy Spirit." It turned out that these "disciples" were, in Paul's mind, in need of a Jesus-specific baptism in water, and phenomenon-producing encounter with his Spirit (Acts 19:3–4).

My potentially provocative suggestion is that this passage presents us with a terrible possibility: nominal "disciples" (apparent believers in Jesus) not fully alive in the Spirit of Christ. Though I refer to this as a mere possibility, Paul experienced it firsthand and took it very seriously. Because of this, I'm of the opinion that this "possibility" should concern all of us—especially those whose calling involves the spiritual, moral, and ministry formation of Jesus' followers.[44]

There really is a pneumatological deficit at work in too many evangelical (and Pentevangelical) congregations. This widespread acceptance of a truncated, impoverished doctrine of the Holy Spirit has created space in our churches for a functional deism/Christian nominalism to take root and flourish. The effect of this encroachment on genuine disciple making

---

44. It should be noted that Karl Barth referred to the "disciples of John in Ephesus" when discussing the phenomenon of "unspiritual theology" produced by what Barth considered the "departure of the Spirit from theology." In the course of this discussion, Barth warned: "Only the Spirit himself can rescue theology! He, the Holy One, the Lord, the Giver of Life, waits and waits to be received anew by theology as by the community. He waits to receive from theology his due of adoration and glorification. He expects from theology that it submit itself to the repentance, renewal, and reformation he effects. He waits to vivify and illuminate its affirmations which, however right they may be, are dead without the Spirit" (Barth, *Evangelical Theology*, 57).

is truly tragic. Indeed, given the discipleship deficit which also seems to be a reality in our contemporary era, I sometimes wonder: were the Apostle Paul to visit some of our churches, if he wouldn't be tempted to ask the folks the same question he put to the "disciples" in Ephesus!

The good news is that in parts two and three of this book we'll discuss at length how we can become the kind of Spirit-empowered disciples Paul wouldn't worry about. However, before we begin those discussions, it's necessary that we gain an even better understanding of what the terrible alternative is. As it happens, that's what the next chapter is all about.

2

Functional Deism: A Surprisingly Pervasive Theological/Ministry Malady

Are you so foolish? After beginning by means of the Spirit, are you now trying to finish by means of the flesh?

—GALATIANS 3:3

EASTERN ORTHODOX THEOLOGIAN KALLISTOS Ware is careful to make clear that: "Christianity is not merely a philosophical theory or a moral code, but involves a direct sharing in divine life and glory, a transforming union with God "face to face." [1] It certainly seems that, without using the term, Ware is describing a Christianity that's grounded in a theological realism.

We've learned already that at the heart of a theological realism are two main contentions: (1) everything that "is" owes its existence to God as the ultimate reality, and (2) because of the revelatory ministry of Jesus the God-man (John 1:18; Heb 1:1–3), and the outpouring of his Spirit upon those who belong to him (1 Cor 2:11–16; 1 John 2:20), it's possible for Christ's followers to know and relate to God in a *real* rather than *merely* theoretical, conceptual, or ritualistic manner.[2]

Unfortunately, however, there's another version of the Christian religion at work in North America; one which, despite its creedal orthodoxy,

---

1. Ware, "Eastern Tradition," 246.

2. For more on this, see the section titled "Revelation as God's Self-Disclosure" in Bird, *Evangelical Theology*, 167–70.

36

is functionally deistic rather than fully realistic in its outworking. In other words, it's possible for members of even evangelical churches to profess a commitment to orthodox Christian doctrines while living day-to-day in an essentially deistic manner. For these folks, the Christian faith is more of a philosophy of life and/or moral code than a real, intimate, interactive, transformational relationship with God the Father, through Christ the Son, by means of the Holy Spirit. Though they may pray, sing, and even serve, it's the *idea of God* these church members are interacting with rather than *God himself.*

Before we can fully appreciate the importance of a pneumatological realism to the spiritual, moral, and ministry formation of contemporary Christians, we need to understand what this deistic alternative to a biblically-informed understanding of Christian faith and life is, and how it negatively impacts a church's ministry fruitfulness. Toward this end, this chapter will present three brief but pungent discussions of: (1) the essence and effect of the "classical" deism put forward by eighteenth century Enlightenment thinkers; (2) the nature and impact of a virulent version of a "functional" deism that's currently at work in the lives of many American Christians; and (3) why the cure for the theological/ministry malady known as Moralistic Therapeutic Deism must involve the recovery of a vigorous, full-throated doctrine of the Holy Spirit. While the contemporary significance of the latter two discussions is obvious, I want to suggest that taking the time to slog through the first one—the one that's more historical in nature—will also pay some rich dividends.

The Essence and Effect of Classical Deism

Deism is a theological perspective—a way of understanding the nature of God and the God-world relationship—that has some huge implications for how its adherents approach the Christian life. Before we discuss the functional deism prevalent within contemporary Christian churches (even some conservative ones), we need to possess a basic understanding of the classical deism which became extremely popular in Europe and North America during the seventeenth and eighteenth centuries.

Originally, says theologian Roger Olson, "Deism was not so much a doctrine of God, as many mistakenly suppose, as *a view of religious knowledge* that placed common principles of human reason and common ideas of humanity at the center and judged all claims to special revelation by them."[3] In other words, at the heart of classical deism was the conviction that *all religious beliefs should be grounded in human reason rather than divine revelation*. If, as many classical deists held, Christianity is superior to all other world religions, it's only because it accords best with right reason—i.e., is more rationally defensible than all the alternatives. Moreover, any Christian doctrine that doesn't accord with human reason should be considered suspect and, at the very least, neglected, if not actually abandoned.[4]

Why did these eighteenth century Christian intellectuals place so much focus on human reason? What effect did this stringent focus on reason have upon their understanding of the Christian faith and Christian living? To what degree is Christian deism a deviant version of the historic Christian faith? These are important questions that, as we'll soon see, really do possess a striking degree of contemporary relevance.

The Historical Causes for Classical Deism

In his book, *Christianity Through the Centuries,* Earle Cairns refers to several historical developments which contributed to the advent of deism in the seventeenth century. These generative developments included: (1) the emergence of modern science and the way it tended, ultimately, to demystify creation (by causing people to "look on the universe as a machine or mechanism that operated by inflexible natural laws"[5]); (2) the way in which international trade enabled Europeans to become acquainted with the religions of other cultures (causing them to "wonder whether there was a basic natural religion that all men had apart from the Bible or priests"[6]); and (3) the manner in which "the new philosophies of empiricism and rationalism also challenged tradition in the name of reason" (leading more and more Europeans to opt for "reason and man's senses" over divine revelation as "the main avenues to knowledge"[7]).

For his part, historical theologian Roger Olson adds to this list of historical causes the observation that another reason why deism caught on was the frustration on the part of many Europeans with the strident

3. Olson, *Story of Christian Theology,* 520, emphasis added.

4. Ibid., 520.

5. Cairns, *Christianity Through the Centuries,* 377.

6. Ibid., 377.

7. Ibid., 377.

sectarianism (infighting) that earmarked Christianity in the aftermath of the Protestant reformation.[8] According to Olson, because deism "emphasized the authority of reason in all matters, including religion," it "dreamed of a reasonable, universal religion that would overcome sectarian strife, superstition and irrational, arbitrary authority, and usher Christianity into a modern age of peace, enlightenment and toleration."[9]

Essentially bringing all of these historical causes together, Olson explains the emergence of deism thusly:

> Disillusioned by sectarian strife, turned off by religious intolerance and controversy, and energized by a new vision of culture, science and philosophy sparked by the Enlightenment, the Deists attempted to reconstruct Christian thought. They were convinced that unless Christianity could be shown to be thoroughly reasonable in terms of the criteria used by Enlightenment thought, it would eventually become irrelevant and die out. They were also convinced that unless it could be shown to be in its essence a universal, rational, natural religion for all thinking people everywhere, it would continue to split apart into warring factions. What the Deists needed was a nonmysterious, rational and universal Christianity that transcended denominational and confessional boundaries and had no need of suprarational faith or internal testimonies of the Holy Spirit to persuade and convince people of its truth. What they ended up with was a generic religion that was a pale theism stripped of almost everything distinctively Christian.[10]

The Main Tenets of Classical Deism

This summative description of deism suggests that the key to understanding it is to focus on the notion of *natural religion*. Renowned Christian historian Kenneth Scott Latourette affirms this suggestion explicitly, and then explains that the natural religion the deists had in mind "was said to be universal, discernible by all men everywhere through their reason, quite apart from special revelation."[11]

8. Olson, *Counterfeit Christianity*, 142; Olson, *Story of Christian Theology*, 519, 521–22.

9. Olson, *Story of Christian Theology*, 519.

10. Ibid., 523.

11. Latourette, *History of Christianity*, 1004. See also Olson, *Counterfeit Christianity*, 145. We should keep in mind, however, that, as Roland Bainton reminds us, once Deism

Furthermore, it appears that one way the deists endeavored to get at the essence of natural religion was to identify those core beliefs that all the major world religions seemed to have in common. According to historical theologian Justo González, deism is what resulted from this "attempt to reduce religion to its basic, most universally held, and most reasonable elements."[12] González, goes on to identify the main forerunner of deism as "Lord Herbert of Cherbury (1538–1648), who rejected the notion of special revelation and attempted to show that all religions have five points in common: the existence of God, the obligation to worship him, the moral character of this worship, the need to repent for sin, and an afterlife of reward and punishment."[13] "These," says González, "were the basic tenets of the English Deists of the eighteenth century."[14]

The Effect Classical Deism Had Upon the Christian Faith

Though the English deists thought they were saving Christianity from the religion-busting effects of the Enlightenment mindset, the faith they created was much different than the one known by Christ's apostles and the church fathers. To be more specific, the description of deism's dogmas presented below demonstrates how a commitment to nothing but natural religion dramatically impacted/altered many of the doctrines central to the Christian faith:

> Deism, a religion without written revelation, emphasized the starry heaven above and the moral law within. One of the main dogmas of deism . . . was the belief in a transcendent God who was the First Cause of a creation marked by evidences of design. The deists believed that God left His creation to operate under natural laws; hence, there was no place for miracles, the Bible as a revelation from God, prophecy, providence, or Christ as a God-man. The deists taught that Christ was only a moral teacher and insisted that worship belonged to God. Another dogma was the belief that "virtue and piety" were the most important worship that one could

"became a widespread phenomenon throughout Europe and in the English colonies," it "developed national varieties" and "was no more able than were the sects to achieve universal concord" (Bainton, *Christianity*, 322).

12. González, *History of Christian Thought*, 306.

13. Ibid., 3:306. See also Olson, *Counterfeit Christianity*, 142–43; and Olson, *Story of Christian Theology*, 524.

14. Ibid., 3:306.

give to God. God's ethical laws are in the Bible, which is an ethical guidebook, and in the nature of man, where they can be discovered by human reason. A person must repent of wrongdoing and have his life conform to ethical laws because there is immortality and each individual faces reward and punishment after death.[15]

Allow me to provide my own summary of some of the ways in which classical deism differed from a biblically-informed understanding of the Christian faith:

- First, the God of deism was viewed primarily not as a divine person capable of and interested in a relationship with human beings created in his image,[16] but as: a philosophical concept (i.e., First Cause);[17] a non-Trinitarian[18] architect of the cosmos;[19] a moral lawgiver/governor;[20] and an absentee landlord who left the world to run on the basis of immutable natural laws that are discernible by reason.[21]

- Second, this view of God as an utterly transcendent[22] (i.e., not personal or relational[23]), non-intervening[24] deity leads to a huge amount of skepticism, if not rejection, of the ideas of miracles and divine providence (i.e., God's gracious involvement in our everyday lives).[25]

15. Cairns, *Christianity Through the Centuries*, 378–79.

16. Bainton, *Christianity*, 322; Olson, *Mosaic of Christian Belief*, 121.

17. Cairns, *Christianity Through the Centuries*, 378; Olson, *Mosaic of Christian Belief*, 122, 188.

18. Latourette, *History of Christianity*, 984, 1004; Olson, *Story of Christian Theology*, 520, 527.

19. Bainton, *Christianity*, 322; Latourette, *History of Christianity*, 984, 1004; Olson, *Counterfeit Christianity*, 145; Olson, *Mosaic of Christian Belief*, 121.

20. Latourette, *History of Christianity*, 984, 1004; Olson, *Counterfeit Christianity*, 145; Olson, *Mosaic of Christian Belief*, 121, 188; Olson, *Story of Christian Theology*, 529.

21. Bainton, *Christianity*, 322; Cairns, *Christianity Through the Centuries*, 378; Olson, *Counterfeit Christianity*, 145; Olson, *Mosaic of Christian Belief*, 121, 188.

22. Cairns, *Christianity Through the Centuries*, 378; Olson, *The Mosaic of Christian Belief*, 121.

23. Bainton, *Christianity*, 322. Cf. Olson, *The Mosaic of Christian Belief*, 120–22.

24. Ibid., 121; Olson, *The Story of Christian Theology*, 531. Cf. Olson, *The Mosaic of Christian Belief*, 188.

25. Cairns, *Christianity Through the Centuries*, 378; Latourette, *A History of Christianity*, 1004; Olson, *Counterfeit Christianity*, 144–45, 148; Olson, *The Mosaic of Christian Belief*, 122; Olson, *The Story of Christian Theology*, 531.

- Third, this in turn leads to either the neglect or rejection of the divine inspiration of the Christian scriptures,[26] and the incarnation of Christ,[27] who is viewed simply as a gifted but merely human social prophet and moral teacher.[28]

- Fourth, since the Christian life is reduced to ethics (i.e., striving to be a good, moral person according to ethical principles that, while presented in the Bible, are also discernible by human reason alone[29]), there was no room in classical deism for the notion of salvation by grace through faith in Christ.[30]

These are just some of the ways in which classical deism differed from historic Christianity. Hopefully, this cursory summary is sufficient for the purpose at hand, which is to help the reader recognize just how damaging any sort of deism is to a biblically-informed Christian discipleship. In his book *Counterfeit Christianity*, Roger Olson makes the following assertion: "I would call anyone *primarily* a Deist who believes: (1) that God exists as the creator and moral governor of the universe but is uninvolved in daily life and never intervenes supernaturally in the courses of nature and history, and (2) religion is primarily, if not exclusively, about morality—living a 'good life' of being nice to others and true to oneself."[31] Olson then goes on to explain why deism should be considered a heresy—a version of Christianity that is "beyond the pale of orthodoxy"[32]:

> It's a heresy because it is "another gospel" than the one we find in the New Testament. The New Testament gospel, understood this way by all branches of historic orthodox Christianity, is *not* that

26. Cairns, *Christianity Through the Centuries*, 378; Latourette, *A History of Christianity*, 984–85, 1004; Olson, *Counterfeit Christianity*, 145.

27. Cairns, *Christianity Through the Centuries*, 378; Latourette, *A History of Christianity*, 985, 1004; Olson, *Counterfeit Christianity*, 144; Olson, *The Story of Christian Theology*, 520, 523.

28. Bainton, *Christianity*, 322; Cairns, *Christianity Through the Centuries*, 378; Olson, *Counterfeit Christianity*, 145; Olson, *The Mosaic of Christian Belief*, 60–61; Olson, *The Story of Christian Theology*, 527–28, 530–31.

29. Cairns, *Christianity Through the Centuries*, 378–79; Latourette, *A History of Christianity*, 984, 1004; Olson, *Counterfeit Christianity*, 145; Olson, *The Story of Christian Theology*, 520, 529.

30. Latourette, *History of Christianity*, 985, 1004; Olson, *Story of Christian Theology*, 529.

31. Olson, *Counterfeit Christianity*, 148.

32. See Olson, *Mosaic of Christian Belief*, 121.

we achieve salvation by living a good moral life but *that* we are sinners who can only be saved by God's grace and that God has reached across the gulf between him and us caused by our sin to bring us salvation through Jesus Christ's death on the cross and his resurrection. In other words, according to Jesus and the apostles who wrote the New Testament, the church fathers and Protestant reformers, the great evangelists and teachers of all denominations in the past, and faithful theologians of the present, true religion is about *sin* and *grace*, not *being good*.[33]

And then, Olson offers this bold summary:

Deism is heresy. It reduces the biblical and Christian picture of God to something small, so insignificant, so banal as to be unimportant. And it can be very dangerous insofar as it leads people to think salvation comes through their own efforts, even if God helps a little (somehow). It is at best a pale reflection of robust "thick" Christianity. It is at best Christianity that has lost its power. It is negotiated and accommodated Christianity if it is Christianity at all.[34]

Moralistic Therapeutic Deism: The Functional Deism at Work in Our Own Era

It's a premise of this work that one doesn't have to refer to oneself as a "Deist" to be one in a *de facto* manner. In other words, there's such a thing as a *functional deism* which occurs when church members who profess orthodox Christian beliefs nevertheless live each day not really expecting to experience God in ways that are personal, interactive, transformational, and ministry-engendering. It goes without saying that such a version of the Christian life will greatly impair the ability of individual Christians and congregations as a whole to impact their culture for Christ.

We've already seen how Roger Olson has characterized deism as a version of Christianity that has "lost its power." Support for this assertion can be found in the findings of a reputable sociological study which suggests that a contemporary version of deism is actually the lived religion of literally millions of North Americans.[35]

33. Olson, *Counterfeit Christianity*, 149, emphasis original.

34. Ibid, 150–51.

35. The ensuing discussion of Moralistic Therapeutic Deism is adapted from my treatment of this topic in Tyra, *Pursuing Moral Faithfulness*, 129–41.

The National Study of Youth and Religion (NSYR) conducted by Christian Smith, Professor of Sociology at the University of Notre Dame, and Lisa Pearce, Assistant Professor of Sociology at the University of North Carolina at Chapel Hill,[36] is an "ambitious study of American teenagers . . . involving extensive interviews of more than 3,300 American teens between the ages of thirteen and seventeen (including telephone interviews of these teenagers' parents)."[37] Though the first phase of the study was conducted between 2002 and 2005, it "also involves an ongoing longitudinal component that has so far revisited more than 2,500 of these young people to understand how their religious lives are changing as they enter emerging adulthood."[38]

The most authoritative work reporting on this landmark study is *Soul Searching: The Religious and Spiritual Lives of American Teenagers*, penned by project leader Christian Smith along with Melinda Lundquist Denton. In this book, the authors make the bold suggestion that "the de facto dominant religion among contemporary US teenagers is what we might call 'Moralistic Therapeutic Deism.'"[39] If what these researchers suggest is true, it provides some powerful (and tragic) support for the thesis of this chapter: there is such a thing as a functional deism, and it constitutes a surprisingly pervasive theological/ministry malady at work in even some conservative, evangelical churches.

The Main Tenets of Moralistic Therapeutic Deism (MTD)

Soul Searching lists five core beliefs which lie at the heart of the worldview to which they've attached the name, "Moralistic Therapeutic Deism." These five principal convictions are:

1. A god exists who created and ordered the world and watches over human life on earth.

2. God wants people to be good, nice, and fair to each other, as taught in the Bible and by most world religions.

3. The central goal of life is to be happy and to feel good about oneself.

---

36. See http://youthandreligion.nd.edu/.

37. Dean, *Almost Christian*, 16.

38. Ibid., 16.

39. Smith, *Soul Searching*, 162.

4. God does not need to be particularly involved in one's life except when God is needed to resolve a problem.

5. Good people go to heaven when they die.[40]

MTD's Essence

Perhaps the best way to wrap our heads around what MTD is and why it should concern us is to allow the principal author of *Soul Searching*, Christian Smith, to explain why he considers this widespread worldview to be a *moralistic* and *therapeutic* version of *deism*.[41]

First, Smith suggests that this worldview is *moralistic* because it "is about inculcating a moralistic approach to life. It teaches that central to living a good and happy life is being a good, moral person."[42] As for what being a good, moral person involves, Smith explains that it means "being nice, kind, pleasant, respectful, responsible, at work on self-improvement, taking care of one's health, and doing one's best to be successful."[43]

Second, Smith goes on to make the critical observation that this belief system as a whole is "about providing therapeutic benefits to its adherents."[44] This explains the adjective *therapeutic*. There's virtually no emphasis in this religious worldview on the need for church-goers to repent of their sins, engage in spiritual disciplines, or to willingly suffer for the cause of Christ. Instead, says Smith, "what appears to be the actual dominant religion among US teenagers is centrally about feeling good, happy, secure, at peace. It's about attaining subjective well-being, being able to resolve problems, and getting along amiably with other people."[45]

This is not to say that the adherents of MTD don't engage in some religious practices. However, according to the thousands of interviews conducted by Smith and his research team, the main reason why many teens and young adults engage in any sort of religious practice is how it makes them feel—good and/or happy.[46] Thus, it appears that the primary goal of

40. Ibid., 162–63.

41. For the sake of convenience, I will sometimes refer to Smith alone as the primary author of this work.

42. Smith, *Soul Searching*, 163.

43. Ibid., 163.

44. Ibid., 163.

45. Ibid., 163–64.

46. Ibid., 164.

MTD is not to serve God or the kingdom's cause, but oneself. Integral to MTD is the conviction that religion is all about enabling people to be happy and successful. *The sovereignty of God has been replaced by the sovereignty of the self.* This is another critical distinction between MTD and a more biblically-informed understanding of the Christian faith and lifestyle.

Third, according to Smith, the reason why MTD is considered a version of *deism* is because of the way it views the nature of God and the manner in which he interacts with human beings. Says Smith, "Moralistic Therapeutic Deism is about belief in a particular kind of God: one who exists, created the world, and defines our general moral order, but not one who is particularly personally involved in one's affairs—especially affairs in which one would prefer not to have God involved. Most of the time, the God of this faith keeps a safe distance."[47] It's this notion of a distance-maintaining deity that causes Smith to see a similarity between the worldview dubbed MTD and the understanding of God put forward by the classical deists.

And yet, Smith is careful to point out that there is an important *dissimilarity* between MTD and classical deism. Referring to this dissimilarity as the "therapeutic qualifier," Smith explains that it evidences itself in the fact that many teens (and adults) believe that "God sometimes does get involved in people's lives, but usually only when they call on him, mostly when they have some trouble or problem or bad feeling they want resolved."[48]

Thus, the distinction between MTD's conception of God and that of classical deism is ultimately not significant. Despite what is confessed or sung about in church, the God of MTD need not be Trinitarian or incarnate in Christ! Accordingly, missing from MTD is any serious notion of Christian discipleship or disciple making. Indeed, Smith explains:

> This God is not demanding. He actually can't be, because his job is to solve our problems and make people feel good. In short, God is something like a combination Divine Butler and Cosmic Therapist: he is always on call, takes care of any problems that arise, professionally helps his people to feel better about themselves, and does not become too personally involved in the process.[49]

The problem is that anyone who knows their Bible will be hard-pressed to square MTD's understanding of God, Christ, the nature of salvation, and the goal of the Christian life with that of historic, orthodox Christianity.

47. Ibid., 164.
48. Ibid., 165.
49. Ibid., 165.

MTD's Extent

Though none of the teens and young adults interviewed as part of the NSYR described themselves as adherents of MTD per se, Smith makes the assertion that "[s]uch a de facto creed is particularly evident among mainline Protestant and Catholic youth" and "is also visible among black and conservative Protestants, Jewish teens, other religious types of teenagers, and even many non-religious teenagers in the United States."[50] In other words, Moralistic Therapeutic Deism is much more prevalent among America's youth than most church-going adults realize.

Moreover, we need to be clear about the fact that Smith is *not* suggesting that MTD is limited to America's teens. No, the startling observation made by the authors of *Soul Searching* is that MTD seems to be a "widespread, popular faith among very many U.S. adults" as well![51] According to Smith and his research team, "[o]ur religiously conventional adolescents seem to be merely absorbing and reflecting religiously what the adult world is routinely modeling for and inculcating in its youth."[52] They go on to assert that "most American youth faithfully mirror the aspirations, lifestyles, practices, and problems of the adult world into which they are being socialized. In these ways, adolescents may actually serve as a very accurate barometer of the condition of the culture and institutions of our larger society."[53] Provocatively drawing attention to the role of church in this inculturation process, Kenda Creasy Dean, Associate Professor of Youth, Church and Culture at Princeton University, offers that "the faith teenagers develop during adolescence serves as a kind of barometer of the religious inclination of the culture that surrounds them."[54] Indeed, in her book *Almost Christian: What the Faith of our Teenagers is Telling the American Church,* Dean boldly asserts that nearly everything that is amiss in the spiritual lives of America's teens can be attributed to a failure on the part of parents and the institutional church to model what a vibrant, biblically-informed Christian discipleship really involves.[55]

50. Ibid., 163.

51. Ibid., 166.

52. Ibid., 166.

53. Ibid., 191. See also Dean, *Almost Christian*, 9; Powell et al., *Growing Young*, 131, 133.

54. Dean, *Almost Christian*, 9.

55. Ibid., 12, 15–16, 18. See also, Smith, *Souls in Transition*, 33; Smith, *Lost in Transition*, 60–61.

MTD's Effect

Perhaps the most shocking conclusion reported on by Smith and his team concerns the long-term impact of MTD on the American religious landscape. The evidence seems to point to the reality that only a tiny minority of US teenagers really understand and are concerned to maintain the historic tenets and practices of the religious tradition to which they claim to belong. Instead, say Smith and his co-authors, "another popular religious faith, Moralistic Therapeutic Deism, is colonizing many historical religious traditions and, almost without anyone noticing, converting believers in the old faiths to its alternative religious vision of divinely underwritten personal happiness and interpersonal niceness."[56] Then, commenting on the impact of MTD on American Christianity in particular, Smith and his team offer this especially dire assessment:

> [W]e can say here that we have come with some confidence to believe that a significant part of Christianity in the United States is actually only tenuously Christian in any sense that is seriously connected to the actual historical Christian tradition, but has rather substantially morphed into Christianity's misbegotten step-cousin, Christian Moralistic Therapeutic Deism. . . . The language, and therefore experience of Trinity, holiness, sin, grace, justification, sanctification, church, Eucharist, and heaven and hell appear, among most Christian teenagers in the United States at the very least, to be supplanted by the language of happiness, niceness, and an earned heavenly reward. It is not so much that U.S. Christianity is being secularized. Rather more subtly, Christianity is either degenerating into a pathetic version of itself or, more significantly, Christianity is actively being colonized and displaced by a quite different religious faith.[57]

The Presence of MTD in Evangelical Churches

In his book *Future Church: Ministry in a Post-Seeker Age*, Jim Wilson shares the following true story:

> Sitting in a window seat, Roger Williams III was looking forward to thumbing through a magazine on a short flight from Sacramento

56. Smith, *Soul Searching*, 171.
57. Ibid., 171.

to attend a national youth ministry conference in San Diego. He'd fastened his seatbelt, made sure his chair was in the full upright position, his tray table locked, and his luggage properly stowed, when two well-dressed Ally McBeal look-alikes sat down next to him. Their conversation competed for attention with his magazine. They talked about the club scene—what they enjoyed drinking, who they were dating, their intimate relationships with men, both single and married. Then it turned into a gripe session.

"Why do guys have such a hard time committing?" one asked. "And why don't they ever leave their wives like they promise to?" another complained. They talked about work for a while, and about the time Williams was tuning out, one of them said, "But you know, if it wasn't for church, my life would really be hell."

By now Williams was only pretending to read his magazine. They had his full attention.

"Wow, you go to church too. I know exactly how you feel. If it wasn't for church, I don't know where I'd be."

"Yeah, I know what you mean," the other woman said. "If I miss more than two weeks of church, everything in my life goes nuts."

The plane started its descent into San Diego, and everything got quiet. Williams sat still—stunned by what he'd just heard. These women weren't genuine seekers—people looking for the truth. Instead they were going to church to get their religious fix.[58]

Though Wilson didn't use the term "Moralistic Therapeutic Deism" to describe the religious experience of these two young women (*Future Church* was published the year prior to the publication of *Soul Searching*), it certainly seems appropriate from our vantage point to do so. And yet, it should be noted that Wilson's goal in sharing this story was not to castigate these women for their rather shallow understanding of the nature of Christian commitment. Rather, his aim was to ask some important questions about the churches they were attending. Wilson continues:

These women on the plane didn't need a sermon on five steps to success. They didn't need a Band-Aid. They needed transformation. They were getting a faith inoculation when they needed an antidote for sin. They needed a church that would confront them, not accommodate them. They needed a church that would get past their felt needs and speak to their greatest need, to confess their sin and turn to Christ.[59]

58. Wilson, *Future Church*, 78–79.

59. Ibid., 80.

At least a year before the results of the NSYR were released, Jim Wilson expressed his concern that, for too many folks, attending church services is about getting a "religious fix" rather than becoming a part of a genuine Christian community that will enable them to experience spiritual and moral transformation into men and women of God. I'll have more to say about the need for churches to do a better job at the spiritual, moral, and ministry formation of their members in the pages that follow. The difficult and perhaps provocative question I want to address at this point is this: To what degree is a discipleship-defeating, faithfulness-frustrating understanding of God and the Christian faith at work among evangelicals? It's one thing to acknowledge that an embrace of MTD might earmark the lives of those who attend non-conservative, non-evangelical churches; it's another to contemplate the possibility that a functional deism could be at work in the membership of churches which pride themselves on not having compromised the historic Christian faith despite the influences of both modernity and late-modernity. So, to be even more precise, the question I'm posing here is this: Can we presume that all the members of all evangelical churches are necessarily immune to the spiritual/ecclesial illness this chapter is about?

Sadly, I'm convinced that the answer to this crucial question must be "no." As someone who works every day with members of the emerging generations, I can attest to the fact that, unfortunately, Moralistic Therapeutic Deism is alive and well in many evangelical homes and churches. Too many of my students, even those who hail from evangelical and Pentevangelical churches, arrive at the university bearing all the earmarks of MTD as described by Smith and his team. These earmarks include: a lack of theological fluency,[60] a troubling degree of biblical and theological ignorance,[61] a profound tendency toward moral autonomy rather than accountability,[62] and virtually no commitment to contend for the historic Christian faith.[63]

Moreover, every semester, and in more than one course I teach, I introduce my university students to the findings of the NSYR. Over the years I've found that once they're made aware of the research indicating the existence and prevalence of MTD within their demographic, the response of many of my students follows a predictable pattern: *alarm*, then

---

60. Smith, *Soul Searching*, 131.

61. Ibid., 131.

62. Ibid., 143.

63. Ibid., 171.

acknowledgement, then *appreciation*. The sense of alarm is nearly universal. But, after acknowledging the presence of at least some aspects of MTD in their own lives and those of their peers, many students go on to state that being made aware of the jaw-dropping specifics of MTD offers them some powerful motivation toward personal spiritual renewal. Indeed, more than a few students have actually expressed appreciation for the exposé, indicating that the findings generated by the NSYR and reported on in *Soul Searching* provides them with language they can use when expressing concern for the spiritual welfare of their family members and friends.

While this evidence is anecdotal in nature, the reader should know that it's not limited to my students. I've shared the material presented in this chapter with numbers of academic and pastoral colleagues as well. Without fail, the response pattern has been the same: alarm, acknowledgment, and appreciation. Put differently, I cannot recall a time I've shared the findings of the NSYR with professional colleagues without the bulk of them appearing to resonate with it. It really does seem to be the case that in the religious lives of way-too-many evangelical teens and young adults, a virulent version of a functional deism is at work, which serves as a huge impediment to a biblically-informed Christian discipleship. This is why I'm so insistent that evangelical pastors of all stripes need to take seriously the possibility that significant numbers of our parishioners are *not* relating to God in the *realistic* manner we see occurring in the Bible.

The Proposed Cure for MTD

Several excellent books have been written which offer practical prescriptions for how the church should respond to the problem of teenagers losing their faith and leaving the church as they enter young adulthood.[64] One such work is the aforementioned *Almost Christian: What the Faith of our Teenagers is telling the American Church* by Kenda Creasy Dean. In this work, Dean offers the following bold diagnosis:

> After two and a half centuries of shacking up with "the American dream," churches have perfected a dicey codependence between consumer-driven therapeutic individualism and religious pragmatism. These theological proxies gnaw, termite-like, at our identity

64. For example, see Dunn and Sundene, *Shaping the Journey*, and Powell et al., *Growing Young*. In addition, an excellent book which focuses on what each family within the church can do to combat the problem stated above is Powell and Clark, *Sticky Faith*.

as the Body of Christ, eroding our ability to recognize that Jesus'
life of self-giving love directly challenges the American gospel of
self-fulfillment and self-actualization.[65]

Dean is insisting that at the heart of Christian MTD is an accommodation to contemporary American cultural values that's made possible by
a shallow, theologically deficient understanding of what genuine Christian
discipleship entails. Indeed, says Dean: "American young people are un-
wittingly being formed into an imposter faith that poses as Christianity,
but that in fact lacks the holy desire and missional clarity necessary for
Christian discipleship."[66]

Essentially agreeing with Dean's analysis of the MTD phenomenon,
Roger Olson makes two prescriptive assertions of his own: (1) "Christians
need to recover a sense of the countercultural nature of the gospel";[67] and
(2) "Christians need to rediscover, without going overboard or to extremes,
the God who is involved, who hears and answers prayer, who is both loving
and just, and who cannot be captured and tamed."[68]

Both Dean and Olson appear to be contending that at the heart of the
functional deism currently plaguing the American church is a *discipleship
deficit*[69] that's enabled by a *deficient theology*. While I concur with this diagnosis, my concern is that it needs to be augmented in an important manner.
Truth be told, it's possible for the members of theologically conservative,
Bible-believing/teaching churches to profess an orthodox (Trinitarian)
understanding of God while at the same time living day-to-day without
any expectation of a real experience of him. What's missing from the faith
orientation of even some evangelicals is the theological realism alluded to
in chapter 1 of this work. In other words, it's not simply a theological defi-
ciency, but the absence of a theologically real approach to the Christian life,
that greatly enhances the likelihood of even evangelical church members
embracing a culture-accommodating, discipleship-defeating functional
deism. Moreover, as the concluding section of this essay will indicate, I'm
concerned that many evangelical church leaders don't properly recognize

65. Dean, *Almost Christian*, 5.

66. Ibid., 6.

67. Olson, *Counterfeit Christianity*, 152.

68. Ibid., 151.

69. For more on the "discipleship deficit" currently observable in even evangelical
churches, see Tyra, *Defeating Pharisaism*, 194–97, and Tyra, *Pursuing Moral Faithfulness*,
15–16.

just how much a theologically real experience of God and Christ depend upon on a doctrine of the Holy Spirit that's dynamic rather than static in character.[70]

Why the Cure for Functional Deism Must Be Pneumatological in Nature

To be more specific, it's my contention that we'll never adequately address the problem of functional deism (MTD) in evangelical churches until we recognize four tremendously impactful realities. First, the fact is that in addition to the discipleship deficit referred to above, there's also a *pneumatological deficit* at work in many of our churches.[71] Second, the problem is that this pneumatological deficit tends to produce within the members of a congregation an attitude or posture of *pneumatological presumption* (or even indifference) rather than expectancy. Third, a very dangerous, reciprocal relationship exists between this posture of pneumatological presumption and the phenomenon of functional deism. Fourth, what makes the relationship just alluded to so very dire is that there's a crucial connection between the attitude or posture of pneumatological *expectancy* and a genuine, empowering *experience* of Christ's Spirit!

Let's take a closer look now at these four very important realities, one at a time.

The Pneumatological Deficit Present in Many Evangelical Churches

As indicated in the previous chapter, the reality is that, in addition to the discipleship deficit referred to above, it's not uncommon for staunch, Bible-believing churches to also experience a pneumatological deficit. In other words, some ecclesial communities can tend to understate the importance

---

70. With this thought in mind, we should note Philip Rosato's observation regarding the manner in which Karl Barth "criticizes aspects of Augustine's theology in terms of their too static pneumatic character." Rosato, *The Spirit as Lord*, 9, referencing Karl and Heinrich Barth, *Zur Lehre vom Heligen Geist*, 95.

71. Karl Barth himself seemed to have acknowledged this in his book *Evangelical Theology: An Introduction*, in which he includes a stark and substantial discussion of the two earmarks of an "unspiritual theology" (56–59).

of the Holy Spirit to the Christian life.[72] Commenting on this neglect of the Holy Spirit within some quarters of traditional evangelicalism, Timothy Tennent, president of Asbury Theological Seminary, writes:

> The Reformation's emphasis on the authority of Scripture, ecclesi-ology, and Christology, as crucial as it was, meant that there was a further delay in a full theological development of the doctrine of the Holy Spirit, and several vital aspects of his work were ne-glected in Post-reformation Protestant theology, which focused on solidifying and organizing the theological developments of the Reformers. Over time, Western theological traditions that devel-oped greatly limited the active role of the Holy Spirit in the life of the church. The result was a pneumatological deficit that is only now becoming painfully apparent.[73]

Painfully apparent indeed! I'm proffering here the idea that another cause for the functional deism present in the lives of many evangelical church members is the pneumatological deficit which earmarks too many theologically conservative churches. In other words, the theological defi-ciency that allows for a functional deism isn't simply the absence of a theo-logical realism generally, but a pneumatological realism specifically. Mark it down: Church members can't give short shrift to the work of the Holy Spirit in their lives and then hope to avoid a functional deism. This is be-cause anything less than a vigorous, realist doctrine of the Holy Spirit tends to produce within a congregation an attitude or posture of pneumatologi-cal presumption (or even indifference) rather than expectation. The three discussions which follow will spell out why this is such a serious situation.

72. Many historical theologians consider the doctrine of the Holy Spirit to be the "orphan doctrine" of Christian theology. See Hunsinger, "Mediator of Communion," 177.

73. Tennent, *Invitation to World Missions*, 94, emphasis original. See also, Olson, *Story of Christian Theology*, 521, 523; Kärkkäinen, *Pneumatology*, 17–18; Loyer, *God's Love through the Spirit*, 1–7. Jürgen Moltmann provides not only a nuanced discussion of the reason for the "reserve in the doctrine of the Holy Spirit" within the established churches in Europe during the modern era, but also an eloquent critique of the tendency among some evangelicals to conflate Word and Spirit, and to conceive of the Spirit only in an intellectual manner. See Moltmann, *Spirit of Life*, 2–3.

The Pneumatological Presumption Produced by a Pneumatological Deficit

The alternative to a pneumatological deficit is a church environment earmarked by the embrace of a pneumatological realism instead. As I've already indicated, such an environment will be one in which church members eagerly expect to interact with the Holy Spirit in ways that are *real* (personal, responsive, and existentially impactful) rather than merely *theoretical* or *ritualistic*. The issue here is the dynamic of *expectancy*—the attitudinal "posture" church members assume (intentionally or not) with respect to the working of the Spirit in their lives. A realist understanding of the Spirit tends to encourage a posture of expectancy toward the Holy Spirit, while a non-realist understanding of the Spirit tends to result in a posture of *presumption* (or even *indifference*) with respect to the Spirit.

FIGURE 5

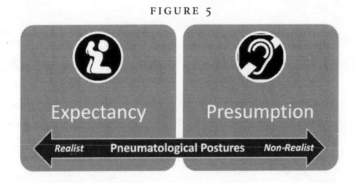

The Reciprocal Relationship between Pneumatological Presumption and Functional Deism

The relationship between pneumatological presumption and functional deism can be considered reciprocal because it's difficult to discern which causes what. On the one hand, an ecclesial environment earmarked by a non-realist pneumatology provides the fertile soil in which a functional deism can take root and thrive. On the other hand, once it becomes established in the life of a disciple or congregation, a functional deism virtually prohibits the assumption of any pneumatological posture other than one of presumption/indifference. At the very least it must be acknowledged that a functional deism certainly does not engender an expectation of genuinely interactive encounters with the Spirit of God. Instead, it facilitates a narcissistic, consumeristic, spectator-oriented version of the Christian life which in no way resembles the full-orbed faithfulness God is looking for and is vital to a fruitful contextualization of the gospel for our place and day.

The *Crucial* Connection between Pneumatological Expectancy and Experience

Building on what we've learned so far, I will offer the bold contention that a lack of pneumatological expectancy regarding the empowerment of the Spirit can't help but result in a diminished experience of the same. If we want to enable our church members to experience the Spirit in truly transformational, ministry-engendering ways, we simply *must* encourage within them a sense of pneumatological expectancy, rather than presumption or indifference.

This provocative notion finds some support from evangelical theologian Gilbert Bilezikian who, commenting on those churches in which the Holy Spirit is "reduced to an item of doctrine," makes a trenchant observation of his own:

> Being practically shut out of the lives of Christians and their churches, the Holy Spirit does not force his way into them. Every instance of the intervention of the Holy Spirit reported in the New Testament indicates that he cooperates actively in situations where he is expected and wanted.[74]

What Bilezikian seems to be suggesting here is that, when it comes to the intervention of the Spirit in the lives of believers, a sense of eager expectancy tends to precede, perhaps even precipitate, experience. If this assertion holds, it serves to explain why a functional deism really must be taken seriously; it's completely oppositional to a Spirit-empowered engagement in the formational ministries of the local church and the ministry fruitfulness these formational ministries contribute to. Moreover, this noteworthy assertion also provides support for my contention that the cure for the functional deism so injurious to the ministry fruitfulness of individual church members and many congregations as a whole is not simply theological but, more precisely, pneumatological in nature. In other words, the remedy for a functional deism requires nothing less than the

74. Bilezikian, *Christianity 101*, 108–9.

recovery of a robust, fully Trinitarian doctrine of the Holy Spirit, leading to an eager embrace of a pneumatological realism which, in turn, encourages believers to expect to interact with Christ's Spirit in truly transformational, existentially-impactful, and ministry-engendering ways.

FIGURE 6

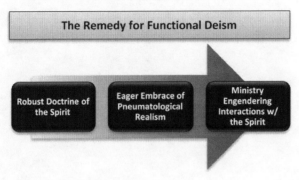

The Remedy for Functional Deism

Robust Doctrine of the Spirit → Eager Embrace of Pneumatological Realism → Ministry Engendering Interactions w/ the Spirit

This is why rank-and-file church members must be encouraged toward a posture of pneumatological expectancy rather than presumption. Once again, what I'm advocating for in this book is a functional-deism-defeating pneumatological realism that's crucial to the threefold faithfulness the Scriptures enjoin upon the followers of Jesus.

This now twice-stated indication of what I'm after in this work explains why the aim of the next three chapters of *Getting Real* is to make the case for the vital importance of a spiritual, moral, and missional faithfulness to a local church's ministry fruitfulness. To be even more precise, the overarching thesis of this next section of the book is that the embrace and promotion of a pneumatological realism in evangelical churches is critical to reaching our post-Christian peers for Christ. Buckle up! Things are about to get real.

Part Two: The Spirit and the Threefold Faithfulness God Desires and Deserves

3

Pneumatological Realism
and a Spiritual Faithfulness

As for you, the anointing you received from him remains in you, and you do
not need anyone to teach you. But as his anointing teaches you about all things
and as that anointing is real, not counterfeit—just as it has taught you, remain
in him.

—1 JOHN 2:27

ACCORDING TO THE GERMAN theologian Jürgen Moltmann, "All of the
works of God end in the presence of the Holy Spirit."[1] Moltmann is rather
famous for maintaining that God's works of creation and reconciliation
through Christ "arrive at their goal" in the "operation and indwelling of
the Spirit." [2] At the risk of greatly oversimplifying a profound theological
observation, Moltmann's rather remarkable contention is that the outpouring of God's Spirit is the grand goal of what God is up to in the world. If
this observation holds, the importance of the Holy Spirit to the Christian
experience simply can't be overstated.

I've argued thus far that the defeat of a functional deism requires the
recovery of an unmitigated doctrine of the Spirit. That said, the actual focus
of the work going forward will be on the issue of *ministry fruitfulness* and

1. Moltmann, *God in Creation*, 96. I'm indebted to my colleague, Frank Macchia, for
bringing this Moltmann quote to my attention.

2. Ibid., 96.

the crucial role which a pneumatological realism plays in it. As indicated in the book's introduction, the cultural context in which we evangelicals currently find ourselves is becoming increasingly post-Christian. The good news is that, while this is a serious development, it's not insurmountable. My experience working with some post-Christian members of the emerging generations is that, with the help of God's missionary Spirit, it really is possible to guide many of these disappointed, disenchanted, disaffected men and women toward a fervent, passionate walk with Christ. It just so happens that what is ultimately required to reach our post-Christian peers with the gospel is a Spirit-enabled threefold faithfulness that's pretty much antithetical to the functional deism / Christian nominalism so prevalent in even evangelical churches. Thus, in the next three chapters I'll explain why a *ministry fruitfulness* requires a *missional faithfulness,* that's supported by a *moral faithfulness,* which flows out of a *spiritual faithfulness.*

FIGURE 7

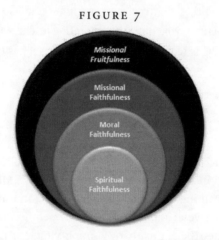

The Essence of a Spiritual Faithfulness

The thesis of this chapter is that the most fundamental type of faithfulness God expects from his people is spiritual in nature. In other words, it's impossible to exhibit a moral or missional faithfulness before God if a spiritual faithfulness isn't also present.

In the Old Testament, a primary way one manifested a spiritual faithfulness toward Yahweh was to remain loyal to the covenant he had graciously effected with Israel (see Pss 25:8–10; 78:32–37). Moreover, the New

Testament also speaks of a covenant—a *new* covenant which centers in the sacrifice of Christ (see Luke 22:20; 1 Cor 11:25; Heb 8:6–13; 9:15–28). Like the old covenant, the new covenant anticipates/expects a faithful response. At the very least, the New Testament makes it clear that fidelity to the new covenant requires that disciples remain steadfast in their devotion to Jesus, God's much beloved son (see Col 1:21–23; 2:6; Heb 3:1–6, 12–14; 4:14; 10:19–39). The question is, what does this steadfast, ongoing devotion to Jesus involve?

The Two Possibilities

In the fifteenth chapter of John's Gospel, we find a passage that seems to provide us with two possible answers to the question just posed. This very familiar passage reads:

> "I am the true vine, and my Father is the gardener. He cuts off every branch in me that bears no fruit, while every branch that does bear fruit he prunes so that it will be even more fruitful. You are already clean because of the word I have spoken to you. Remain in me, and I will remain in you. No branch can bear fruit by itself; it must remain in the vine. Neither can you bear fruit unless you remain in me.
>
> "I am the vine; you are the branches. If a man remains in me and I in him, he will bear much fruit; apart from me you can do nothing. If anyone does not remain in me, he is like a branch that is thrown away and withers; such branches are picked up, thrown into the fire and burned. If you remain in me and my words remain in you, ask whatever you wish, and it will be given you. This is to my Father's glory, that you bear much fruit, showing yourselves to be my disciples." (John 15:1–8)

This passage is famous for its call for Christ's followers to "continue," "remain," or "abide" (*menō*) in him. Some Christians tend to interpret this call as an exhortation to maintain a *volitional-intellectual commitment* to Christ. In other words, to continue in Christ is to be careful to maintain an orthodox understanding/profession of who Jesus is and what he's about. Other Christians tend to interpret the call presented in John 15 as an exhortation to maintain a *mystical-experiential communion* with the risen Jesus—to interact with him daily in some sort of spiritual/devotional manner.[3] So, which is it? Does a steadfast devotion to Christ involve a volitional-intellectual commitment or a mystical-experiential communion?

There's no doubt that the apostolic authors evidenced a concern that Christian believers stand strong in their faith concerning Christ.[4] Thus, the notion that a steadfast devotion to Jesus involves a volitional-intellectual commitment to him is not lacking in scriptural support. Indeed, passages such as John 20:30–31 and 1 John 5 indicate that John, himself, had this concern.

That said, we must also acknowledge that passages such as John 14:23 and Revelation 3:20 indicate that John was also open to the notion of a mystical communion with Christ. These two representative passages read:

> Jesus replied, "Anyone who loves me will obey my teaching. My Father will love them, and *we will come to them and make our home with them.*" (John 14:23, emphasis added)

> Here I am! I stand at the door and knock. If anyone hears my voice and opens the door, *I will come in and eat with that person, and they with me.* (Rev 3:20, emphasis added)

3. An indication that Karl Barth, though not a card-carrying Charismatic in the contemporary sense of the term, might have nevertheless been at least cautiously comfortable with the notion of an "experiential" relationship with Christ through the Spirit is provided by Joseph Mangina who writes: "Attention to Barth's pneumatology can help correct the misapprehension that there is no room for human experience in his thought. Already in I/1, we learn that the word of God is humanly knowable, and that if this is so we must certainly affirm that it can be experienced" (Mangina, *Karl Barth*, 44). Moreover, Barth himself seems to refer to an experiential (theologically real) aspect of the Spirit-filled life that must be renewed daily when he states: "To receive the Spirit, to have the Spirit, to live in the Spirit means being set free and being permitted to live in freedom. . . . To have inner ears for the Word of Christ, to become thankful for His work and at the same time responsible for the message about Him and, lastly, to take confidence in men for Christ's sake—that is the freedom which we obtain, when Christ breathes on us, when He sends us His Holy Spirit. If He no longer lives in a historical or heavenly, a theological or ecclesiastical remoteness from me, if He approaches me and takes possession of me, the result will be that I hear, that I am thankful and responsible and that finally I may hope for myself and for all others; in other words, that I may live in a Christian way. It is a tremendously big thing and by no means a matter of course, to obtain this freedom. We must therefore every day and every hour pray *Veni Creator Spiritus* [Come, Creator Spirit] in listening to the word of Christ and in thankfulness. That is a closed circle. We do not 'have' this freedom; it is again and again given to us by God" (Barth, *Dogmatics in Outline*, 138–39).

4. For example, see Acts 14:21–22; 1 Cor 16:13; 2 Cor 9:13; 13:5; Phil 1:27; 2 Thess 2:15; 1 Tim 1:18–19; 3:8–9; 4:1, 6; 6:12, 20–21; Heb 3:12–14; 4:14; 1 Pet 5:8–9; 2 Pet 3:17–18; Jude 1:3.

In a succeeding section of this chapter I'll have more to say about John's support for a mystical-experiential communion with Christ that's to be experienced here and now, as well as for eternity. But at this point, I want to shift attention away from John to the Apostle Paul and a set of passages from his pen that I believe are especially helpful when it comes to forging a biblically-informed response to the question that arises from the call to continue presented in John 15.

The Wholistic Spirituality of the Apostle Paul

While John 15 is very well-known, I've found that many of my students are much less familiar with Colossians 3:1–4. I find this highly ironic since, in my estimation, this passage is at the very center of Paul's understanding of Christian spirituality.

An Initial Look at Colossians 3:1–4

This often overlooked and underestimated passage reads thusly:

> Since, then, you have been raised with Christ, set your hearts on things above, where Christ is, seated at the right hand of God. Set your minds on things above, not on earthly things. For you died, and your life is now hidden with Christ in God. When Christ, who is your life, appears, then you also will appear with him in glory. (Col 3:1–4)

Before I launch into a rather involved discussion of this text, I want to provide a rationale for it. Leslie Weatherhead, writing a generation ago in his book *The Transforming Friendship*, indicated what he believed should be the main priority of Christian ministers and educators. According to this Anglican churchman:

> There is no greater need in our time than that those who teach religion should concern themselves, not with tightening up the machinery, developing organization, or arranging more meetings; but rather to make Jesus real to men [and women]; to invite them into that *transforming fellowship* which cannot be proved save by personal experience, but which, when realized, brings men [and women] that glorious exhilaration, that sense of ineffable peace,

and that escape from all bondage which are promised in the New Testament.[5]

Weatherhead was convinced that one of the most critical things a local church can do is encourage and enable its members to experience what he referred to as a transforming fellowship/friendship with the risen Jesus. Another couple of passages from *The Transforming Friendship* enable us to gain a clearer picture of what its author had in mind by his use of this phrase. First, he presents his readers with a litany of questions:

> Is it a real fact, practicable for everyday life in the twentieth century, that we may have communion with Jesus Christ as really as we have communion with our earthly friends? Can we know that same Jesus of Nazareth who walked about in Galilee two thousand years ago? I do not mean can we treasure His words, can we follow His way of life, can we, following His example, be heroic as He was, can we benefit by His ideas; I do not mean can we imaginatively reproduce a picture of Him clearly enough to form a substitute for His actual presence; but can we really meet Him, know Him, commune with Himself?[6]

Then, a few pages later, Weatherhead presents to his readers this bold answer:

> What Jesus once was, He is eternally. He comes to us, not only in His temple, or in the room when the door is shut, but as He came to Mary and Martha in the midst of household tasks, and as He came to Peter mending his nets and doing his daily work; and He comes with the same offer, the offer of His transforming friendship. There are no conditions save the imaginative faith to believe that He is, and that fellowship with Him is possible.[7]

It would certainly seem that this Anglican churchman was advocating for a mystical-experiential communion with Jesus. But, we might inquire, where did this idea that it's possible for Christian disciples to experience a transforming friendship with the risen Christ come from? Actually, the notion of a mystical-experiential communion with Jesus is one that shows up quite often in the writings of Christianity's spiritual masters both ancient

5. Weatherhead, *Transforming Friendship*, 37.

6. Ibid., 29.

7. Ibid., 35.

and contemporary.[8] I'm suggesting here that, ultimately, all of Christianity's spiritual masters got the idea from the New Testament in general, and passages such as Colossians 3:1–4 in particular. Just the possibility that this is true, I believe, justifies a careful examination of this text and the bold thesis that it represents the very center of Pauline spirituality.

Of course, to fully understand what Paul was doing in this pivotal passage, we need to pay some careful attention to its context—the verses that immediately precede and succeed this text so very critical to the Apostle Paul's understanding of Christian spirituality. For reasons that will soon become apparent, I'll treat these two sections of Paul's letter in reverse order.

The Verses That Immediately Succeed Colossians 3:1–4

Colossians 3:5–17 is a very important passage, where Paul describes the kind of life that's made possible by following the instructions he's presented in the first four verses of the chapter. It's on the heels of Colossians 3:1–4 that Paul exhorted the members of the church in Colossae thusly:

> Put to death, therefore, whatever belongs to your earthly nature: sexual immorality, impurity, lust, evil desires and greed, which is idolatry. Because of these, the wrath of God is coming. You used to walk in these ways, in the life you once lived. But now you must also rid yourselves of all such things as these: anger, rage, malice, slander, and filthy language from your lips. Do not lie to each other, since you have taken off your old self with its practices and have put on the new self, which is being renewed in knowledge in the image of its Creator. Here there is no Gentile or Jew, circumcised or uncircumcised, barbarian, Scythian, slave or free, but Christ is all, and is in all.
>
> Therefore, as God's chosen people, holy and dearly loved, clothe yourselves with compassion, kindness, humility, gentleness and patience. Bear with each other and forgive one another if any of you has a grievance against someone. Forgive as the Lord forgave you. And over all these virtues put on love, which binds them all together in perfect unity.
>
> Let the peace of Christ rule in your hearts, since as members of one body you were called to peace. And be thankful. Let the message of Christ dwell among you richly as you teach and admonish one another with all wisdom through psalms, hymns, and songs from the Spirit, singing to God with gratitude in your

8. For more on this, see Tyra, *Christ's Empowering Presence.*

hearts. And whatever you do, whether in word or deed, do it all in the name of the Lord Jesus, giving thanks to God the Father through him. (Col 3:5–17)

At first glance, the many ethical exhortations which make up this passage might strike us as just another impatient pastoral rant. However, I want to suggest that this admittedly sobering, challenging passage actually serves as an encouraging indication that it's possible for those of us who profess to be followers of Christ to begin living our lives in ways that, deep down inside, we've always dreamed of. Please pardon the redundancy but, according to the Apostle Paul, it's possible for us as Christ's followers to become the kind of people who are:

- overcoming our natural tendencies toward sexual immorality, impurity, lust, evil desires, and greed (3:5);

- no longer given to anger, rage, malice, slander, and filthy language (3:8);

- not in the habit of lying to one another (3:9);

- overcoming our prejudices (and critical, dismissive attitudes) toward individuals and members of entire cultures (3:11);

- so secure, ourselves, in God's merciful love that we're able to manifest compassion, kindness, humility, gentleness, and patience toward others (3:12);

- willing to forgive others in just the same way that the Lord forgives us (3:13);

- proactively demonstrating genuine love for our brothers and sisters in Christ (3:14);

- routinely functioning as peacemakers (rather than troublemakers) in the church, grateful for the privilege just to belong (3:15);

- speaking prophetically into the lives of others in encouraging, edifying ways (3:16a; cf. Eph 5:19a);

- offering to God Spirit-enabled expressions of sincere praise and thanksgiving (3:16b; cf. Eph 5:19b); and

- continually endeavoring to imitate and honor Christ in everything we say and do, thereby offering our entire lives to God as an act of grateful worship (3:17; cf. Eph 5:20).

I'm suggesting that what we find in Colossians 3:5–17 is a vivid description of something I refer to as the "Colossians 3 Kind of Life." Seriously, wouldn't it be wonderful to be able to live this way—in a truly Christ-honoring, Christ-like manner? The good news is that the Apostle Paul was dead serious about the possibility of the original readers of this letter experiencing the Christian life as depicted in this passage.[9]

But this, of course, raises the following question: How? Where does the empowerment come from to actually live this kind of life? Here's some more good news: the key to living the kind of life described in verses 5–17 of Colossians 3 is found in verses 1–4 of the same chapter. And yet, before we examine what Paul was up to in that pivotal passage, let's continue our consideration of its context.

The Verses That Immediately Precede Colossians 3:1–4

I have in mind here the entirety of Colossians 1 and 2. Because space won't permit a thorough, verse-by-verse exposition, I'm going to ask the reader to bear with me as I attempt to summarize what I see Paul doing in these two chapters.

To begin, we should note that, very early in the letter, Paul indicates that the ultimate goal of Christian discipleship should be nothing less than a *lifestyle* that's "worthy of the Lord" and pleasing to him in "every way" (Col 1:9–10). Knowing what we know about where Paul is headed in this missive—a vivid description of the "Colossians 3 Kind of Life"—it's difficult not to surmise that Paul might have had this topic in mind from the very outset. If this is true, it would mean that one of the apostle's aims in chapters 1 and 2 of Colossians was to specify for his readers the type of spirituality required for the realization of the rather daunting set of pastoral exhortations presented in chapter 3.

That said, we should also take note that in these two chapters we find Paul emphasizing the need for Christian disciples to maintain a strong faith commitment to what eventually became the orthodox understanding of the nature of Christ and his importance to God's plan of redemption (Col 1:21–23; 2:1–7). But does this mean that Paul believed that a volitional-intellectual commitment to Christ, by itself, is the key to the realization of

---

9. Some support for this assertion can be found in Romans 6:1–14 and 2 Corinthians 5:14–21—two other Pauline passages that refer to Christian disciples becoming new themselves, and then living a new kind of life.

a "Colossians 3 Kind of Life"? Or is there also room in Paul's spirituality for a mystical-experiential communion with Christ as well? I'll submit that the rest of chapter 2 helps us answer this latter query in the affirmative.

This contention is based on the fact that later in chapter 2 we find Paul expressly encouraging his readers to recognize that the key to living fully in God is not the human traditions which lie at the heart of both philosophy (Col. 2:8) and religiosity (Col. 2:16–19), but the wisdom and power available to them through an ongoing (spiritually real) relationship with the risen Jesus (Col. 2:9–15). While this relationship is founded on (or presumes) an orthodox opinion concerning Christ (Col 2:9–10), Paul's lyrical references to the readers being "circumcised by Christ," and "buried" but also "raised" with him suggests that the apostle had room in his spirituality for a mystical-experiential communion as well (Col 2:11–15).

Then, becoming even more precise, Paul indicates at the end of chapter 2 that the problem with a religiosity which focuses on anything other than Christ (i.e., religious rules, rituals, and regulations) is that it fails miserably when it comes to "restraining sensual indulgence" (Col. 2:20–23, cf. 3:5–10). In the process, Paul provides a stunning critique of any spirituality that doesn't understand how important it is to maintain a wholistic connection to Christ (Col 2:16–19). While it's possible to think that Paul only had in mind here the need to maintain a correct creedal profession, his reference to those who have "lost connection with the head, from whom the whole body, supported and held together by its ligaments and sinews, grows as God causes it to grow," seems to suggest the need for a relationship with Jesus that's dynamic rather than static, transformational rather than conceptual, spiritually real rather than merely ideal.[10]

Ultimately, then, the big takeaway from Colossians 2 is that we need something more than human philosophy or religiosity if we're going to live a life worthy of God, pleasing him in every way. We're also going to need more than an intellectual-volitional commitment to Jesus as Lord, as important as this is.

---

10. I might also suggest that, given Paul's reference to "the whole body" in Colossians 2:19, the connection to Christ he has in mind can also be said to be corporate rather than private in nature. Thus, the communion of each individual disciple with Christ will necessarily also involve a communion with the other members of Christ's body. a prominent theme of the chapter which follows.

A Second Look at Colossians 3:1–4

This brings us back again to Colossians 3:1–4 and my thesis that, given where these four verses are situated in this letter—after Paul's critique of philosophy and religiosity, and prior to his discussion of the Colossians 3 Kind of Life—their importance to the apostle's understanding of Christian spirituality should be quite apparent. Once again, these four very important verses read thusly:

> Since, then, you have been raised with Christ, set your hearts on things above, where Christ is, seated at the right hand of God. Set your minds on things above, not on earthly things. For you died, and your life is now hidden with Christ in God. When Christ, who is your life, appears, then you also will appear with him in glory. (Col 3:1–4)

What's not so apparent, at least at first glance, is what Paul was encouraging the Colossian Christians to do in this passage. I suspect it's the mysterious nature of this pericope (thematically-related range of verses) that has caused it to be so often overlooked by rank-and-file believers. So, for the sake of clarity as well as expediency, I'll simply offer two big exegetical observations. First, Paul seems to be suggesting here that there's a *mystical union* between earth-bound believers and the risen and ascended Christ (see also Rom 6:1–14). Second, it appears that Paul was calling for the Colossian Christians to set their hearts and minds—that is, to focus their devotion and attention—on the risen Christ, as if this would have an empowering effect (see also Rom 8:5; 13:12–14; Eph 4:21–24; Heb 3:1; 12:1–3). It's these two very basic observations, along with a careful consideration of the totality of Paul's writings on Christian spirituality, that stand behind my contention that in Colossians 3:1–4, the apostle was encouraging the Colossian church members to cultivate and maintain a persistent, moment-by-moment mentoring relationship with the risen Christ—an intimate, interactive relationship that could and would empower them to live a "Colossians 3 Kind of Life."[11]

---

11. Some additional support for the notion of a mentoring relationship with the risen Christ is inherent in the way 1 Corinthians 2:6–16 connects the Spirit with the wisdom of God, and then indicates that, through the Spirit, Christian disciples are enabled to possess the "mind of Christ." I want to suggest that, given the content of John 14:25–26 and 16:12–15, a Spirit-enabled acquisition of the mind of Christ might actually mean that the Spirit not only mediates a real knowledge of God, but also makes it possible for Christian disciples to, more and more, have their worldviews approximate that of Christ

In sum, I'm convinced that the authors of the New Testament, especially the apostles John and Paul, were convinced that a spiritual faithfulness to Jesus involves *both* a volitional-intellectual commitment *and* mystical-experiential communion.[12] In other words, the apostolic authors present us with the possibility of an ongoing mentoring relationship with Jesus—an intimate, interactive relationship that's designed to have a *transformational, fruit-bearing* effect upon our lives.[13]

FIGURE 8

A Spiritual Faithfulness

John 15:1–8 / Colossians 3:1–4

Continuing in Christ

Volitional-Intellectual Commitment	Mystical-Experiential Communion

An Ongoing Mentoring Relationship w/ the Risen Jesus

The Critical Role the Holy Spirit Plays in a Spiritual Faithfulness

Moving forward, it's worth noting that the New Testament contains many passages which indicate the crucial role the Holy Spirit plays in assuring Christian disciples of God's faithfulness toward them.[14] However, the topic at hand is not the Spirit's role in assuring Christ's followers of the faithful-

---

Jesus himself. In other words, perhaps it's possible for Jesus' followers to, over time, grow in their ability to see and feel about almost everything the way he does!

12. For more on this, see Tyra, *Christ's Empowering Presence*, 101–3.

13. For more on this, see ibid., 99, 108–9, 184.

14. For example, the Apostle Paul taught that it's the Spirit who assures Christ's followers that they belong to God (Rom 8:15–16; Gal 4:6), are loved by God (Rom 5:5), have an eternal inheritance awaiting them in heaven (Eph 1:13–14), and can be counted on to function as a resource when weary, beleaguered believers in Jesus find themselves in desperate need of a hope renewal (Rom 15:13).

ness of God, but the ways in which the Spirit can be counted on to enable them to render to God the spiritual faithfulness he desires and deserves.[15] It's toward that important topic we now turn.

Paul, the Spirit, and a Spiritual Faithfulness before God

Though Paul seems to refer in many of his letters to the role the Holy Spirit plays in helping disciples embody a spiritual faithfulness,[16] my focus here will be on his epistles to the Colossians and Ephesians. As we've already seen, the vital role the Holy Spirit plays in enabling Christians to "live a life worthy of the Lord" is explicitly indicated in Paul's prayer for the Colossian Christians presented in the opening paragraphs of his letter to them:

> For this reason, since the day we heard about you, we have not stopped praying for you. We continually ask God to fill you with the knowledge of his will through all the wisdom and understanding that *the Spirit gives*, so that you may live a life worthy of the Lord and please him in every way. (Col 1:9–10, emphasis added)

If it's true, as previously argued, that this summary of Paul's praying for the Colossians located in Colossians 1 anticipates the more detailed description of the "Colossians 3 Kind of Life" which appears later in the letter, it can be deduced that the importance of the Holy Spirit to the spiritual faithfulness described in Colossians 1 is true also of the spiritual faithfulness elaborated upon in Colossians 3. In other words, it's through the Spirit that we engage in the mystical-experiential communion prescribed by Paul in Colossians 3:1–4.[17]

---

15. The ensuing discussion is biblical in nature. For a more theological treatment of this theme, see Hunsinger, "Mediator of Communion," 181–82.

16. I'll have more to say about this in chapter 6.

17. Some theological support for this exegetical take might be adduced from the manner in which Karl Barth boldly argued for the critical importance of the Holy Spirit not only to the *union* of the divine and human natures in the incarnate Christ, but also the *communion* which does (*de jure*) and may (*de facto*) exist between the risen Christ and the members of his body here on earth. Barth scholar, Philip Rosato, explains that, for Barth, "The Spirit's temporal mission is that of *continually* unifying in individual men what is already unified in Jesus Christ: divine and human nature. The Spirit carries out his unique role not only for but also in the Christian, by *conjoining him to the risen Son of God*. This *union* take place when man hears, believes in and witnesses to the gracious self-revelation of God in Jesus Christ through *a life of faith*" (Rosato, *The Spirit as Lord*, 67, emphasis added). And again, Rosato writes that, according to Barth, "Just as the Spirit is the only possibility, the only real ground of the Word's becoming man in Jesus

Moreover, a similar exercise in exegetical deduction will reveal that an even more pronounced emphasis on the importance of the Spirit to Christian spirituality appears in several passages located in Paul's letter to the Ephesians—passages which seem to echo and elaborate upon what we just observed in his letter to the Colossians. In Ephesians, too, Paul refers to the direction of his prayers for its readers. Actually, two Pauline prayers are presented in his letter to the Ephesians: one in 1:15–23; the other in 3:14–19. Please note the reference to the Holy Spirit in both:

> For this reason, ever since I heard about your faith in the Lord Jesus and your love for all God's people, I have not stopped giving thanks for you, remembering you in my prayers. I keep asking that the God of our Lord Jesus Christ, the glorious Father, may give you *the Spirit of wisdom and revelation*, so that you may know him better. I pray that the eyes of your heart may be enlightened in order that you may know the hope to which he has called you, the riches of his glorious inheritance in his holy people, and his incomparably great power for us who believe. (Eph 1:15–19, emphasis added)

> For this reason I kneel before the Father, from whom every family in heaven and on earth derives its name. I pray that out of his glorious riches he may strengthen you with power *through his Spirit* in your inner being, so that Christ may dwell in your hearts through faith. And I pray that you, being rooted and established in love, may have power, together with all the Lord's holy people, to grasp how wide and long and high and deep is the love of Christ, and to know this love that surpasses knowledge—that you may be filled to the measure of all the fullness of God. (Eph 3:14–19, emphasis added)

Just as in his letter to the Colossians, I see a thematic connection between both of Paul's prayers for the Ephesian disciples and the much more detailed descriptions presented in Ephesians 4:1–6, 25–32 and 5:1–20 of the kind of life the Spirit wants to enable Christ's followers to live. If this observation holds, then it's possible to deduce that in this letter also, Paul

---

of Nazareth, the Spirit alone is responsible for the Word's *union* with the believer in and through faith. The Holy Spirit, the same divine power at work in the incarnation of the Word of God, is at work in the believing Christian" (ibid., 68, emphasis added). I want to suggest that the language used in these quotes, especially the phrase "a life of faith," connotes a union with Christ that's dynamic rather than static in nature.

was indicating the importance of the Holy Spirit to a lifestyle of spiritual faithfulness before God.[18]

John, the Spirit, and a Spiritual Faithfulness before God

In addition to several other non-Pauline passages which indicate the importance of the Holy Spirit to Christian living in general,[19] there is the way John 14 and 16—the two chapters which frame or "bookend" the *call to continue* (or *abide*) sounded in John 15—suggest how important a pneumatological realism is to a spiritual faithfulness. In John 14 and 16, we discover that the Holy Spirit is "another" *advocate, counselor, or mentor* (*paraklētos*) (John 14:15–18), whose role is to bring to the minds of Jesus' disciples everything that he has taught them (John 14:26), and wishes (in an ongoing way) to teach them (John 16:13). In sum, what I'm proposing is that a careful consideration of the pneumatology presented in John 14–16 provides support for the notion that one of the primary tasks of the Holy Spirit is to make it possible for Christian disciples to experience that ongoing mentoring relationship with Christ that John 15 exhorts us toward![20]

Simply put, there's ample evidence in the New Testament, especially in the writings of the apostles John and Paul, that we're not experiencing the *fullness* of Christ's Spirit in our lives if we're not allowing him to enable us to interact with Jesus in a moment-by-moment mentoring manner.[21]

18. The fact that, according to Karl Barth, a pneumatological realism lies behind not just the faith of the believer, but his or her faithfulness as well is indicated when Philip Rosato makes the cogent observation that: "The obvious, yet mysterious, *reality* of the conscious faith of the Christian induces Barth to investigate the various *observable* aspects of this faith before he can adequately explain their possibility. The first of these *concrete* aspects is that the individual Christian is in fact capable of *acting publicly* as a man who has heard the Word of God addressed to him and accepted that Word with the trust of a child. The believer discovers that he both is and *acts* in a way which his own powers could not account for. He has become the recipient of *a new capacity*. This central fact of Christian existence constitutes for Barth the subjective reality of revelation, the work of the Holy Spirit, God present in man creating in him the freedom to *become obedient* to the Father through faith. When a man believes, God receives a new son through the power of the Holy Spirit, who alone makes it possible first that a man is a child of God and thus that he can subsequently *become* so" (ibid., 71).

19. For example, see 1 Pet 4:12–14; Jude 1:17–20.

20. Moreover, some explicit support for this assertion can be discerned by comparing Matthew 10:19–20 and Luke 21:14–15. For more on this, see Tyra, *Christ's Empowering Presence*, 99. See also, Tyra, "Proclaiming Christ's Victory."

21. I'm going to suggest that this is an important point that even many Pentecostal-charismatics need to take into account.

Moreover, since a posture of pneumatological expectancy rather than presumption or indifference is obviously necessary for this type of enablement to occur, it would certainly seem that a pneumatological realism is crucial to the ability of Christ's followers to render to God the spiritual faithfulness he desires and deserves.

But what of my previously stated assertion that more Christians exhibiting a spiritual faithfulness is also a dynamic which our post-Christian peers desperately need to witness? The final section of this chapter will explain why this is so.

How a Spiritual Faithfulness Contributes to Ministry Fruitfulness

My experience with post-Christians tells me that very few of them have actually rejected Christianity. What most post-Christians are struggling with is not Christianity per se, but "churchianity"—the sometimes egregiously imperfect manner in which many church members tend to represent the faith to one another and those outside the ecclesial community.

To be more specific, my research into the post-Christian dynamic, along with my personal experience with thousands of students over the past two decades, tell me that one of the biggest reasons why so many of our contemporaries claim to be over Christianity and done with the church is because of the *Christian Pharisaism* they've experienced within conservative Christian congregations. While I include a brief discussion of what I refer to as "conservative Christianity's image problem" in my book *A Missional Orthodoxy: Theology and Ministry in a Post-Christian Context*,[22] I devote an entire chapter to this topic in an earlier work titled *Defeating Pharisaism: Recovering Jesus' Disciple-Making Method*.[23] In both books, I cite the research reported on by David Kinnaman in his *unchristian: What a New Generation Really Thinks about Christianity—and Why It Matters*.[24] Unfortunately, Kinnaman's findings indicate that conservative Christianity does indeed have an image problem, especially among the members of the emerging generations. Kinnaman summarizes his findings thusly:

22. Tyra, *Missional Orthodoxy*, 38–42.
23. Tyra, *Defeating Pharisaism*, 53–76.
24. Kinnaman and Lyons, *unchristian*.

> Our research shows that many of those outside of Christianity, especially younger adults, have little trust in the Christian faith, and esteem for the lifestyle of Christ followers is quickly fading among outsiders. They admit their emotional and intellectual barriers go up when they are around Christians, and they reject Jesus because they feel rejected by Christians.[25]

More precisely, I'll offer that while Jesus exhorted his followers time and again to display grace and mercy toward others (e.g., Matt 5:7; 12:7; 18:21–35; 23:23), what many post-Christians report having experienced among conservative church members instead are some of the same graceless attitudes and actions the New Testament ascribes to Jesus' ministry antagonists—the Pharisees. Some of these missionally problematic attitudes and actions include:

- *legalism* (e.g., Luke 18:9–14; John 5:39);
- *dogmatism* (e.g., Luke 7:29–35; John 9:24–34);
- *judgmentalism* (Luke 7:36–39; John 9:16);
- *separatism* (Matt 9:10–13); and especially
- *hypocrisy* (Matt 23:1–36; Luke 12:1).

Now, based on my experience with university students, this phenomenon of graceless Christianity is a very big deal! On the one hand, there seems to be an inverse relationship between Christian Pharisaism and ministry fruitfulness, especially with respect to our post-Christian peers.

FIGURE 9

Ministry Fruitfulness

Christian Pharisaism

25. Ibid., 11.

On the other hand, I'm also convinced that an ongoing mentoring relationship with Jesus can't help but continually remind us of our need to *embrace* God's grace and mercy for ourselves, and *extend* this grace and mercy to others (e.g., Matt 5:7; Luke 6:36). This more grace-oriented approach to Christian life and ministry is absolutely crucial to our attempts to influence our post-Christian peers for Christ.

A very important component in my life as a university professor is cooperating with the Spirit of mission in the endeavor to woo university students who've adopted a post-Christian orientation (or are on the way to doing so) back into a fervent and faithful relationship with Jesus. You might be surprised at just how many of my students fall into this category, even though I teach at a private, Christian, liberal arts university. [26] Each semester I teach a theology course titled "Developing a Christian Worldview." Since this course is part of the university's core curriculum, it's required of all students regardless of their major. The goal of this course (and a couple of other religion courses like it) is to help university students integrate their "faith" (at whatever level it is) with their learning and living so that once they graduate they can impact the world for Christ.

Not long ago I had a student approach me after the initial class session of this "Christian Worldview" course to indicate a concern. In a manner that was both courteous and bold at the same time, she alerted me to the fact that, not only did she not consider herself a Christian, she didn't even believe in the existence of God! So, she wondered, how was she going to fare in a class that presumes an interest in cultivating a Christian worldview? I assured her that I would work with her. She could write the final paper, being honest about her present level of commitment, while at the same time interacting with the content of the texts, lectures, and class discussions. She left that initial class session feeling a sense of relief.

It was in a subsequent conversation that I learned the reason for her rather strident unbelief: she had been bitterly disappointed by life and the Christians she had known growing up, both inside and outside her family. We met in my office several times during the semester to discuss the content

---

26. According to research reported on by Kara Powell and Chap Clark, "40 to 50 percent of kids who graduate from a church or youth group will fail to stick with their faith in college" (Powell and Clark, *Sticky Faith*, 15, 213–14). While this same research indicates that "somewhere between 30 and 60 percent of youth group graduates who abandon their faith and the church return to both in their late twenties," these authors go on to lament "the 40 to 70 percent who won't" (ibid., 16). See also Powell et al., *Growing Young*, 15–18.

of the course. Mostly, I just listened as she related to me her "story," and elaborated upon all the reasons why she didn't feel that she could take the Christian message seriously. Rather than try to fix or correct her, I simply did my best to engage in some empathic "hearing" and promised to keep praying for her regardless of whether she considered it a waste of my time or not.[27] In other words, I endeavored to prayerfully model for this student what a thoughtful yet grace-oriented version of the Christian life looks like.

The final week of the course I received an email from her, indicating that she had not only changed her mind about the existence of God, but had prayerfully surrendered her life to the lordship of Christ. *What had happened?*

After our most recent conversation, she had, at my encouragement, been reading the Gospel of Matthew while pondering this question: What is it about Jesus that causes so many people to be enamored with him? I had also encouraged her, as an "experiment" based on Psalm 34:8, to offer the prayer: "Jesus, if you're real, reveal yourself to me."

She hadn't gotten very far in this "taste and see" exercise before something dramatic occurred. The Spirit of Christ came upon this troubled university student in a remarkable way as she read the story in Matthew 8 of Jesus calming a *troubled* sea, and then exhorting his disciples to overcome their *unbelief*. This young woman, so very disenchanted with the Christian faith, is one of many I've seen be led by the Holy Spirit to take another look at Christ and his church. Indeed, during the past year (at the time of this writing) I've interacted with this student on several occasions. I'm happy to report that in each conversation she's spoken of the progress she's making in her new life as a Christian disciple.

So here's the bottom line with respect to the importance of a spiritual faithfulness to reaching post-Christians for Christ: since it's the lack of grace experienced by many that's at the heart of the post-Christian dynamic, it's precisely a grace-embracing, grace-extending, theologically real approach to the Christian faith that needs to be lived out if we're to succeed at encouraging our cultural peers to give Christ and the church a second look![28]

27. I tell my ministry-bound students that while the words "listen" and "hear" can be used interchangeably (see Prov 1:5; 20:12), some qualifications need to be made. It's possible to hear without really "listening." It's also possible to listen without really "hearing." The goal should be to engage in a process of active, intentional "listening" that leads to genuine "hearing." Whatever the relationship, this empathic attending to the other is crucial to it.

28. Some tacit support for this assertion is provided by *Growing Young: Six Essential*

Thus, the spiritual faithfulness I'm promoting in this chapter (at the heart of which is an ongoing mentoring relationship with Christ made possible by the Holy Spirit) is indeed very important to reaching post-Christians for Christ!

Chapter 4 of *Getting Real* will focus even more intently on the way a spiritual faithfulness contributes to ministry fruitfulness by impacting the character and ministry manner of Christ's followers. In other words, an authentic *spiritual faithfulness* will, with the help of the Holy Spirit, produce a *moral faithfulness* also. This, too, is a cardinal component of a Spirit-empowered Christian discipleship. Sadly, a serious, balanced, effectual engagement in the moral training of church members is often neglected in evangelical approaches to disciple making. My message is that we can do better. In the next chapter I'll indicate how.

Strategies to Help Young People Discover and Love Your Church. In this work Kara Powell, Jake Mulder, and Brad Griffin emphasize the need for churches to "take Jesus' message seriously" (126–62), "fuel a warm community" (163–95), and "be the best neighbors" (234–70). Although, as far as I can tell, the term "Pharisaism" doesn't appear in *Growing Young*, I'll suggest that taking these three exhortations promoted by Powell et al. seriously will serve to mitigate the presence of it in a congregation. Indeed, with respect to the last exhortation, these authors state, "Churches striving to be the best neighbors reflect this selfless mercy toward the people outside their congregations whether those neighbors are friends, strangers, or enemies. They demonstrate compassion and forgiveness, even when it is within their power to turn away or inflict harm. Churches that grow young practice this mercy in a myriad of forms—in their service and social justice efforts, in their political engagement, in discussions about race and ethnic identity, and in response to pop culture. Doing so earns these churches a hearing in a culture that often otherwise dismisses them as judgmental or closed-minded" (ibid., 240). Intended or not, the implicit allusion to a Christian Pharisaism is hard to miss.

4

Pneumatological Realism
and a Moral Faithfulness

In order that the righteous requirement of the law might be fully met in us,
who do not live according to the flesh but according to the Spirit.

—ROMANS 8:4

IF MY STUDENTS ARE any indication, the moral training provided in many
evangelical (and Pentevangelical) churches, if occurring at all, doesn't
amount to much more than a periodic rehearsing of a laundry list of ethical dos and don'ts (with a primary focus on the don'ts). What's *not* being
provided in enough congregations is an intentional engagement in *moral
formation* which aims at producing church members eager and able to
make ethical choices and form moral opinions in a way that's distinctively
Christian.

A few years back I experienced an epiphany while grading the final
papers which some ministry-bound students had written for a course titled
"Foundations of Christian Ethics." One intelligent student in his mid-
twenties confessed in his paper that, prior to taking this ethics course, he
had been quite cavalier with respect to the moral dimension of his life, not
giving much attention at all to the process by which he had been making ethical decisions. As a result, his confession continued, he'd been guilty
of making moral choices just as many non-Christians do: from the gut
and/or based on what his friends would think of him. Recognizing how

representative this student's moral manner was, my eyes were opened to the distressing reality referred to in the previous paragraph. In sum, the typical evangelical church member is not sufficiently aware of three critical facts: (1) there is such a thing as a *moral faithfulness*—Christians committed to honoring the heart of God in their ethical lives (rather than simply going with their gut or being driven by cultural convention); (2) such a moral faithfulness requires a lifestyle of surrender to the Holy Spirit's endeavors to help Christ's followers discern and do the will of the Father; and (3) such a moral faithfulness, because it lies at the heart of a genuine Christian discipleship, is crucial to a ministry fruitfulness.

This chapter will elaborate upon these three critical facts one at a time. The goal is to both inspire and inform. That said, here's some good news right off the bat: with the help of the Holy Spirit, a moral faithfulness is possible—a moral faithfulness that can support, rather than undermine, the church's missional endeavors.

The Essence of Moral Faithfulness

At the heart of moral faithfulness is a commitment on the part of the moral agent to make ethical decisions by striving to "hear" and then honor the heart of God.[1]

---

1. Some support for the theological realism present in Barth is provided by Nigel Biggar in an essay which focuses on his trinitarian ethic. Biggar states that at the heart of Barth's theology was his conception of God as "not just a symbolic epitome of human achievement but as an active, living transcendent *reality* whose nature is unsettlingly strange to humans" (Biggar, "Barth's Trinitarian Ethic," 213, emphasis added). Moreover, some support for a theologically real approach to Christian ethics is provided when Biggar goes on to explain Barth's suggestion (contra Kant) that "we do not discover what is right simply by means of a process of autonomous reasoning; that is by deducing from the universal moral law of reason what is required in particular situations. Rather, we discover it in a unique event of *encounter* with the *living God* and his special command to us here and now. . . . The focus here is also very strongly on the interpersonal relationship between the human individual and God, a focus which never allows us to treat God merely as a useful concept, but always presents him as a *reality* at least as *free, spontaneous,* and *living* as human persons" (ibid., 214, emphasis added).

FIGURE 10

However, before elaborating upon what moral faithfulness is and why it is so integral to ministry fruitfulness in our increasingly post-Christian cultural context, we must first endeavor to understand what it's not. In a book titled *Lost in Transition: The Dark Side of Emerging Adulthood,* Christian sociologist Christian Smith and a team of co-authors include a chapter titled "Morality Adrift."[2] Based on the National Study of Youth and Religion (NSYR) referred to in chapter 2 of this work, Smith and his coauthors suggest that the moral lives of many of America's emerging adults seem to be earmarked by: an embrace of *moral relativism,* a commitment to *moral autonomy,* and a capacity for *moral compromise.* To be more specific, according to the NSYR:

- 30 percent of America's emerging adults profess a belief in a strong moral relativism—the notion that "morals are relative, there are not definite rights and wrongs for everybody."[3]

- The other two-thirds of America's emerging adults should be thought of as "reluctant moral agnostics and skeptics" who can't clearly explain why moral relativism is wrong.[4]

- 60 percent of emerging adults surveyed expressed a highly individualistic approach to morality: "morality is a personal choice, entirely a matter of individual decision. Moral rights and wrongs are essentially matters of individual opinion."[5]

2. Smith et al., *Lost in Transition,* 19–69.

3. Ibid., 27.

4. Ibid., 27.

5. Ibid., 21.

- One in three (34 percent) of those interviewed said they might do certain things they considered morally wrong (e.g., lying, cheating, and stealing) if they knew they could get away with it.[6]

Obviously, what we're talking about here is just about the opposite of the moral faithfulness described above. Furthermore, while I'd like to be able to say that this antithesis to a moral faithfulness only shows up in the lives of those outside the church, I can't. The truth is that the ethical lives of many of my students, even those who profess to be fervent Christ-followers, have been significantly influenced by the increasingly morally relativistic cultural context in which we currently find ourselves!

Keeping in mind what was said in chapter 2 about the way the "almost Christianity" that earmarks many members of the emerging generations seems to be at work in not a few members of the prior generations as well, this really is some distressing news. Indeed, it was this awareness of the effect a functional deism is having upon a multitude of Christian adults, their generational status notwithstanding, that prompted within me the haunting question: Shouldn't there be something distinctively Christian about the way Jesus' followers make ethical decisions and form moral opinions? Based on my understanding of the moral manner and message of Jesus, I'm of the opinion that a biblically-informed answer to this crucial question must be *yes!* Thus, I teach my students (and parishioners) that we don't have to allow our cultural context to completely determine us. A moral faithfulness is possible: Christians can learn to, like Jesus, make important moral choices by hearing and then honoring the heart of God! Such a moral faithfulness, I contend, will be distinguished by four criteria:

- a careful, rather than cavalier, attitude toward the moral dimension of life;

- a moral realism that works against a moral relativism;

- a commitment to moral accountability rather than autonomy;

- a commitment to Christ that enables a moral consistency rather than compromise.[7]

6. Ibid., 47.

7. For a detailed discussion of each of these criterion, please see Tyra, *Pursuing Moral Faithfulness*, 148–58.

FIGURE 11

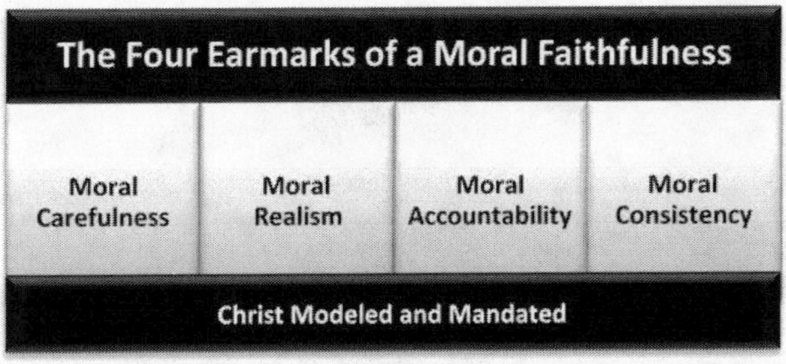

The Four Earmarks of a Moral Faithfulness			
Moral Carefulness	Moral Realism	Moral Accountability	Moral Consistency
Christ Modeled and Mandated			

Now, thus far we've merely glanced at the big picture of what a moral faithfulness is and isn't. Much more detail will be unveiled in subsequent sections of this chapter. At this point, however, I want to underscore several crucial contentions: First, I'm absolutely convinced that it's possible for evangelical Christians of all ages to render to God the moral faithfulness he desires and deserves. Second, for this to happen, the local church simply must become proactive about engaging in a much more intentional approach to the moral formation of congregation members, viewing this as a crucial component of Christian discipleship. Third, this moral formation ministry, to be effective, must be conducted in an ecclesial environment that's earmarked by a realist rather than non-realist understanding of Christ's Spirit.

The Critical Role the Holy Spirit Plays in a Moral Faithfulness

It's with the goal in mind of helping Christian disciples forge a moral faithfulness before God that I've put forward a moral model I refer to as the "ethic of responsible Christian discipleship."[8] I'd like to think that one of the things that makes this approach to making ethical decisions and forming moral opinions somewhat unique is the way it strives to be not only biblically-informed and Christ-centered, but genuinely *Spirit-empowered* as well!

---

8. See Tyra, *Pursuing Moral Faithfulness.*

FIGURE 12

Proverbs 2 is one of many biblical passages which indicate that the God we serve is both willing and able to impart moral wisdom into the lives of people who are eager to receive it.[9] Based upon both the Scriptures and my own experience as a moral agent, I'm proffering the notion that as we engage in certain spiritual discernment practices (Scripture study and prayer practiced in a theologically real manner)[10] and engage in an ethical deliberation process that strives to be both responsible and responsive,[11] we put ourselves in a place where God's Spirit is able to help us "hear" or sense the heart of God with respect to this or that moral matter, virtually "speaking" wisdom, understanding, and insight to us through the Scriptures, the community of faith, and/or directly to the self by means of his still small voice.[12] What this means is that the Bible not only supports the notion of

9. For more on this, see ibid., 183–88.

10. To engage in any spiritual discipline in a theologically real manner is to be careful to do so in a way that reckons with God's real presence. For example, to pray in a theologically real manner is to see ourselves conversing with God, himself, rather than simply talking toward the idea of God.

11. In a nutshell, to make an ethical decision in a "responsible" manner is to engage in a deliberation process that is responsible rather than irresponsible, being careful to do so as a responsible, rather than irresponsible, moral agent. To make an ethical decision in a "responsive" manner is, essentially, to prayerfully wait upon God for any specific guidance he deigns to provide with respect to the moral matter at hand. (For more on responsible and responsive ethical decision-making, see ibid., 229–53.)

12. For more on this, see ibid., 189. I must acknowledge here that, despite Barth's commitment to the possibility of Christians "hearing" the special command of God "here and now," his understanding of how this "hearing" occurs is decidedly less "prophetic" or charismatic than mine. For Barth, it's a vocation or general sense of "calling"

a theological realism, but a moral realism as well. Even as God himself is knowable to us by virtue of the revelatory ministries of Christ and the Holy Spirit, so is his heart concerning moral matters (see Eph 5:8–10, 15–17; Phil 1:9–11; Col 1:9–10).

When this embrace of a theological and moral realism is combined with a pneumatological realism, we have the potential for something I refer to as Spirit-enabled (or prophetic) moral guidance: the Holy Spirit in one way or another communicating divine moral guidance to Christ's followers in a way that's situation specific.[13] One way this can happen is when the Holy Spirit "brings to life," as it were, some portion of the Scriptures, impressing upon the Christian disciple the pertinence of this story or didactic (teaching) passage to the moral dilemma he or she is currently facing. Another way the phenomenon of "prophetic" moral guidance can occur is even more specific (and *charismatic*) in nature. A fully realist understanding of the Holy Spirit won't rule out the possibility of the risen Jesus "speaking" through his Spirit directly to the disciple, essentially prescribing a specific course of action with respect to the moral matter at hand. While this prompting can and often does result from the disciple's prayerful study of the Scriptures, it might also derive from the Spirit-inspired counsel provided by fellow church members, or the Spirit "speaking" directly to the disciple through his still small voice heard deep within (see John 14:26; Acts 10:19; 13:2).[14]

---

that will inform the manner in which a particular biblical principle or paradigm might play out in this or that situation (see Biggar, "Barth's Trinitarian Ethic, 222). As I indicate in the next paragraph presented above, while I'm willing to stipulate that divine moral guidance may indeed take this form, I also believe it can go beyond this, on occasion, to include ethical instruction more specific in nature and communicated by means of the Spirit speaking to us in one or more of the three ways referred to above.

13. In *Pursuing Moral Faithfulness,* I include an excursus discussion titled "The Two Ways of Understanding the Prophetic Phenomenon" (166–67). In that discussion, I explain how that, in general, the Scriptures seem to describe the prophetic phenomenon as occurring in two stages. The first stage is charismatic in nature and involves *discernment*—the Spirit enabling the prophet to somehow "hear" from God so as to receive a message and/or ministry assignment from him. The second stage is confrontational in nature and involves *deployment*—the Spirit empowering the prophet to speak and/or act into the lives of people on God's behalf. Most often these two aspects of the prophetic phenomenon occur in tandem: the prophet hears from God, then speaks and/or acts on behalf of God. As it relates to the notion of a "prophetic" moral guidance, I refer to it thusly because of the *charismatic* manner in which it is discerned. I elaborate some on this charismatic discernment process later in this book.

14. For more on the notion of "prophetic moral guidance," see Tyra, *Pursuing Moral Faithfulness,* 188–204.

FIGURE 13

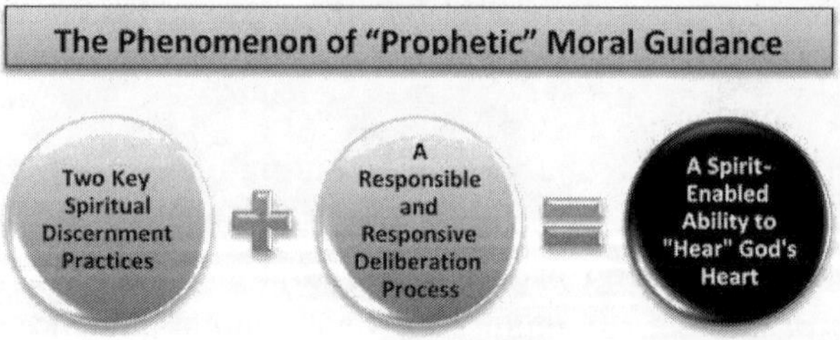

The Phenomenon of "Prophetic" Moral Guidance

In more than one of my books I've included a story from my ministry files which provides a powerful real-life illustration of how the Holy Spirit can "speak" into the lives of Christ's followers, providing them some quite specific moral guidance.[15]

> A young couple came to faith in Christ in one of the churches I pastored. One day the husband (I'll call him Rich) called the church office to let me know that he and his wife (I'll refer to her as Miranda) would not be attending the small group meeting that was scheduled to occur at my home that evening. He went on to indicate the reason why. He and Miranda were in the midst of a significant disagreement over a serious matter and did not think it would be a good idea to be around other couples that evening. They both felt that it would seem hypocritical to come to the meeting, pretending that everything was fine in their lives when the reality was otherwise.
>
> When I asked Rich if he wanted to talk about what was going on, he told me the story. In brief, Miranda had recently received news from her OB/GYN confirming a suspicion that she might be pregnant. Immediately, without discussing the matter with Rich, she had scheduled an appointment to have the pregnancy terminated. My wife Patti recollects that there was some sort of health concern at work in the situation. All I remember is Rich explaining that Miranda did not want to be pregnant again at that point in her life. Their daughter was just emerging from the "terrible twos" and they had both been looking forward to certain changes in their lifestyle which that development would bring. Rich indicated to me that though he was sympathetic to Miranda's desire not to be pregnant again, he felt that such a huge decision merited a discussion between the two of them and some serious consideration of

15. I'd like to express my appreciation here to IVP for allowing me to make this story available to the readers of this work.

where God's heart was on the matter. Becoming more and more heated, the disagreement had begun to spiral out of control. According to Rich, they had come to the point where they were not communicating at all.

Though I indicated to Rich that it's often during such tough times that a Christian couple most needs the love and support of a caring community, I put no pressure on him with respect to the small group meeting scheduled that evening. I told him I would be praying for him and Miranda and would, of course, keep the matter we had just discussed to myself.

Later that evening, the small group meeting was about to begin when, to my surprise, Rich and Miranda arrived, filling two empty chairs to my immediate left. Pleased that this young couple, new in the faith, had made the decision to attend the meeting after all, I began the meeting in the usual way by asking the members of the group to "check in," sharing what they sensed the Lord was currently "up to" in their lives based on their experiences the previous week, their study of Scripture, or perhaps what the Spirit of the Lord had spoken to them by means of his still small voice. It seemed wise at the time to begin with the person on my right who happened to be Patti, my wife. As Patti explained briefly what she sensed the Lord might be doing in her life at the moment, I took note of the fact that what she shared had an amazing degree of relevance for Rich and Miranda. Apparently Miranda sensed this as well; she began to dab at tears welling up in her eyes.

The really astounding thing is that this dynamic of the Holy Spirit speaking to Rich and Miranda through the "innocent" sharing of the others in the group repeated itself over and over again as everyone else checked in, commenting on what they felt like God was saying to or doing in them. And what was happening was not lost on this couple, especially Miranda. Before long she was a mess, mascara running down both cheeks!

Eventually, it came to be Rich's turn to weigh in. He simply deferred to Miranda. Everyone in the room sensed that God was, at that moment, effecting some work within her. When she was finally able to speak, she slowly articulated what was going on: that she had discovered that week that she was pregnant; that she had wasted no time in scheduling the procedure that would end the pregnancy. "But," she went on to say, "God has spoken to me through the sharing of each and every one of you tonight. I now know that I can't go through with the procedure. God wants me to have this baby."[16]

16. Tyra, *Missional Orthodoxy*, 252–54; Tyra, *Pursuing Moral Faithfulness*, 250–52.

Walking around somewhere today is a young woman in her early thirties who owes her very existence, at least in part, to the way in which the Holy Spirit spoke through that group of Christian disciples, without their even realizing it, providing her mom and dad with some very specific moral guidance. It has been experiences such as this that have encouraged me to believe that if our moral deliberation is going to do the *best* job possible of hearing and honoring the heart of God (Phil 1:9–11), it should strive to be responsive as well as responsible—that is, sensitive to any guidance the Spirit deigns to provide.

Some Biblical Support for the Notion of Spirit-Enabled Moral Guidance

Now, to be sure, any sort of spiritual prompting, regardless of how it comes to us, must be validated against the Scriptures. However, this important caveat notwithstanding, there's a good amount of biblical support for the notion of Spirit-enabled (prophetic) moral guidance (even though one of the signs of the pneumatological deficit at work in many evangelical churches is a lack of expectation with respect to it). For example, in Proverbs 2:1–6 we find a reference to God's willingness to communicate moral guidance to his people in response to their *waiting upon him* for it:

> My son, if you accept my words and store up my commands within you, turning your ear to wisdom and applying your heart to understanding—indeed, if you call out for insight and cry aloud for understanding, and if you look for it as for silver and search for it as for hidden treasure, then you will understand the fear of the LORD and find the knowledge of God. For the LORD gives wisdom; from his mouth come knowledge and understanding. (Prov 2:1–6)

Likewise, when we consider the fact that some scholars have argued that the Spirit of God is sometimes personified in the Hebrew Scriptures as Lady Wisdom,[17] we might also find some tacit biblical/theological support for the notion of a Spirit-enabled moral guidance in those several passages in Proverbs 8–9 which portray a personified wisdom "calling out," eager to provide moral guidance to those who will "listen" (e.g., Prov 8:1–6, 32–34; 9:1–6).

Such support can also be found in the Psalms. For instance, I'm inclined to believe that in Psalms 32:8–9 we ultimately hear God, himself,

17. Murphy, *Tree of Life*, 118–20, 144. See also Whybray, *Book of Proverbs*, 51; and Keener, *IVP Bible Background Commentary*, 301.

beseeching us to pay attention to the guidance he wants to provide. On this reading, it's possible to see God, through David, virtually pleading with his people to be responsive rather than resistant to the counsel and guidance he's eager to provide them:

> I will instruct you and teach you in the way you should go; I will counsel you with my loving eye on you. Do not be like the horse or the mule, which have no understanding but must be controlled by bit and bridle or they will not come to you. (Ps 32:8–9)

And then, there's Psalm 143:10 with its rather explicit reference to the Holy Spirit's role in providing divine moral guidance:

> Teach me to do your will, for you are my God; may your good Spirit lead me on level ground. (Ps 143:10)[18]

Moreover, additional Old Testament support for "prophetic" moral guidance can also be discerned in Ezekiel 36:24–27, a forward-looking passage which anticipates what appears to be an expanded role of the Spirit in the ethico-religious lives of God's people:

> For I will take you out of the nations; I will gather you from all the countries and bring you back into your own land. I will sprinkle clean water on you, and you will be clean; I will cleanse you from all your impurities and from all your idols. I will give you a new heart and put a new spirit in you; I will remove from you your heart of stone and give you a heart of flesh. And I will put my Spirit in you and move you to follow my decrees and be careful to keep my laws. (Ezek 36:24–27)

Some support from the New Testament for the possibility of a Spirit-enabled moral guidance is also available. Functioning as the epigraph for this chapter was a reference to the way Romans 8:4 indicates a moral enablement provided by the Holy Spirit. I'll also suggest that the way 1 Corinthians 2:6–16 connects the Spirit with the wisdom of God, and then indicates that, through the Spirit, Christian disciples are enabled to somehow possess the "mind of Christ" is surely relevant to our current discussion. As well, we must take into account the manner in which the Apostle Paul connects the moral life of Christians with the Holy Spirit in Galatians 5:16–26. Finally, I want to encourage evangelical readers to take a closer

18. Some other passages from the Psalms that support the notion of divine moral guidance include Pss 5:8; 16:7; 23:3; 25:4–5, 8–9; 27:11; 43:3; 51:6, 12; 73:24; 86:11; 119:18, 19, 26–27, 33–37, 64, 66, 68, 73, 108, 125, 133, 135, 144, 169, 171; 143:8.

look at how Paul's prayer for the Colossian Christians explicitly refers to the notion I'm advocating for: "For this reason, since the day we heard about you, we have not stopped praying for you. We continually ask God to fill you with the *knowledge of his will* through all *the wisdom and understanding that the Spirit gives*" (Col 1:9, emphasis added).

In sum, I'm convinced that the notion of a *Spirit-enabled moral guidance* is not only a possibility which enjoys biblical support, but is nothing short of a game changer when it comes to Christian ethics.[19] It's not just that evangelical church leaders need to be more intentional about the moral formation of their members. The moral model promoted in evangelical churches, to really be effective, must not only strive to be biblically-informed and Christ-centered, but genuinely Spirit-empowered as well!

How a Moral Faithfulness Contributes to Ministry Fruitfulness

Given what we've discovered about the rather cavalier manner in which many emerging adults approach morality, we might be tempted to assume that more and more Christians endeavoring to hear and honor the heart of God would be off-putting rather than compelling to them. But I've discovered that just the opposite is true. There are four reasons why I'm convinced that the ethic of responsible Christian discipleship I'm promoting possesses missional legs and can enhance any church's ministry fruitfulness. As it happens, all of these reasons are related either directly or dialectically to the sensibilities at work among huge numbers of our post-Christian peers—especially those from the emerging generations.

First, according to the research alluded to earlier (NSYR), most of our cultural peers aren't philosophically trained moral relativists, abjectly committed to an ethical nihilism. Indeed, most of the emerging adults I interact with each semester seem to be *conflicted*—intrinsically frustrated by the fact that the only two alternatives they see being presented to them are: their culture's embrace of an *abject moral relativism;* or a *strident ethical legalism* they associate with fundamentalist Christianity.

The problem is that this false dichotomy suggests to members of our society that they only have two options when it comes to making ethical decisions and forming moral opinions: by focusing on how their decisions affect *people*, or doing their duty with respect to some biblical *principles.*

19. For even more on the notion of "prophetic moral guidance," see Tyra, *Pursuing Moral Faithfulness*, 188–204.

FIGURE 14

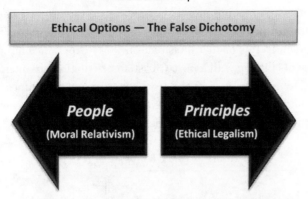

It should come as no surprise that, when confronted with such a false antithesis, very few of our contemporaries, especially those who are moving toward a post-Christian perspective, are going to prioritize principles over people. Thus, they feel that moral relativism is their only option, and Christianity as a belief system (and way of life) takes yet another hit!

However, here's the good news: the Gospels seem to portray Jesus resolving moral dilemmas in a way that strived to do justice to both principles and people.[20] A classic example of this can be found in the story of the woman caught in the act of adultery that's related in John 8:1–11.[21] Jesus responded to this contrived ethical dilemma in a way that, at the same time, honored the biblical principle (i.e., he didn't deny that the woman was guilty of a capital crime per Moses), but also demonstrated a profound degree of concern for the person involved (i.e., he refused to cast the first stone himself). Indeed, knowing that this poor, humiliated woman, though genuinely guilty of having transgressed the Mosaic law, was being used by his adversaries—the Pharisees—as a pawn in an attempt to try to trip him up, Jesus' concluding comments to her were pregnant (as it were) with both grace and truth: "Then neither do I condemn you. Go now and leave your

20. For more on this, see chapters 7 and 8 of Tyra, *Pursuing Moral Faithfulness*, 205–53.

21. Though fully aware that the authorship, date, and original placement of this pericope is highly disputed (see for example, Bruner, *Gospel of John*, 507–8; Ridderbos, *Gospel of John*, 285–87; Morris, *Gospel According to John*, 778–79; Bruce, *Gospel of John*, 413), I make use of it, having embraced the notion put forward by Ridderbos, Morris, and others that even if this passage was not an original part of the Fourth Gospel, it was, nevertheless, an insertion that was reflective of a real incident from Jesus' life. See Ridderbos, *Gospel of John*, 287; Morris, *Gospel According to John*, 779.

life of sin" (see John 8:11).[22] This is just one example, but it's apparent that Jesus' focus when making moral choices was on the original intention of God's moral commands and how this could be achieved in the life of this or that person in this or that life situation.[23] My experience has been that when students flirting with a post-Christian orientation are offered a third alternative to moral relativism and legalism—a moral faithfulness that, like the one embodied by Jesus, is *balanced* in its emphasis upon principles and people—they resonate with it big time!

FIGURE 15

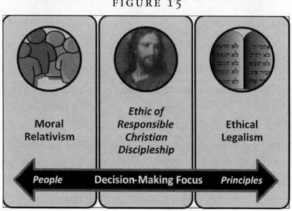

I've actually had students comment in class sessions (before their peers) that becoming aware of how Jesus embodied a moral faithfulness before God that's balanced and wholistic rather than unbalanced and myopic has caused them to "want to study more about how Jesus lived" and to "fall in love with him all over again."[24] It's difficult not to see some ministry value in an ethical model that elicits from students this kind of visceral response to the moral message and manner of Jesus!

A second reason for confidence in the fruit-bearing potential of this moral model, closely related to the first, derives from the somewhat

22. For more on the manner in which I make use of this story as a paradigm of sorts for an ethical decision-making approach which strives to be both responsible and responsive to the heart of God, see Tyra, *Pursuing Moral Faithfulness*, 222–28, 238–49.

23. Nowhere is Jesus' focus on the original intention of God's moral commands more apparent than in Matthew 5:17–48. Passages such as Mark 3:1–6 and John 7:14–24 (cf. John 5:1–18) indicate that this focus ultimately worked to his own detriment.

24. These are actual statements uttered by students during in-class discussions of the ethic of responsible Christian discipleship.

provocative way in which I approach the matter of moral absolutes. I've already indicated that most of my students, though greatly impacted by the widespread embrace of moral relativism, aren't studied, die-hard ethical antinomians (i.e., moral anarchists). Nor do they seem to be prepared to live with a full-blown moral relativism. Instead, many (if not most) of my students not only understand but actually appreciate the emphasis the ethic of responsible Christian discipleship places on the three moral virtues/behaviors articulated in Micah 6:8. Set in its immediate context, this classic passage, so very important to a biblically informed ethic, reads:

> With what shall I come before the LORD and bow down before the exalted God? Shall I come before him with burnt offerings, with calves a year old? Will the LORD be pleased with thousands of rams, with ten thousand rivers of olive oil? Shall I offer my first-born for my transgression, the fruit of my body for the sin of my soul? *He has shown you, O mortal, what is good. And what does the LORD require of you? To act justly and to love mercy and to walk humbly with your God.* (Micah 6:6–8, emphasis added)[25]

Just today (at the time of this writing) I was grading some final papers written by students for that "Developing a Christian Worldview" course I referred to in the previous chapter. The final unit of this required course focuses on Christian ethics. In this unit of study, I present to my students the idea that at the heart of the ethic of responsible Christian discipleship is not only Jesus' call to love God supremely and our neighbors as ourselves (Matt 22:34–40), but the ethical exhortations presented in Micah 6:8.

It's not at all uncommon in this course-concluding assignment to have students express their appreciation for having been made aware of how the Scriptures seem to indicate that the three virtues/behaviors enunciated in Micah 6:8 are not only grounded in the very character of God,[26] but also embodied in the moral message and manner of Jesus (e.g., Matt 23:23). To be sure, I'm careful to tell my students that all the moral commands articulated in Scripture should be taken seriously (see Matt 5:17–19). However, that said, I go on to pose to them three possibilities that, if accepted, are nothing short of game-changing when it comes to Christian ethics:

25. The tremendous importance of Micah 6:8 to biblical ethics has been underscored in such works as Maston, *Biblical Ethics*, 58.; Lovin, *Introduction to Christian Ethics*, 5–6; Holmes, *Ethics*, 55; Stassen and Gushee, *Kingdom Ethics*, 82; Nullens and Michener, *Matrix of Christian Ethics*, 149.

26. Some Old Testament passages that support this notion include Exod 34:6–8; Pss 36:5–6; 89:14; Hos 2:19–20.

1. What if, though all the divine commands in the Bible should be taken seriously, in God's moral economy there are only three transcendent, universally applicable moral absolutes—the ones articulated in Micah 6:8?

2. What if, rather than pit Micah 6:8 and Jesus' emphasis on love for God, neighbor, and self against one another, the three virtues of Micah 6:8 can and should be thought of as the biblically-informed key to discerning what a neighbor and self-love that's genuinely pleasing to God will and won't entail?[27]

3. Could it be, then, that in any given ethical dilemma, the response that's going to be closest to the heart of God is *always* going to be the one that does the best job of heeding (at the same time) the call to do justice, love with mercy, and walk humbly/faithfully before God?[28]

Please note: this doesn't make Christian ethics *easy*; there's still need for a Spirit-enabled contextualization of Micah 6:8 in this or that moral situation—a "*prophetic* word/impulse," as it were, through which a call by Jesus to specific ethical action might be discerned.[29] The point I'm endeavoring to make in the preceding paragraphs is simply that we shouldn't allow ourselves to believe that an ethic which takes seriously the notion of transcendent, universally applicable moral absolutes will necessarily be a nonstarter when encouraging our post-Christian cultural peers to reconsider the validity of a Christian worldview. My experience tells me that it doesn't have to be that way. Not at all.

A third reason for the conviction that the ethic of responsible Christian discipleship will prove attractive rather than repelling to many emerging adults, even those who consider themselves post-Christian, is because of the way its emphasis on the moral message and manner of Jesus (and the

27. In his commentary on the Gospel of Matthew, R. T. France references a rabbinic discussion located in the Babylonian Talmud (*Makkot*) which identifies Micah 6:8 as a summary of the law in three principles. See France, *Gospel of Matthew*, 844. For more support for this possibility see the discussion of the role of rules in the moral life presented in Lovin, *Christian Ethics*, 57–60.

28. Some support for this bold but profoundly important assertion can be found in Holmes, *Ethics*, 55.

29. For more on this notion, and the similarities which exist between the model I'm proffering and the "prophetic casuistry" promoted by Donald Bloesch, see Tyra, *Pursuing Moral Faithfulness*, 164–67. See also Bloesch, *Freedom for Obedience*, 19-20, 55–57; and Rae, *Moral Choices*, 47.

virtues prescribed in Micah 6:8) accords with the emerging generations' passion for *justice* (rather than exploitation), *mercy* (rather than judgmentalism), and *humility* (rather than arrogance or demagoguery). Whether this correspondence between the virtues of Micah 6:8 and the innate moral sensibilities present in the hearts and minds of many members of the emerging generations is providential or a fluke, I'll allow the reader to decide. My suggestion is simply that this very real correspondence needs to be acknowledged and leaned into by Christian disciples eager to influence their post-Christian peers for Christ.

A final reason for my confidence in the missional utility of the ethic of responsible Christian discipleship is the manner in which my students seem to appreciate the model's emphasis on community and accountability rather than an abject moral autonomy. I provide my students with nine questions they can ask themselves as part of a moral deliberation process to test how responsible and responsive it really is. Four of these nine self-reflection questions have the effect of encouraging the moral agent to *avoid* making a moral choice entirely on their own and without giving some serious consideration as to how it will affect those around him or her. Specifically, one of these questions has the moral agent asking himself or herself: *Am I willing to have the people most important to me know about this decision, and to accept the consequences for it without trying to shift blame to someone else?*[30]

---

30. The entire set of reflection questions includes: (1) Have I done a really good job of gathering all the facts so that I might accurately discern what's going on in front of me? (2) Have I identified the most significant moral issue at work in this situation and what all of my options are with respect to it? (3) Have I been careful to engage in a thoughtful examination of what God's word has to say about this kind of situation—what moral principles presented in Scripture might apply? (4) Have I done a really good job of trying to predict what the consequences of each possible response to this situation are likely to be? (5) Which of the actions I'm considering allows me to function with the strongest degree of integrity—to behave in a manner congruent with the virtues I've always espoused, the various roles I've been called to play in life, and the most important commitments I've made to the people who depend on me? (6) Am I willing to have the people most important to me know about this decision—to accept the consequences for it without trying to shift blame to someone else? (7) What does acting justly, loving with mercy, and walking humbly before God look like in this particular situation? (8) Have I been careful to bathe this entire moral deliberation process in some serious prayer offered in a theologically real manner? (9) Have I consulted with other members of my community of faith, humbly seeking their counsel and prayers regarding this issue? For more on the nature and effect of these questions, see Tyra, *Pursuing Moral Faithfulness*, 236–53.

I'll acknowledge here that while I was still working on the manuscript for *Pursuing Moral Faithfulness*, I toyed with the idea of paring this particular question from the list out of concern for brevity. However, it just so happened that this editorial move was being contemplated at the same time I was teaching an evening course on Christian ethics. I still remember telling the class one evening that I was thinking about removing this particular query from my list self-reflection questions. Immediately, a young woman who did not tend to be outspoken in class, spoke up and virtually pleaded with me not to make that editing move. Her take was that, for all the talk of how the members of her generation prize community, she was a witness to a tendency in many of her peers toward a radical individualism and penchant for privacy. She went on to comment on how important it is, in her opinion, for people her age to be challenged to make themselves accountable to others for their moral choices. It was in large part due to that student's passionate intercession that this question showed up in the published text and continues to play a vital role in the moral model it proffers. To the degree this young woman spoke for others in her demographic, I have reason to believe that the moral faithfulness I'm espousing does indeed possess the potential to resonate deeply in the hearts of at least some of our post-Christian peers.[31]

In sum, as counterintuitive as it may seem, my experience has been that one way to encourage post-Christians to take another look at Christ and the church is to "talk turkey" with them about the possibility of (and need for) a moral faithfulness, and then to humbly invite these spiritually-open-but-frustrated folks to investigate how a participation with our faith community might enable them to become responsible ethical actors on the stage of human history. This ideal—becoming responsible rather than irresponsible moral agents—possesses more intrinsic appeal than we may think. Of course, there is no magic bullet. Still, it really does seem to be true that many post-Christians, especially those from the emerging generations, are eager to discover that there's more to the faith than what they've seen

31. This is yet another personal observation which reeks of irony since the findings of the NSYR presented above indicate that a hefty majority (60 percent) of the emerging adults surveyed indicated a preference for a highly individualistic approach to morality. An alternative, however, to the conclusion that even my most religiously jaded students are nevertheless radically atypical, is the possibility that what I'm witnessing in their lives is the Spirit of mission at work, readying them for a fresh, compelling presentation of the Christian faith that, while thoughtfully and prayerfully contextualized for the emerging culture, avoids an over-accommodation to it. I'll have more to say about the contextualization dynamic at the heart of a missional faithfulness in the next chapter.

going on in churches rife with a functional deism and the "almost Christi-anity" it produces. Increasing numbers of church members doing their best, with the help of Christ's Spirit, to embody the ethic of responsible Christian discipleship can't help but encourage this missionally fruitful dynamic.

The preceding paragraph functions as a near-perfect segue to that third form of faithfulness which God desires (and our post-Christian peers desperately need to witness). My argument is that a genuine spiritual faithfulness will contribute greatly to the rendering of a moral faithfulness which, in turn, is crucial to a missional faithfulness. But what is a missional faithfulness? And why is a realist (instead of a non-realist) understanding and experience of the Holy Spirit crucial to it? These two very important queries will be discussed in the chapter which follows.

5

Pneumatological Realism and a
Missional Faithfulness

But you will receive power when the Holy Spirit comes on you; and you will
be my witnesses in Jerusalem, and in all Judea and Samaria, and to the ends of
the earth.

—ACTS 1:8

MISSIONARY PASTOR AND THEOLOGIAN J. H. Bavinck once made the following observation:

> People wish to remain quiet, in the peaceful little church under the
> high Gothic arches; they would brood about God and be preoc-
> cupied with the needs of their own souls. They do not want to be
> shocked by the bewildering idea that there are still many hundreds
> of millions of people who have never heard the gospel.[1]

As important as spiritual and moral faithfulness are to impacting our
culture for Christ, they must be combined with yet another type of fidelity
for God's ultimate purposes to be achieved. The "Cape Town Commitment"
(created at Cape Town 2010: The Third Lausanne Congress on World Evan-
gelization) refers to the Holy Spirit thusly: *"He is the missionary Spirit sent
by the missionary Father and the missionary Son, breathing life and power
into God's missionary Church."*[2] One of the implications of this extraordi-

1. Bavinck, *Introduction to the Science of Missions*, 277.
2. Lausanne Movement, "Cape Town Commitment," Part 1, §5, emphasis original.

nary pneumatological statement would seem to be that to experience a ministry fruitfulness at this critical time in the history of North American culture, we simply must allow the Holy Spirit to help us embody a faithfulness that's missional in nature!

Just what is a missional faithfulness, and why is a pneumatological realism so very crucial to its cultivation? These are the two main questions I'll provide responses to in this essay as I discuss the essence of a missional faithfulness and the importance of the Holy Spirit to it. Most of us know that Pentecostal Christianity is "blowing up" around the world, especially in the Global South. This chapter will conclude with the bold assertion that an enthusiastic embrace of the missional pneumatology presented in these pages can take an evangelical engagement in missional ministry here in the West to an entirely new level.

The Essence of Missional Faithfulness

Speaking broadly, a missional faithfulness requires that Christ's followers do justice, simultaneously, to Jude's exhortation to *keep contending* for the historic Christian faith (Jude 3) and Paul's implicit encouragement to *keep contextualizing* the gospel in compelling ways within various cultural settings (1 Cor 9:20–22).[3] Unfortunately, church history tells us that Christians have not always done an adequate job of remaining faithful to both Jude 3 and 1 Corinthians 9:20–22. Traditional churches can focus so much on the contending task that they fail to adequately contextualize the faith for new cultural groups. On the other hand, Progressive/Emerging churches can so focus on the contextualizing task that they fail to adequately contend for the faith that was "once for all entrusted to God's holy people." But according to the Bible: "It is good to grasp the one and not let go of the other. The man who fears God will avoid all extremes" (Eccl 7:18). In other words, a missional faithfulness occurs when we embrace the tension between the contending and contextualizing tasks and *faithfully* engage in both—at the same time.

---

3. For more on this, see Tyra, *Missional Orthodoxy*, 11–12. See also Newbigin, *Gospel in a Pluralist Society*, 153–54.

FIGURE 16

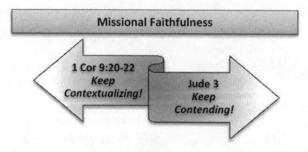

In *A Missional Orthodoxy,* I suggest that it's possible to see a conceptual analogy between Christ's incarnation (the divine Son assuming human flesh) and an *incarnational* approach to ministry contextualization on the part of his church. The Chalcedonian definition hammered out by the church fathers in 451 AD insisted that, for Christ's twin ministries of revelation and redemption to be theologically coherent and truly transformational, it was necessary for him to be fully God and fully man at the same time. The technical term for this perfect balance between the divine and human natures of Jesus is *hypostatic union.* I'm arguing that, similarly, an *incarnational* approach to ministry contextualization that's truly transformational (that truly transforms individual lives and cultures) will require a balanced sensitivity to both the *divine* element inherent in the gospel—the christological verities (truths about Jesus) which "underwrite the Christian gospel"[4]—and the *human* element inherent in the conditions "on the ground" within any given ministry context (the specifics of this or that individual or culture). In other words, just as a hypostatic union (of the two natures of Jesus) is necessary for a theologically coherent conception of the revelatory and redemptive ministries accomplished by Christ, a carefully balanced sensitivity to both the contending and contextualizing tasks is crucial if we are to avoid an under-contextualization of the gospel on the one hand (contra 1 Cor 9:20–22), or an over-contextualization of the gospel

---

4. These four christological doctrines are: Jesus is both God and man (see John 20:31; 1 John 5:5, 11–12; 2 John 1:7–9); Jesus' death on the cross possessed an atoning significance (see 1 Cor 15:1–3; 1 John 2:2; 4:10); Jesus rose bodily from the grave (see Rom 10:9–10; 1 Cor 15:1–5); and Jesus is now Lord of all (see Rom 10:9–10; cf. Rom 14:9–12; 1 Cor 12:3; Phil 2:9–11; Heb 3:1, 15). For more on the importance of the verities to a missional faithfulness, see Tyra, *Missional Orthodoxy,* 15, 49–51, 72–79, 80, 85n67, 86, 95–96, 102–109, 114, 121–22, 168, 184, 196, 208, 211, 249–50, 349, 356–57, 368.

on the other (contra Jude 1:3).[5] I apologize if this paragraph came off as overly technical, and therefore required an extra-careful reading. The point of it is that, because we're after a contextualization of the gospel that's *truly transformational* rather than merely theoretical or conceptual, a missional faithfulness needs to be understood for what it is: a really big deal!

The Critical Role the Holy Spirit Plays in a Missional Faithfulness

Confident that some additional understanding of the essence of a missional faithfulness will be achieved by doing so, I'm going to shift the focus of our discussion at this point to the reason why a pneumatological realism is so very important to it. In truth, the importance of the Holy Spirit to the missional endeavor has been underscored by some of the major voices in the missional conversation.[6] It's my contention that there are two primary ways the Spirit of mission contributes to missional ministry:

- first, by enabling the missional community to *discern* what God is up to in this or that ministry context (Prov 19:21); and

- second, by empowering the missional community to adequately *represent* the kingdom of God to people who are hurting within the target community.

I'm convinced that if we want church members to become fully missional in the way they live out their faith, we need to help them possess a keen understanding of these two principal ways the Holy Spirit (and a realist rather than non-realist understanding and experience of him) really are crucial to the missional endeavor.

The Holy Spirit and the Ministry Discernment Dynamic

Some missional experts have insisted that a contemporary engagement in the process of ministry contextualization, to qualify as missional, must involve an *imaginative dialogue* between the biblical text and the cultural context. These missional experts go on to stipulate that the purpose of this

---

5. Ibid., 95–110.

6. For example, see Newbigin, *Gospel in a Pluralist Society*, 118–19; Guder, *Missional Church*, 142, 145; Roxburgh and Boren, *Introducing the Missional Church*, 122.

dialogue is to help the members of the missional community discern what God is already up to in this or that ministry location so they can cooperate with him in it (Prov 19:21).[7] More precisely, implicit in this assertion is the conviction that such a dialogue will enable the members of the missional community to discern the ministry leading of the Holy Spirit for this or that ministry milieu.[8] Such discernment is considered crucial to the ministry contextualization task.

Thus, one of the main reasons why a pneumatological realism can make a huge contribution to missional ministry is that at the heart of missional ministry is a contextualization question that's pneumatological in nature. This crucial question is: What's the Spirit of mission up to in this ministry context, and how might/ought we cooperate with him in the fulfilling of God's purposes within it?[9] I hold firmly to the idea that if a Spirit-sensitive approach to ministry discernment is to be authentically engaged in, it will require that the members of the missional community actually believe that it's possible to interact with Christ's Spirit in a personal, interactive, "prophetic" manner.[10] After all, it makes no sense to pose this pneumatological question if we don't actually *expect* the Holy Spirit to in some way *respond*, providing some situation-specific ministry direction in the process. What this suggests, therefore, is that for an ecclesial community to adequately discern the leading of the Spirit with respect to missional ministry, something akin to what I'm referring to as pneumatological realism is required.

In their book *Introducing the Missional Church*, Alan Roxburgh and Scott Boren tell of a retired white couple who, wanting to become more missional and less consumeristic in the way they approached their faith, moved closer to their church's building even though the neighborhood around it was now "primarily Black-American." Wanting to impact the

---

7. For example, see Roxburgh and Boren, *Introducing the Missional Church*, 99.

8. Tyra, *Missional Orthodoxy*, 85.

9. Roxburgh and Boren, *Introducing the Missional Church*, 20, 52, 70, 86.

10. Commenting on Barth's doctrine of the word of God, John Franke asserts: "God speaks, and, by a miracle enacted by God through the work of the Holy Spirit, this speech is actually heard and received by human beings who are made alive and enabled by the grace and mercy of God to live lives of faith and obedience to God as an act of God's covenant faithfulness" (Franke, *Barth*, 117). While I, like most Pentevangelicals, make a distinction between the authority of the revelation provided in Scripture and any "revelations" contemporary members of Christ's body might receive from the Spirit, I'm committed to the idea that the prophetic dynamic at work in the inscripturation process persists into the post-apostolic era and functions in essentially the same manner.

neighborhood for Christ, the wife (her name was Mary) began a journey down the main street, speaking to shopkeepers about ways in which the church might be of help to the community. When one shopkeeper "unceremoniously told her to leave and not come back" she was understandably shaken. But, as she and her small group prayed about this situation, Roxburgh and Boren explain, "God gave Mary a new imagination." In other words, in some way or another, the Spirit spoke to this woman, providing her with an innovative approach to building relationships with her new neighbors. In response to what I hold to be an experience of some "prophetic" (i.e., Spirit-provided) ministry guidance, this retired couple took up the habit of routinely traveling down the main street with garbage bags picking up litter along the way. As time passed, the members of the community began to nod in acknowledgement of what this retired couple was doing. A full year later, the shopkeeper who had been so rude to Mary invited her in for some coffee. A conversation began that eventually turned into a coalition of community members and a plan to develop housing within the neighborhood.[11]

Roxburgh and Boren cite this story to indicate how ordinary church members can engage in an imaginative process of ministry contextualization. I contend that it also serves as an example of how important it is for the members of missional communities to not only pray to the Spirit of mission for ministry guidance, but to do so actually expecting the Holy Spirit to respond to this appeal for divine wisdom (see Jas 1:5).

The Holy Spirit and the Kingdom-Representing Dynamic

Pressing further, many missional thinkers contend that, per the New Testament, the strategic goal of a properly contextualized missional ministry should be a faithful representation of the kingdom of God to a given neighborhood, community, or people group. But this critical observation then raises the following questions: what does this kingdom representation involve and how does it occur?

For his part, the venerable missional theologian Lesslie Newbigin famously insisted that, in the first century, Christian proclamation was not so much a lecture forced on uninterested ears, but an enthusiastic response to a question continually being put to the church by those in the surrounding

11. I also relate this story in only a slightly different manner in Tyra, *Holy Spirit in Mission*, 142. My thanks to IVP for their willingness to allow me to adapt it for use here.

community: "What is going on?"[12] Newbigin went on to explain that this crucial, ministry-generating question was prompted by a "new reality" at work in the church and perceptible to those outside it.[13] Moreover, said Newbigin, this all-important "new reality" was the *presence* and *activity* of the Holy Spirit—the *arrabōn* or foretaste of God's coming kingdom (Eph 1:13–14).[14] This identification of the Holy Spirit as the "new reality" in the church would seem to provide some impressive support for the emphasis I'm placing on the need for a realist rather than non-realist understanding and experience of the Spirit by rank-and-file church members.[15]

Now, as for how this "new reality" is to be manifested in the local church, the multiple authors of the widely read *Missional Church: A Vision for the Sending of the Church in North America* contend that the approach should be Christocentric. It is by studying "Jesus' way of carrying out God's mission," say these authors, that "we discover that the church is to represent God's reign as its *community*, its *servant*, and its *messenger*."[16] Thus, this much-respected work issues a call for churches in the post-Christian West to engage in the missional endeavor by means of three Christ-modeled, kingdom-representing ministry activities: community, service, and proclamation. Just as Jesus was careful to embody God's reign by (1) creating a winsome community earmarked by both inclusion and instruction, acceptance and accountability; (2) serving the poor, the sick, and the demonized with works of provision, healing, and exorcism; and (3) proclaiming the message of the kingdom to all who would listen, so should his Spirit-empowered followers. In other words, the *koinonia* (community), *diakonia* (service), and *kerygma* (proclamation) of local churches can and should, in the power of the Spirit, serve to embody in the here and now the reality of Christ's coming kingdom.[17]

12. Newbigin, *Gospel in a Pluralist Society*, 117.

13. Ibid., 116–17.

14. Ibid., 120.

15. For more on the emphasis Newbigin placed on pneumatology in his Trinitarian missiology, see Amos Yong, "Pluralism, Secularism and Pentecost," 147–59.

16. Guder, *Missional Church*, 102.

17. Though I won't presume to know the extent to which Barth exercised an influence on the authors of *Missional Church*, I will point out that the book's emphasis on the church's engagement in *koinonia*, *diakonia*, and *kerygma* reminds me of a discussion by Eberhard Busch of the role Barth saw the Spirit playing in the missional "sending" of the Christian community into the world (see Busch, *The Great Passion*, 234–37). And yet, the irony is that though Barth scholar Philip Rosato can on the one hand refer to Barth's

FIGURE 17

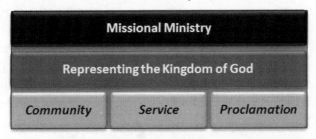

One of my favorite passages from *Missional Church*—one that I would encourage all evangelical pastors to incorporate into their ecclesiology (understanding of the church's nature and mission)—reads thusly:

> In summary, the church in mission may be characterized as the sign of Messiah's coming. Our being, doing, and speaking are signs that his coming is "already" and "not yet." He is here already or the signs would not be present. He is coming still or the signs would not be muted. Broken though they may be, the signs persist in the world by the Spirit's insistence, and they spell hope for the renewal of the human community in the final reconciliation of all things to God through the Lord Christ. In this respect, the Church is the preview community, the foretaste and harbinger of the coming reign of God.[18]

theology as a "Spirit theology" and opine that Barth's pneumatology "leads the reader to the core of his thought on every major dimension of Christian theology" (Rosato, *The Spirit as Lord*, 181), in the epilogue of his book-length examination of this Spirit theology, Rosato offers the following critical observation as it relates to Barth's concept of mission: "Although the Spirit is *theoretically* given much space in the treatment of the Christian community in *Church Dogmatics,* Christ so controls the being of the Christian that the Spirit's mediating function becomes rather lifeless. There is no prophetic thrust to the ecclesial dimensions of Barth's pneumatology. . . . The work of the church is essentially that of witnessing to the reconciliation won by Christ and not that of furthering the but incipient victory by cooperating in the transforming action of the Spirit who first anointed Jesus and who enabled Him to become the inaugurator of liberation for the oppressed. . . . The dangerous tendency in Barth's ecclesiology is that . . . the Church is huddled around Christ the Victor, but not sent out on the liberating mission of the Kingdom's harbinger, the Lord and Giver of Life [i.e., the Holy Spirit]" (ibid., 185). The contrast between Busch and Rosato couldn't be more striking! Finally, it should be noted that fellow Barth scholar, John Thompson—not at all reluctant to critique some of Rosato's conclusions—offers a rather substantial critique of the complaint presented above, essentially echoing Busch's take with respect to this topic (see Thompson, *The Holy Spirit,* 198–200).

18. Guder, *Missional Church*, 108.

The role of the Holy Spirit in the mission of the church is indicated in this passage by the assertion that "the signs persist in the world by the Spirit's insistence." Indeed, to the authors' credit, scattered throughout *Missional Church* are numerous references to the importance of the Holy Spirit to the church's ministry of kingdom representation.[19] And yet, I humbly maintain that, while the allusions to the importance of the Spirit to missional ministry in *Missional Church* are a step in the right direction, they're nevertheless insufficient. Given the fact that Newbigin—the doyen of the missional movement—was careful to describe the "new reality" at work in the church in pneumatological as well as christological terms, a much more explicit understanding of just how crucial a pneumatological realism is to an ecclesial environment productive of a missional faithfulness is warranted. Indeed, what's required in our place and day is a *missional pneumatology* which properly emphasizes the missionary nature of the Holy Spirit and the crucial need for a realist experience of him! Presented below are four lines of argument which I believe support this bold assertion.

The Biblical Case for Prophetic Capacity

A carefully constructed biblical theology of the Spirit will, I contend, indicate the connection which exists between the coming of the Spirit and the phenomenon of prophetic activity (Spirit-inspired speech and action).

FIGURE 18

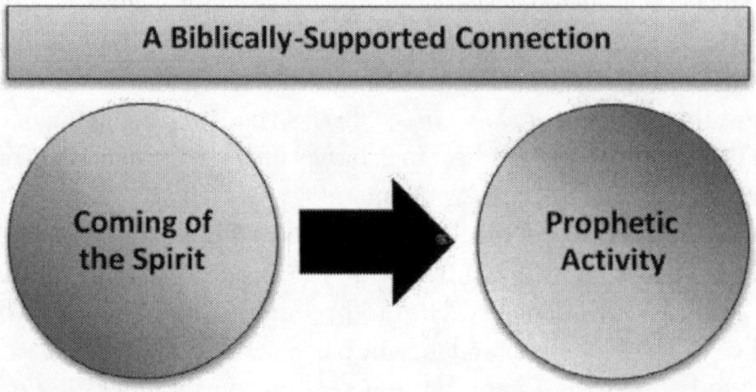

A Biblically-Supported Connection

Coming of the Spirit → Prophetic Activity

19. Over and over again, *Missional Church* speaks of the importance of the Holy Spirit to missional ministry. For example, see ibid., 4, 8, 12–13, 69, 82, 86–87, 96, 108, 114, 123, 134, 140–41, 142–82, 183–84, 199–200, 214, 223, 226, 231, 236, 238–39, 242, 247, 255–56, 259, 265, 267.

Scattered throughout the Bible are passages which seem to connect the coming of the Spirit upon God's people with the phenomenon of prophetic speech and action—people being compelled by the Spirit to speak and act in God's name. Actually, what we find spread across both testaments is a coherent, extremely meaningful *pneumatological* drama comprised of three main acts, each filled with one or more story-advancing scenes.

In the first act of this drama, we discover how that at a pivotal moment near the beginning of the Old Testament era, Moses, himself a prophet (Deut 34:10), expresses a wish that all of God's people would be filled with God's Spirit and become involved in prophetic activity (Num 11:29; cf. 11:25–28). Then, as if to illustrate this connection between the Spirit and the prophetic phenomenon Moses had in mind, throughout the rest of the Old Testament are many passages which seem to indicate that prophetic activity—both prophetic speech and action—routinely occurs when God's Spirit comes upon people who belong to him.[20]

In the second act of the drama, the setting of which is near the end of the Old Testament era, we find God inspiring the prophet Joel to announce that Moses' wish (that all of God's people might be filled with God's Spirit and become involved in prophetic activity) will someday come true! Because of the importance of this passage, I'll cite it here: "And afterward, I will pour out my Spirit on all people. Your sons and daughters will prophesy, your old men will dream dreams, your young men will see visions. Even on my servants, both men and women, I will pour out my Spirit in those days" (Joel 2:28–29). There's a sense that this is how the Old Testament ends with respect to its pneumatology—with this promise of a future outpouring of the Spirit upon all of God's people, regardless of traditional gender, generational, and class distinctions.

However, after a not-so-brief intermission, the drama resumes as we discover in the New Testament, as well, many passages which seem to evidence a connection between the Holy Spirit and prophetic speech and action. Functioning as sort of a segue between the second and third acts of the pneumatological story are several sections in the Gospel of Luke which seem to emphasize such a "connection":

- The prophetic activity in the infancy narratives of Luke (Luke 1:41–45, 67; 2:25–28).

20. For example, see 1 Sam 10:6, 9–10; 19:19–20, 23; Num 24:2–3; 1 Chr 12:18; 2 Chr 15:1–2; 20:14–15; 24:20; Isa 61:1; Ezek 11:5.

- The prophetic activity in the inauguration narrative of Luke (Luke 3:21–22; 4:1–13; 4:14–30; 4:31–44; cf. Isa 61:1).

- The prophetic activity alluded to in Jesus' preparation of his disciples (Luke 12:11–12; cf. Matt 10:18–20).

And yet, it's in the second chapter of the book of Acts that we witness the formal unveiling of the third act of the drama as an inspired apostle Peter boldly announces to a curious crowd that, with the coming of the Holy Spirit on the day of Pentecost, both Moses' wish and Joel's promise have finally been fulfilled![21] Again, because of its importance, I'll cite this passage here:

> Then Peter stood up with the Eleven, raised his voice and addressed the crowd: "Fellow Jews and all of you who live in Jerusalem, let me explain this to you; listen carefully to what I say. These men are not drunk, as you suppose. It's only nine in the morning! No, this is what was spoken by the prophet Joel: 'In the last days, God says, I will pour out my Spirit on all people. Your sons and daughters will prophesy, your young men will see visions, your old men will dream dreams. Even on my servants, both men and women, I will pour out my Spirit in those days, and they will prophesy.'" (Acts 2:14–18)

Noteworthy is the fact that Peter seems to be underscoring here the connection between what was happening to the one hundred twenty believers on the day of Pentecost and the phenomenon of prophecy. Though Peter would go on to explain to the crowd of onlookers that what they were seeing and hearing was indicative of Christ's resurrection and exaltation to the right hand of God (Acts 2:32–33), apparently, the first thing the Spirit did, having come upon the church, was to impart to *all* of Christ's followers a new *prophetic capacity* to speak and act on God's behalf.[22]

But this is not the end of the pneumatological story per se. Many more passages supportive of the "connection" are provided in the remainder of

21. Actually, it should be noted that even before its depiction of the outpouring of the Holy Spirit on the church in Acts 2, the book of Acts provides some initial support for the connection between the Holy Spirit and prophetic speech (see Acts 1:8, 16).

22. Referring to how Luke-Acts as a whole characterizes the relationship between Jesus' ministry and that of his first followers, charismatic theologian Roger Stronstad states: "The Gospel is the story of Jesus, the unique Charismatic Prophet; the Acts is the story of His disciples, a community of Charismatic prophets. As Luke describes it, their respective ministries of salvation are possible only through the anointing, empowering, and leading of the Holy Spirit" (see Stronstad, *Charismatic Theology of St. Luke*, 34–35).

the New Testament. For example, the rest of the book of Acts is replete with stories of Christ-followers being empowered by the Holy Spirit to engage in prophetic speech and action. Indeed, in no fewer than twenty-one of the twenty-eight chapters which make up the book of Acts, I can identify an explicit reference to some form of prophetic activity. Over and over again in Acts we find people being filled or re-filled with the Holy Spirit and, as a result,

- praising God with prophetic speech;
- receiving from God personal words of encouragement;
- receiving from God special ministry assignments;
- speaking and acting into the lives of others in Christ's name;
- making a difference in people's lives; and (in the process)
- being used by the Holy Spirit to achieve God's missional purposes in the world!

Moreover, we should also take note of how the "connection" we see presented in the rest of the Bible shows up in some of Paul's letters as well. Despite the fact that Paul's pneumatology seems to be more soteriological (oriented toward the experience of salvation) than the "vocational," "charismatic," or "missional" pneumatology apparent in Luke-Acts,[23] I believe it's possible nevertheless to identify several passages in Paul's writings which seem to connect the phenomenon of prophetic activity with the coming of the Spirit,[24] and which suggest that the activity of the Spirit in the lives of believers can and should exercise a missional effect (e.g., Rom 8:15–16; cf. Gal 4:6; Rom 8:26–27; 1 Cor 12–14; Eph 5:15–20).[25]

In sum, the Bible seems to evidence a dynamic connection between empowering encounters with the Holy Spirit—the Spirit of mission—and the phenomenon of prophetic activity (Spirit-prompted and enabled speech and action). Passage after passage in both the Old and New Testaments demonstrate a pattern that's simply too apparent to ignore: when the Spirit of God comes upon a person or persons, a divinely enabled ability to speak and/or act into the lives of others on God's behalf is often the result. Put differently, my thesis is that both the Old and New Testaments teach

23. See Tyra, *Holy Spirit in Mission*, 68–69.

24. For more on this, see ibid., 68–74.

25. Certainly, this was the case with Paul himself, as Acts 13:9–12 makes clear.

that when the Spirit of mission comes upon God's people in an empowering manner, something missionally significant occurs: *the impartation of
prophetic capacity.* This prophetic capacity involves a Spirit-enabled ability
to—like Ananias of Damascus—hear God's voice, receive ministry assignments from him, and speak and act into the lives of hurting people on his
behalf, making disciples, and building up Christ's church in the process
(see Acts 9:10–22).[26]

FIGURE 19

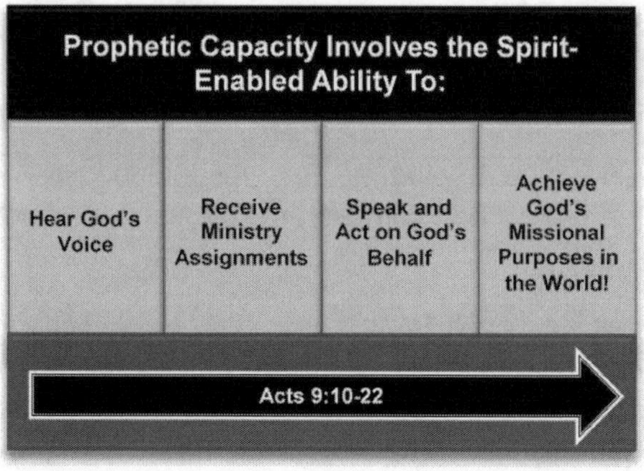

Prophetic Capacity Involves the Spirit-Enabled Ability To:

| Hear God's Voice | Receive Ministry Assignments | Speak and Act on God's Behalf | Achieve God's Missional Purposes in the World! |

Acts 9:10-22

The Connection between Prophetic Activity and Missional Faithfulness

Pressing further, I'll suggest that a carefully constructed biblical theology
of the Spirit will also disclose the crucial connection between the prophetic activity just described and the missional faithfulness we observe
in the book of Acts. According to Luke's account, it was in an undeniably
"prophetic" (i.e., Spirit-prompted and empowered) manner that the earliest Christians proceeded to turn their world upside-down for Christ (Acts
17:6, KJV). To be more specific, on nearly every page of Luke's record of the
earliest church, we find references to believers engaging in what I refer to
as *prophetic evangelism, edification,* and *equipping*: apostles and rank-and-
file disciples (like Ananias of Damascus) ministering to others in Spirit-
prompted ways as they speak and/or act into their lives at the behest of the
risen Christ. To be even more precise, it's my contention that prophetic

26. See Tyra, *Holy Spirit in Mission,* 68, 98, 129.

evangelism, edification, and equipping occur when Christ's followers are enabled by Christ's Spirit to speak and/or act into the lives of others in an impromptu, ad hoc manner with evangelizing, edifying, and equipping effects.[27]

FIGURE 20

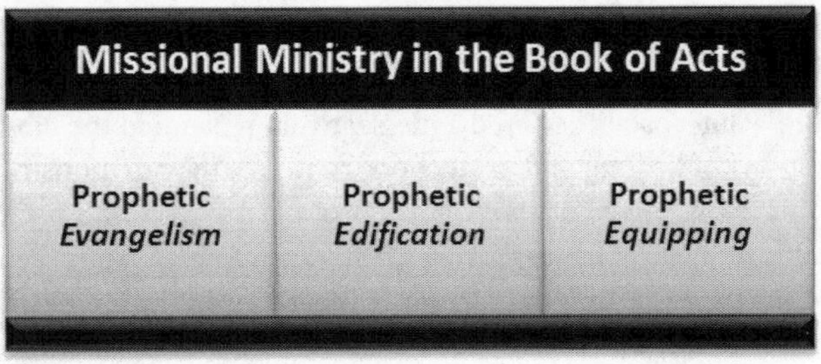

Missional Ministry in the Book of Acts		
Prophetic Evangelism	Prophetic Edification	Prophetic Equipping

Now, because I see a correlation between the ministries of edification, equipping, and evangelism with an engagement in the kingdom-representing ministries advocated for by the authors of *Missional Church*—community, service, and proclamation—I'm suggesting that one can't study the book of Acts without being made aware of how big a role prophetic speech and action played in the missional faithfulness of the first followers of Jesus!

The Connection between Prophetic Activity and the Global Growth of Pentecostalism

An argument can also be made for the idea that, in the modern era, the prolific growth of Pentecostalism around the globe (especially in the majority world) has been due, at least in part, to a similarly "prophetic" engagement in these three ministry activities.[28]

Traditionally, the proposed explanations for the phenomenal growth of Pentecostalism[29] worldwide emphasize: (1) the ease with which the Pen-

27. For more on this, see ibid., 80–97.

28. Ibid., 102–7.

29. Though I'm using the term "Pentecostalism" in an umbrella-like manner to refer not only to Classical Pentecostals, but to Charismatic, Neo-Pentecostal, and Neo-Charismatic believers as well, I'll point out here that Pentecostal scholar Cecil Robeck has observed that, when speaking of Pentecostalism in a global context, we should actually speak of "Pentecostalisms." See Robeck, "Taking Stock of Pentecostalism," 45. See also Synan, *Holiness-Pentecostal Tradition*, 282–85; and Yong, *Spirit Poured Out*, 18.

tecostal version of the Christian faith is contextualized in various Majority World cultures,[30] and/or (2) the physical, spiritual, and psychological/ sociological *benefits* which Pentecostalism tends to produce in the lives of those who embrace it.[31] In the quote presented below we find a synthesis of these two traditionally popular explanations:

> Pentecostals responded to what they experienced as a void left by rationalistic western forms of Christianity that had unwittingly initiated what amounted to the destruction of traditional spiritual values. Pentecostals declared a message that reclaimed the biblical traditions of healing and protection from evil, they demonstrated the practical effects of these traditions and by so doing became heralds of a Christianity that was really meaningful. Thus, Pentecostalism went a long way towards meeting physical, emotional and spiritual needs of people in the Majority World, offering solutions to life's problems and ways to cope in what was often a threatening and hostile world.[32]

At the same time, there are other scholars who contend that the traditional explanations are insufficient because they don't fully explain Pentecostalism's amazing ability to see remarkable numbers of rank-and-file church members move past a consumeristic preoccupation with the gospel's benefits toward an enthusiastic and fruitful missional engagement in their homes, neighborhoods, workplace, marketplace, and so on.[33] The question is, how do we explain this unique ability on the part of Pentecostal and charismatic churches to motivate their members toward a vigorous missional ministry engagement with their cultural peers?

The best answer seems to be that, because of their embrace of a pneumatological realism, multitudes of rank-and-file Pentecostal believers have been willing to follow the personal leading of the Spirit of mission to speak and act prophetically (in an Ananias-like manner) into the lives of hurting people living in their communities. In addition to some demographic evidence for this assertion,[34] and evidence from the literature devoted to

---

30. Anderson, *Introduction to Pentecostalism*, 201–2, 212–13, 215–16, 223–24, 283–84.

31. For more on this, see Tyra, *Holy Spirit in Mission*, 107–12.

32. Anderson, *Introduction to Pentecostalism*, 212.

33. For example, see McClung, "Truth on Fire," 78, 81. See also Pomerville, *Introduction to Missions*, 95–97.

34. See Tyra, *Holy Spirit in Mission*, 118–19.

global Pentecostalism,[35] are ministry anecdotes from the field which indicate how common it is for rank-and-file church members to feel prompted by the Spirit of mission to go to certain people, humbly yet boldly speaking and acting into their lives on behalf of the risen Christ. According to these anecdotes, this pneumatologically real version of prophetic speech and action often creates opportunities for *ministry conversations* that end up resulting in *ministry conversions* as well—people joyously coming to faith in Christ, undergoing water baptism, and then commencing a life of Christian discipleship.[36] It appears to be true that when those who are hurting sense that the risen Jesus has sent someone to them, speaking and acting into their lives in a grace-imbued manner, it's hard for the recipients of these mercy-saturated words and deeds to continue to ignore or relativize the Jesus of the Christian scriptures. Thus, the phenomenon of a pneumatologically real version of prophetic speech and action really must be understood to be at the heart of one of the most plausible explanations for the growth of Pentecostalism around the world.

The Unrecognized Prophetic Activity Occurring in the West

Finally, I'm absolutely convinced that the same type of prophetic evangelism, edification, and equipping we find in the book of Acts and currently at work in the majority world is, though often unrecognized, actually occurring here in the West as well.[37] I'm sometimes invited to speak in churches on the topic of the Holy Spirit in mission, some of which are anything but Pentecostal-charismatic in orientation. When addressing the provocative notion of non-Pentecostal evangelicals opening themselves to the possibility that the Holy Spirit might want to use them to speak and act into the lives of others in a missional manner, I try to make the point that this type of prophetic ministry is already occurring much more often than many of them realize. In such settings I routinely pose this question: Have you never felt a strong impression deep within to speak and/or act extemporaneously into someone's life in an evangelizing, encouraging, or equipping manner? At first there may be some reluctance to acknowledge that this is happening. But then I press further. Gently, I pose the question, "Really, you've *never* offered to pray for someone you were pretty certain didn't even believe in

35. See ibid., 119–21.

36. See ibid., 122–26.

37. For more on this, see ibid., 129–58.

God, or felt led to intercede for a particular missionary at a particular time, or to send a note of encouragement to someone without knowing precisely why such a note might be needed, or to give in an especially generous manner in a particular offering, or to stop and actually converse with a particular homeless person, or suddenly decide to partner with a ministry designed to alleviate human suffering in the world?" Then, I'll go on to ask the church members I'm addressing if they're absolutely certain that they've *never* had the experience of feeling like God was speaking through them as they counseled someone, advised someone, or made a suggestion in a ministry meeting, or offered an observation in a Bible study, etc. Often, this type of gentle probing has the effect of enabling rank-and-file evangelicals to recognize the prophetic activity that's already occurring in their lives. "What if we were to lean into this phenomenon?" I go on to ask. "What if we were to prayerfully commit ourselves to taking seriously any ministry promptings the Spirit of mission might produce within us? What kind of ministry opportunities/fruitfulness might such a pneumatological realism produce?"

For what it's worth, my own spiritual journey convinces me that, if we'll allow it, this type of prophetic ministry can occur in our place and day. As it happens, I experienced this phenomenon only a few weeks ago (at the time of this writing). I had just concluded the final four-hour class session for a required course titled Foundations of the Christian Life. The level of Christian commitment for this group of returning adult students ranged from nil to nominal to strong. It was right at 10:00 p.m. and the last student to leave that night paused at the classroom door, indicating a desire to chat just a bit about something that was on her mind. An oncology nurse with thirty years of experience, she was hoping I could speak to a work-related issue that had been bothering her for some time. She explained that she often witnesses people at the end stages of their illness "clawing for God," while at the same time acknowledging that prior to this time of crisis they haven't paid him any serious attention. After confiding to me that she hasn't been especially religious herself, she went on to indicate that it has always struck her as odd that people can live their entire lives ignoring God and then expect to suddenly find him as death approaches. She indicated that, though she wants to be of encouragement to her patients, she's hasn't known what to say to those who seem compelled to communicate their sense of spiritual desperation. It was apparent to me that this was an is-sue of real concern for this essentially post-Christian (lapsed Catholic) student. Indeed, she gave the impression that she'd been agonizing for some time over what she considered to be a particularly perplexing professional dilemma.

Though I obviously didn't have a prepared answer to her query, and was somewhat weary due to the lateness of the hour, I also got the impression that the Spirit of mission was up to something in this woman's life. This inkling was confirmed when the words making up my prompt, yet prayer-bathed response just seemed to flow, not so much from my head but from somewhere else deep within. I don't want to overly-spiritualize what happened, but, once again, I had the somewhat surreal experience of *hearing myself* minister to someone in an impromptu manner, communicating concepts "on the fly" that, though unprepared, nevertheless seemed remarkably coherent, relevant, even eloquent.

First, I indicated to my student that I understood why she might consider it odd, even hypocritical, for some of her patients to think that they could spend the majority of their lives in an irreligious, perhaps even immoral manner, and then hope to be reconciled to God in the final days of their earthly existence. Then I put to her this question: "But what if the Bible were to actually suggest that, because God is so very gracious, merciful, and forgiving, some of these patients might actually end up in heaven?" Not at all familiar with the Bible herself, she looked surprised. I went on to tell her the story of the two criminals who were crucified alongside Jesus. I described the way one of the criminals mocked and castigated Christ while the other, in a sincerely repentant manner, said to him: "Jesus, remember me when you come into your kingdom" (Luke 23:42). When I related to my student that Jesus' response to this man's desperate "clawing for God" at the very end of his life was to say "Truly I tell you, today you will be with me in paradise" (Luke 23:43), she seemed shocked, but pleasantly so. Then, without having thought about this matter before this moment, I essentially heard myself saying to her: "Maybe there's a significant difference between those dying patients who are simply scared, and those who are sincerely sorry. Maybe something you can say to encourage those patients "clawing for God" at the end of their lives is this: "You know, I've come to believe that because God is so very merciful, gracious, and forgiving, we really can find peace with him *if,* in addition to being *scared,* we're also *sorry,* truly sorry for having failed to honor him in the way he deserves. The Bible tells us that we experience forgiveness from God when we humbly come to his

Son, Jesus, requesting mercy for ourselves, and then beginning in earnest the process of forgiving those who've sinned against us."[38]

The look on her face changed immediately. Whereas, before, her countenance had evidenced serious consternation, it now reflected intense relief. Apparently, she had experienced an epiphany she considered truly profound. After dabbing at her eyes and expressing her appreciation for our after-class chat, she departed with what appeared to be a genuine sense of hope in her heart.

Here's the irony I couldn't help but reflect upon as I drove home that night: While the counsel my student received was couched in a conversation ostensibly about how she might aid others, I'm fairly sure it was designed by the Spirit of mission to impact her own spiritual journey as well. Thus, I humbly offer this as a contemporary example of the type of prophetic evangelism, edification, and equipping we see in the book of Acts, and hear about by way of many ministry anecdotes from around the world.

The upshot of all this is that a posture of pneumatological expectancy rather than presumption (or indifference) seems to earmark some of the most fruitful missional endeavors the Christian church has ever engaged in. If this observation holds, it provides some solid support for my contention that the importance of the Holy Spirit to the Kingdom-representing dynamic deserves a much closer look. If those of us involved in missional ministry really want to do an adequate job of representing the kingdom of God in our place and day, the embrace of a pneumatological realism would seem to be critical to our doing so.

In this second section of *Getting Real*, the focus has been on the importance of a realist, instead of a non-realist, pneumatology to the threefold faithfulness so very critical to reaching our post-Christian peers for Christ. Imagine with me a multitude of evangelical church members fully empowered by the Spirit to exhibit a spiritual, moral, and missional faithfulness before God and a watching world. I'm convinced we can do this. In the final section of this work, we'll discuss what the leaders of evangelical congregations can do to encourage their members toward an eager embrace of a pneumatological realism.

---

38. See Rom 10:9–10; Matt 6:14–15.

Part Three: Getting Real about Getting Real

6

Encouraging a Pneumatological Realism in the Local Church

> My message and my preaching were not with wise and persuasive words, but
> with a demonstration of the Spirit's power, so that your faith might not rest on
> human wisdom, but on God's power.
>
> —1 CORINTHIANS 2:4–5

IT'S MY HOPE THAT the pneumatological perspective proffered in this book
will serve to facilitate among evangelical church leaders a *Spirit-empowered*
engagement in ministry, not only in the evangelistic, church planting ministry Paul was referring to in the passage cited above, but also the equipping
ministry he alluded to when he wrote to the church in Ephesus:

> So Christ himself gave the apostles, the prophets, the evangelists,
> the pastors and teachers, to equip his people for works of service,
> so that the body of Christ may be built up until we all reach unity
> in the faith and in the knowledge of the Son of God and become
> mature, attaining to the whole measure of the fullness of Christ.
> (Eph 4:11–13)

What if it were possible for church leaders to cultivate an ecclesial
environment that greatly enhanced the likelihood of rank-and-file church
members interacting with the Holy Spirit in real, personal, transformational, ministry-engendering ways? How would one put a value on such a
ministry move—a move so very critical to the defeat of functional deism

in our churches and the nominal Christianity it produces? If a genuinely Spirit-empowered engagement in the formational ministry prescribed in Ephesians 4:11–13 were possible, wouldn't such a cultivation endeavor be of immense importance?

Questions such as these are at the heart of my understanding of a pneumatological realism. They also drive my motivation for its promotion. Given everything presented thus far about the importance of church members interacting with the Holy Spirit in ways that will nurture within them a spiritual, moral, and missional faithfulness, here's a pivotal question which all pastors concerned about reaching this generation for Christ should be asking themselves: to what degree am I being careful to encourage the members of my congregation to adopt a "posture" of expectancy rather than presumption (or even indifference) with respect to the working of the Holy Spirit in their lives? It's because I'm absolutely convinced that this question should be taken very seriously, that I want to bring this book to a close with a chapter in which I identify and briefly discuss several practical suggestions regarding how the leaders of evangelical churches (of all stripes) can succeed at the cultivation of an ecclesial environment marked by that *realist* understanding and experience of the Spirit which makes a God-pleasing faithfulness possible.

Prayerfully Partnering with the Spirit

In his book *True Spirituality,* the very evangelical Francis Schaeffer wrote: "If I woke up tomorrow morning and found that all that the Bible teaches concerning prayer and the Holy Spirit were removed . . . what difference would it make *in practice* from the way we are functioning today? The simple tragic fact is that in much of the church of the Lord Jesus Christ—the evangelical church—there would be *no difference whatsoever*. We function as though the supernatural were not there."[1] I'm struck by the way Schaeffer associates prayer with the Holy Spirit in this quote, as well as the fact that he seems to be encouraging the leaders of evangelical churches to take both seriously. Indeed, I'm going to suggest that the very first step in the process of cultivating a pneumatological realism in evangelical (and even some Pentevangelical) churches will involve some serious praying on the part of the church's leadership. It only makes sense that if the goal is to see the members of a church become more aware of the crucial need for

1. Schaeffer, *True Spirituality*, 150–51.

a theologically real partnership with the Holy Spirit as it relates to their spirituality, morality, and missionality, those endeavoring to achieve this shift in church culture need to prayerfully enter into such a partnership with the Spirit themselves. Attempting to alter the culture of a church is a huge undertaking, and not for the faint of heart. To accomplish this significant endeavor, we're going to need wisdom and empowerment from above. Ongoing prayer offered in a theologically real (interactive) manner is the key to experiencing both.[2]

Raising Awareness Regarding Pneumatological Realism

Moving forward in this cultivation process, church leaders will also need to help their congregants understand what "pneumatological realism" is and why it's so very critical to avoiding the "almost Christianity" produced by functional deism. I'd like to think that *Getting Real* can help with this important endeavor. A sermon series on the threefold faithfulness God is looking for, and the crucial importance of the Holy Spirit to this faithfulness would be something I'd heartily recommend.

That said, I also want to encourage the leaders of local churches to be careful to contextualize the message of this work for their parishioners. Obviously, not all churches are the same in terms of their demography, denominational affiliation (or lack thereof), theological heritage, and liturgical practices. All of these factors can greatly affect a congregation's theological and ministry vocabulary. The central contention of *Getting Real* is that the Holy Spirit is more than an idea, concept, or article of faith. He's the third *person* of the Trinity who can and should be interacted with in ways that are *real, personal,* and, *genuinely impactful.* However, perhaps the term "pneumatological realism" isn't the best way to refer to this crucial dynamic in your ministry context. If not, how will you do so? How will you explain to the members of your congregation what it means for them to assume a posture of pneumatological expectation rather than presumption or indifference? Helping church members understand the importance of these

---

2. One version of prayer offered in a theologically real manner is the practice of "praying in the Spirit" (Rom 8:26; Eph 6:18; Jude 1:20). However one conceives of this practice—as merely extemporaneous prayer, literally groaning before God in prayer (Rom 8:26), or glossolalic prayer (cf. 1 Cor 14:13–15)—it would seem appropriate for church leaders wanting to forge and model a theologically real partnership with the Holy Spirit, to take seriously the multiple exhortations provided in the New Testament to engage in it.

alternative possibilities is crucial to seeing a congregation move toward a corporate embrace of a realist experience of Christ's Spirit. There's no time like the present to begin enabling our church members to better understand the tremendous value of getting real with respect to Christ's Spirit!

Acknowledging Any Pneumatological Presumption

Of course, the kind of awareness-raising needed to change a church's corporate ethos might require some prophetic *critique* as well as *vision-casting*.[3] According to Walter Brueggemann, at the heart of the prophetic ministry portrayed in the Old Testament scriptures was an attempt on the part of the prophets to effect change in the covenant community by nurturing, nourishing, and evoking "*a consciousness and perception alternative*."[4] Applied to the topic at hand, this begs the question: What precisely is a posture (or attitude) of pneumatological expectation an alternative to? The answer to this critical question needs to be made clear to our congregants.

The good news is that my experience as a pastor has been that, if a congregation knows that its leaders genuinely love them, it's amazing how much truth-speaking they'll tolerate. Indeed, done in the right manner and with the right spirit in place, I've found that a congregation will not only tolerate, but will ultimately appreciate some prophetic challenge now and then. So, my suggestion here is that one of the ways in which both evangelical and Pentevangelical leaders can succeed in encouraging their parishioners toward a more realist experience of the Spirit is to make them aware of the presence and impact of any pneumatological non-realism (or functional deism) that may currently be at work in their lives. Our congregants need to know how amazingly easy it is for any of us to adopt a posture of pneumatological presumption (or even indifference), with the result that we live our everyday lives not really expecting to interact with the Spirit of Christ in ways that will help us cultivate a spiritual, moral, and missional faithfulness before God. To the degree that the New Testament seems to indicate that a sense of pneumatological expectancy is crucial to pneumatological experience, and given what the New Testament has to say about the possibility of the Holy Spirit being *resisted* (Acts 7:51); *grieved* (Eph 4:30); *rejected* (1 Thess 4:8); *quenched* (1 Thess 5:19); and even *insulted* (Heb

3. We find the Apostle Paul modeling this leadership principle for us in Ephesians 4:14–16.

4. Brueggemann, *Prophetic Imagination*, 3, emphasis original.

10:29), any pneumatological presumption/indifference present in the local church really does need to be recognized, repented of, and then replaced. This "prophetic," awareness-raising ministry in the local church needs to be undertaken in a careful, prayerful, humble manner, but it does need to occur. This constitutes yet another reason why church leaders endeavoring to effect change in their congregation's cultural ethos simply must learn to lead from their knees!

Recovering a Robust Pneumatology

Building on the previous suggestion, and speaking now in a more positive manner, I'll go on to offer that, to create a genuine sense of pneumatological expectancy, church members need to be routinely reminded of how important the Holy Spirit is to just about every aspect of their walk with Christ. What I'm arguing for here is a recovery within the local church of a vigorous, comprehensive doctrine of the Holy Spirit. For an ethos of genuine pneumatological expectancy to be cultivated in a church, the members must be made aware of the full scope of the Spirit's work in their lives, and what this portends for their cultivation of a comprehensive, wholistic faithfulness before God. By means of sermons, seminars, retreats, Sunday School studies, worship themes, counseling sessions, hallway conversations, etc., church members can be encouraged to reckon with just how crucial the Spirit is to a fully devoted and empowered Christian discipleship.

Wanting to be of some help here, presented below is a less-than-exhaustive list of the various roles the apostolic authors ascribed to the Holy Spirit vis-à-vis a Spirit-empowered walk with Christ. This bulleted list also includes some biblical passages supportive of each role. Moreover, the copious set of footnotes tied to the list provides some important exegetical observations, and some reasons why only a realist understanding of the Spirit makes sense of the pneumatology presented in the New Testament.

According to Jesus and his apostles, it's the Holy Spirit's job to

- enable us (Christ's followers) to experience the *new birth* and *new life in Christ* (John 3:3–8; 6:44; 16:7–11; Eph 2:18, 22; 3:16–17; and Gal 5:25);[5]

5. Commenting on John 3:3–8, Leon Morris makes an observation which simultaneously supports the notion of a pneumatological realism and belies one of the major tenets of Moral Therapeutic Deism: "Jesus is stressing the truth that spiritual regeneration is indispensable if we would be God's. It is the perennial heresy of the natural man to think

- assure us that we've become God's children (Rom 8:15–16; Gal 4:6);[6]

- lead us into a deeper and ongoing interaction with the risen Christ (John 14:15–26; 16:12–15);[7]

- serve as a guarantee of our heavenly inheritance (2 Cor 1:22; 5:5; Gal 4:6–7; Eph 1:13–14; 4:30);[8]

---

that he can fit himself by his own efforts for the kingdom of God. Jesus makes clear that no man can ever fit himself for the kingdom. Rather he must be completely renewed, born anew, by the power of the Spirit. These solemn words for ever [sic] exclude the possibility of salvation by human merit. Man's nature is so gripped by sin that an activity of the very Spirit of God is a necessity if he is to be associated with God's kingdom" (Morris, *Gospel According to John*, 218–19).

6. Commenting on Romans 8:15, C. K. Barrett suggests that, while Paul may have had a worship setting in mind when referring to the Spirit-enabled cry "*Abba*, Father," the apostle may have also been referring to "Spirit-inspired prayers (cf. 1 Cor. xiv. 15)." "The use of the violent word, 'cry out,'" says Barrett, might suggest "a free prayer spontaneously inspired by the Spirit" (*Epistle to the Romans*, 164.) Obviously, such an interpretation, which opens the door to construing the "*Abba*, Father" utterance as ecstatic or "prophetic" in nature, provides some significant support for a pneumatological realism.

7. The idea being communicated in these complementary passages is that the Holy Spirit is to function as "another counselor"—a theologically real representation of Jesus in the lives of his disciples, enabling them to adequately comprehend everything that the Master had taught them (John 14:26) and would in an ongoing way communicate to them (John 16:14). See Morris, *Gospel According to John*, 656–57, 701. Commenting on John 16:14, Gary Burge writes, "Jesus discloses that the Spirit will have a revelatory role, unveiling things that the disciples have not yet heard. These verses complement what we read in 14:26, and the two sections must be read closely together. John's understanding of revelation has two foci: (1) There is historical remembering, in which the words from Jesus' earthly ministry are recalled accurately by the Spirit. (2) There is ongoing illumination, which either (a) *applies* these historic words to new contexts or (b) *opens up new vistas*, new ideas, that the church has not known before" (*John*, 446, emphasis original). I'll point out that Burge is careful to clarify this ongoing revelatory role of the Spirit in a way that should assuage the fears of most evangelicals. In other words, though these "new ideas" may not have previously occurred to the church, there's antecedent support for them in God's word. See Burge, *John*, 450–52. See also my discussion of this dynamic in Tyra, *Holy Spirit in Mission*, 139–41 (especially n. 30).

8. Please note that in his commentary on Ephesians 1:13–14, New Testament scholar Francis Foulkes seems to refer to a presence and activity of the Spirit in the believer's life that is phenomenal rather than theoretical in nature. In the process, he offers an explanation as to how an overly ritualized understanding of the Spirit emerged in the life of the church. The implied question in this discussion is, how can the Spirit function as a "seal" or "guarantee" of anything if his presence in the disciple is merely assumed on the basis of a liturgical ritual? Foulkes writes, "'The Jews thought of circumcision as a seal. The Holy Spirit is the Christian's seal. The *experience* of the Holy Spirit in his life is the final *proof* to him, and indeed a *demonstration* to others, of the genuineness of what he has believed, and provides the inward *assurance* that he belongs to God as a son (cf. Rom. Viii. 15f.;

- inspire us toward a vital, joyful, prophetic, theologically real worship experience (John 4:24; Eph 5:18–20);[9]

- manifest the risen Christ's presence and power in our lives in various edifying, community-building, ministry engendering ways (1 Cor 12:4–8; 14:24–25);[10]

Gal. iv. 6). Later on, perhaps because of the analogy of circumcision, perhaps because of the language used for initiation in the Mystery Cults, baptism came to be known as the seal of the Spirit. It is indeed 'an outward and visible sign' given to the Christian of the inward work of God. But here it is clearly intended that *the Holy Spirit's presence* is the seal. The *Spirit in the believer's life* is the *undeniable mark* of God's work in and for him" (Foulkes, *Ephesians*, 56, emphasis added). Foulkes goes on to say: "The Christian's *experience* of the Spirit now is a *foretaste* and *pledge* of what will be his when he fully possesses his God-given inheritance" (ibid., 57, emphasis added).

9. A couple of exegetical observations supportive of a pneumatological realism are in order here. First, referring to the command in Ephesians 5:19 to be filled with the Spirit, Foulkes writes, "The tense of the verb, present imperative in the Greek, should be noted, implying as it does that the experience of receiving the Holy Spirit so that every part of life is permeated and controlled by Him is not a 'once for all' experience. In the early chapters of the Acts of the Apostles it is repeated a number of times that the apostles were 'filled with the Holy Spirit.' The practical implication is that the Christian is to leave his life open to be filled *constantly and repeatedly* by the divine Spirit" (Foulkes, *Ephesians*, 152, emphasis added). Second, Foulkes also provides support for my associating the exhortations found in 5:19–20 with the act of worship when, in his notes on this passage, he writes, "The fullness of the Spirit will find manifestation in fellowship whenever Christians are found together, and will be given joyful expression in song and praise. The *psalmos* was originally that which was sung to the harp, and here perhaps includes not only the psalms of the Old Testament, but those (like Lk. i. 46–55, 68–69 and ii. 29–32) which were of the new, but in the spirit and manner of the old psalms. . . . A number of New Testament passages like this (e.g., Acts xvi. 25; I Cor. xiv. 26; Col. Iii. 16; Jas. v. 13) indicate the place of song in the early Church; in the second century Pliny and Tertullian give the same testimony. Singing has always had a great place in the Church's life and worship, and every new movement of the Spirit has brought a fresh outburst of song" (ibid., 152–53).

10. Perhaps nowhere in the Bible is the Apostle Paul's commitment to a pneumatological realism more apparent than in 1 Corinthians 12 and 14. With respect to 1 Corinthians 12, New Testament scholar Gordon Fee asserts that the "gifts" listed in this chapter are "above all *manifestations* of the Spirit's presence" in the midst of the Christian assembly "because they are, like tongues itself, extraordinary phenomena" (Fee, *God's Empowering Presence*, 165, emphasis original). Concerning 1 Corinthians 14, it's here we discover that Paul viewed the ability to prophesy an especially important, valuable spiritual gift (ibid., 215). Moreover, Paul goes on in the chapter to explain why he holds the gift of prophecy in such high esteem. First, there is its ability to bring messages to fellow church members that result in their "strengthening, encouragement, and comfort" (1 Cor 14:3) (ibid., 217–19). Second, says Paul, *when conducted properly*, a charismatic worship service earmarked by valid prophetic utterances will have a positive missional

- empower us to obey God's moral commands (Rom 8:1–4) by enabling us to overcome our habitual sinful tendencies (Gal 5:16–21), and producing within us the character traits and ethical virtues of Jesus instead (Gal 5:22–25);[11]

- intercede for us and through us according to the will of the Father (Rom 8:26–27);[12]

- empower us to boldly bear witness to the risen Christ (Acts 1:8; cf. Matt 10:18–20);[13]

---

effect upon any unbelievers who happen to be in attendance (1 Cor 14:24–25). Third, Paul concluded the chapter by admonishing the Corinthians to be eager to prophesy and not to forbid speaking in tongues (1 Cor 14:39).

11. It's my suggestion that the character/personality traits listed in Galatians 5:22–25 were manifestly present in the life of Jesus, himself. Moreover, it appears, based on this passage, that one of the principal aims of the Holy Spirit is to produce these ethically significant attributes in the lives of Christ's followers (see Tyra, *Pursuing Moral Faithfulness*, 274). Support for this interpretive take can be adduced from the fact that Ronald Fung describes these nine attributes as "ethical graces" and "graces of character" (Fung, *Epistle to the Galatians*, 271–72), and, according to F. F. Bruce, this list of "nine graces" is Paul's way of describing "the lifestyle of those who are indwelt and energized by the Spirit" (Bruce, *Epistle to the Galatians*, 251). With this thought in mind, the need for an ongoing posture of pneumatological expectancy is suggested by the following assertion: "While these virtues are presented as the product of the Spirit, it is worth emphasizing again . . . that the believer is not without responsibility, 'by attentive openness to God,' to allow the Spirit to produce these graces in him" (Fung, *Epistle to the Galatians*, 272–73). The upshot of all this is that it's hard to conceive of this existentially-impactful work of the Spirit in the lives of Christian disciples apart from a realist understanding of the Spirit.

12. Most scholars agree that the plain sense of Romans 8:26–27 is that, in one way or another, the Holy Spirit assists believers by enabling them to pray in accordance with God's will. The scholarly debate centers on the question of whether Paul had *glossolalia* (speaking in tongues) in mind here, or a literal groaning inspired by the Spirit. Eminent evangelical scholars F. F. Bruce and C. K. Barrett both acknowledge the possibility that Paul may have had *glossolalia* in mind in verse 26 (see Bruce, *Romans*, 165; Barrett, *Romans*, 168). For his part, Gordon Fee is less ambivalent, asserting that "Origen probably had it right, in understanding these sentences as a whole and this phrase in particular to refer to a kind of private ('to oneself') praying in tongues that Paul speaks about as part of his resolution of the practice of uninterpreted tongues in the worshiping community in Corinth" (Fee, *God's Empowering Presence*, 580). Moreover, according to Fee, Ernst Käsemann also sees a reference to prayer in tongues at work in this passage (see Käsemann, *Perspectives on Paul*, 135). Regardless of whether Paul had *glossolalia* in mind or not, it appears that Paul meant to suggest that at times the Spirit will actually pray *through* the believer, offering effective intercession on his or her behalf in the process. Either way, only a realist understanding of the Spirit makes sense of this provocative passage.

13. I'd like to think that chapter 5 of this work, and the entirety of *The Holy Spirit in Mission*, will be helpful here. That said, I'll also draw attention to the fact that, in

- provide us with an amazingly precise degree of ministry guidance (Acts 10:17–20; 13:1–3; 16:6–10);[14]

- motivate us to stand firm in the faith and to intercede for others in this regard (Eph 6:10–18, cf. Jude 1:17–21; 2 Tim 1:13–14);[15] and

---

commenting on Acts 1:8, I. Howard Marshall opines that the promise of spiritual empowerment referenced here (and in Luke 24:49) was not fulfilled only on the day of Pentecost (in a one-off manner), but also "on many other occasions" (Marshall, *Acts*, 61). Moreover, in his note on Matthew 10:18–20, Michael Wilkins writes: "In their future mission, the disciples are to depend on the Holy Spirit to *speak through them*. . . . The Holy Spirit is the creative, empowering, guiding force in Jesus' own life ([Matt] 1:18, 20; 3:11, 16; 4:1; 12:18, 28). Through this same Spirit his disciples will find their own *empowering* and *guidance* to give them witness (Wilkins, *Matthew*, 393, emphasis added). The note by Marshall supports the notion of a pneumatological realism while the one by Wilkins, to have any real meaning, requires it!

14. As it happens, I reference each of these Acts passages in *The Holy Spirit in Mission* as part of a bulleted summary of the prophetic activity observable in the book of Acts as a whole (Tyra, *The Holy Spirit in Mission*, 65–67). Some additional support for the apostolic experience of Spirit-enabled missional guidance is provided by I. Howard Marshall's note on Acts 13:2. Indeed, we can't help but infer a pneumatological realism from the way Marshall refers to the agency and authority of the Holy Spirit, and the responsiveness of the church to it, as he writes: "To a church waiting on the Lord his word now came. The *Spirit* is named as the author, since it is he who appoints leaders in the church (20:28) and guides the church at crucial points. But the Spirit speaks through human agencies (4:25), and it must be assumed that one of the prophets in the church received the message which called the church to be willing to give up the service of two of its most outstanding teachers for the sake of God's work elsewhere" (Marshall, *Acts*, 216).

15. Since I've already referred in this list to the dynamic of "praying in the Spirit," my focus here will be on the way both Paul and Jude refer specifically to this type of prayer as a resource for persevering in the faith. Actually, the point I want to make is one filled with irony. My research suggests that nowhere does a less-than-fully-real (i.e., non-phenomenal, overly intellectualized) pneumatology reveal itself than in the way many evangelical scholars exegete Ephesians 6:18 and Jude 1:20. What I mean is that, though many words have been spent discussing what Paul had in mind when he used the qualifying phrase "in the Spirit" in these passages, many of these treatments, because they divorce 6:18 and Jude 1:20 from their immediate contexts, end up so generalizing what it means to pray in the Spirit, that the sense of urgency and personal agency communicated in these passages is essentially ignored. Thus, the connotation of many of these exegetical treatments is that praying in the Spirit is simply to pray as a Christian committed to the authority of the Spirit-inspired Scriptures. (For example, see part two of the two-part series by John Piper titled "Learning to Pray in the Spirit and the Word" [Piper, "Learning to Pray in the Spirit"].) So common is this tendency among evangelical scholars to ignore the possibility that there's something about praying "in the Spirit" that's crucial to resisting the evil one, keeping oneself in the love of God, and, thus, persevering in the faith, that I'm tempted to wonder about a possible connection between a non-realist pneumatology and those versions of evangelical theology which either downplay the reality of the

- endow us over and over again with a dynamic, despair-defeating sense of hope (Rom 15:13).[16]

All of the effects listed above indicate how very important the Holy Spirit is to the Christian life. Even some decidedly non-Pentecostal evangelicals have been willing to acknowledge this reality. The British churchman and biblical scholar John Stott once opined: "The Christian life is essentially life in the Spirit, that is to say, a life which is animated, sustained, directed, and enriched by the Holy Spirit. Without the Holy Spirit, true Christian discipleship would be inconceivable, indeed impossible."[17] So, here's the big takeaway: To create an *environment of expectancy* with respect to the Spirit, all evangelical church members must be continually reminded of how crucial the Spirit of Jesus is to true Christian discipleship. We simply must take the Spirit seriously in order to live the Christian life. This is what a pneumatological realism is all about!

---

demonic, or hold that the perseverance of Christian disciples is a discipleship dynamic that can simply be assumed (the following passages notwithstanding: Rom 11:17–22; 1 Cor 9:24—10:12; 15:1–2; 16:13; 2 Cor 1:24; Gal 4:8–20; 5:2–6; Col 1:21–23; 1 Thess 3:5; 1 Tim 1:18–19; 3:6–7; 4:1–10; 5:8; 6:9–12, 20–21; 2 Tim 2:11–13, 16–21; 2 Tim 4:7–8; Heb 2:1–4; 4:1–2; 6:4–12; 10:26–39; 12:15–17; Jas 5:19–20; 1 Pet 5:8–9; 2 Pet 1:5–11; 2:20–22; 3:17; 1 John 2:24–28; 2 John 1:9; Jude 1:3–5, 20–25).

16. The benediction Paul pronounces in Romans 15:13 is so beautifully stated that it's easy, I tell my students, to approach it in such an idealized or romanticized manner that we miss the practical implications of Paul's linking the experience of hope with work of the Spirit. The fact is that the value of hope as a theological virtue is a pervasive theme in this letter (Rom 4:18; 5:1–5; 8:20, 24–25; 12:12; 15:4, 12–13). Indeed, Paul had referred to hope earlier in chapter 15, associating it with the spiritual encouragement Christian disciples need to live lives which succeed in glorifying God (Rom 15:4–5). As Paul concludes what constitutes a major section of his letter to the Romans (12:1—15:13), a section that focuses on the practical implications of the theology presented in Romans 1:1—11:36, he prays for them, asking God to fill them with joy, peace and, most importantly, hope. And, how would this prayer be answered? Apparently, by a fresh encounter with God's Spirit! Thus, I routinely remind my students that a practical implication of Paul's prayer for the Roman Christians in 15:13 is that whenever we or our Christian brothers and sisters are running low in terms of spiritual encouragement, we have reason to believe that our praying in the Spirit, for the Spirit, can make a real, life-story shaping difference. This is yet another indication of the importance of a pneumatological realism to the spiritual, moral, and ministry formation of contemporary Christians.

17. See Stott, *Message of Romans*, 216.

Advocating for a Spirit-Sensitive Spirituality

Obviously, a Christian spirituality should be Christ-centered. In chapter 3 of this work, I argued that at the heart of a spiritual faithfulness is the experience of a moment-by-moment mentoring relationship with the risen Jesus.

However, I also indicated in that essay how very crucial Christ's Spirit is to this Christ-centered spirituality. This being the case, another step in the culture-changing process being discussed here calls for some rather consistent reminders of the need for Christ's followers to continually surrender themselves to the leadership of the Holy Spirit.

Such an observation is validated by the fact that the writings of Jesus' apostles are replete with passages which not only underscore the prominent roles the Holy Spirit is to play in the Christian life (see above), but also how important it is for Christ's followers to actively cooperate with him. The Apostle Paul, in particular, was emphatic about the need for church members to *live according to the Spirit* (Rom 8:5–13), *keep in step with the Spirit* (Gal 5:24–25), and *continually be filled with the Spirit* (Eph 5:18).[18] Thus, crucial to a theologically real experience of the Spirit is a spirituality which facilitates an ongoing surrender to his leadership. Because of the paradoxical relationship which exists between a Spirit-sensitive spirituality and the phenomenon of a pneumatological realism (such a spirituality is, ironically, both the root and the fruit of a pneumatological realism), it's imperative that both evangelical and Pentevangelical pastors encourage their congregation members to develop a daily devotional practice of prayerfully, sincerely surrendering their lives to the leadership of Christ's Spirit.[19] Just because there's no biblically prescribed method for engaging in this daily

18. Commenting on the exhortation found in Ephesians 5:18 to be filled with the Spirit, Frances Foulkes writes: "the tense of the verb, present imperative in the Greek, should be noted, implying as it does that the experience of receiving the Holy Spirit so that every part of life is permeated and controlled by Him is not a 'once for all' experience. In the early chapters of the Acts of the Apostles it is repeated a number of times that the apostles were 'filled with the Holy Spirit.' The practical implication is that the Christian is to leave his life open to be filled constantly and repeatedly by the divine Spirit" (Foulkes, *Ephesians*, 152).

19. I'll also suggest here that being careful to obey the several biblical exhortations to pray/intercede "in the Spirit" (Rom 8:26; Eph 6:18; Jude 1:20) should also be considered a vital part of a Spirit-sensitive spirituality. At the very least, such prayer has the effect of encouraging a sense of pneumatological expectancy (rather than presumption or indifference). Because of this, it's my custom to encourage students and congregants to incorporate this type of Spirit-enabled prayer into their everyday spirituality.

act of surrender, doesn't mean that it shouldn't happen. Indeed, it's difficult to overstate how important this pastoral instruction is toward the promotion of a pneumatological realism and the Christ-honoring faithfulness it facilitates.[20]

Promoting the Notion of Prophetic Capacity

Because, rightly understood, the prophetic phenomenon is at the heart of the faithfulness Jesus himself rendered to the Father,[21] I will also stress here the importance of some serious study of what the Bible has to say about the relationship between the indwelling of the Spirit and the impartation of prophetic capacity. Once again, when I speak of "prophetic capacity" I'm referring to a Spirit-enabled ability to: hear God's voice, receive ministry assignments from him, and then speak and act into hurting people's lives in a way that achieves God's missional purposes in the world.[22] Biblical passages supporting such a notion really are there (e.g., Acts 9:10–22), but church members need to be exposed to them.[23]

Having expounded on this theme in various settings, even in some decidedly non-Pentecostal ones, I can attest to the fact that it's possible to make a compelling case for the notion that the Spirit of mission can and will use everyday church members in missionally fruitful ways if we'll take seriously those occasional promptings of the Spirit to speak and act into the lives of hurting people as he directs. Getting this message out is crucial! Encouraging our church members to embrace rather than ignore the

20. Commenting on Galatians 5:18, Ronald Fung has written: "This conditional sentence clearly shows that Paul does not regard the believer as a helpless spectator or an unwilling pawn in the fierce battle between the flesh and the Spirit; the assumption is rather that the Christian can overcome the flesh by siding with the Spirit. Being 'led by the Spirit' is in form passive; in its actual meaning, however, it is not entirely passive. The active leading of the Holy Spirit does not signify the believer's being, so to speak, led by the nose willy-nilly; on the contrary, he must let himself be led by the Spirit—that is actively choose to stand on the side of the Spirit over against the flesh" (see Fung, *Epistle to the Galatians*, 251–52).

21. The prophetic, responsive nature of Jesus' intimate, interactive relationship with the Father is evidenced in those Johannine passages where we find him asserting that everything he does is at the behest of his Father (see John 14:10, 31), because he only does the kinds of things he sees his Father doing (see John 5:19; 10:37) and only says the kinds of things he hears his Father saying (see John 5:30; 8:28; 12:49; 14:24; 15:15).

22. See Tyra, *Holy Spirit in Mission*, 98.

23. For more on this, see ibid., 39–74 and 75–101.

phenomenon of Spirit-imparted prophetic capacity is not only integral to a missional faithfulness before God, it's the key to avoiding a Christianity that's merely nominal in nature. It's very hard, if not impossible, to relate to the risen Christ as a mere idea, concept, or creedal article when we're experiencing a moment-by-moment mentoring relationship with him by means of the Holy Spirit![24]

Confronting the Demand for Certainty and Control

The problem is that the story of Ananias in Acts 9 also demonstrates how unpredictable the Christian life can become once a pneumatological realism is embraced. Who knows when the Spirit might speak, prompting us to engage in some unanticipated ministry assignment? Therefore, it's also important for church leaders to keep reassuring anxious church members that, while the adoption of a pneumatological realism can make those of us who tend to obsess over *certainty* and *control* a bit uneasy, it's for this very reason critical to our spiritual (and psychological) development.

The story of the fall related in Genesis 3:1–7 seems to portray the first couple trading in a life of trust and obedience for one earmarked by a quest for certainty and control (see Gen 3:4–5). Going further, I believe that, ironically, it's an inherent craving for certainty and control with respect to spiritual matters that explains the ubiquity of the religious impulse. In other words, religion is all about gaining a sense of certainty and control in our lives vis-à-vis the spiritual world, and the psychological safety before God such a sense of certainty and control provides.

My experience has been that it's somewhat common for church members to bring this innate religious impulse with them into their walk with Christ. Indeed, I'll offer that to some degree we're all prone to this: We talk and sing about walking by faith, while at the same time desperately questing to be certain about those things we say we believe, and in control of how this belief system affects our daily lives. However, it's one thing to merely crave a sense of certainty and control in our religious lives; it's another to go beyond *desiring* these two dynamics, to virtually *demanding* them. For a variety of reasons, this is a serious problem. As I've argued elsewhere, it's my belief that an inordinate and unbridled demand for a sense of certainty

---

24. I've spoken of the possibility of this type of relationship with Jesus at several places in this work. For more on this, see Tyra, *Christ's Empowering Presence*, 10, 12, 99, 109, 162.

and control is at the heart of not only the fall and the religious impulse in general, but the phenomenon of Christian Pharisaism as well.[25] Thus, I contend that one of the most loving things a caring pastor can do is to gently, humbly encourage those church members who tend to obsess over certainty and control to learn to live with some divinely ordained (purposeful) ambiguity in their lives.[26] As it happens, our doing our best to steer church members away from a religion of rules and rituals, toward a sensitivity and obedience to the Spirit whose movements (workings) defy human management (cf. John 3:8), is an important, divinely-ordained way to do this.

Encouraging Pneumatological Nuance

Following up on the last two suggestions, I will also offer that church leaders committed to the type of culture change we're discussing here need to be prepared to deal with the lack of pneumatological balance in the lives of many evangelical and Pentevangelical congregants. I have in mind, on the one hand, enthusiastic church members who tend to over-spiritualize just about everything going on in the church, and, on the other hand, those reluctant congregants who are deathly afraid that the church cannot take the Holy Spirit seriously without things getting weird. The fact is that sometimes the prophetic working of the Spirit *can* strike us as strange! This impression is exacerbated when church members insist on referring to themselves as prophets, and/or engaging in prophetic activity in a super-spiritual manner.[27] Still, the instruction of the Apostle Paul is clear: "Therefore, my brothers, be eager to prophesy, and do not forbid speaking in tongues. But everything should be done in a fitting and orderly way" (1 Cor 14:39–40). In other words, there are two extremes which must be avoided: first, given what we've learned about the role of prophetic capacity

25. In my book *Defeating Pharisaism,* I argue that at the heart of a pharisaical reduction of the Christian faith to a myopic focus on the obedience of rules and observance of rituals, is a deep-seated, obsessive need for certainty and control (see Tyra, *Defeating Pharisaism*, 68–74). Unfortunately, Christian Pharisaism is rife in many conservative churches, causing much pastoral burnout, the loss of members, and a great deal of missional dysfunction. See ibid., 53–67.

26. For more on the notion of a divinely ordained, purposeful ambiguity and the manner in which it chases us away from a religion of rules and rituals into an intimate, interactive with the living God, see Tyra, *Pursuing Moral Faithfulness*, 258–69.

27. I'm of the opinion that both of these behaviors are unnecessary and should be lovingly discouraged.

in all three forms of faithfulness God desires of us, it's simply not okay to *reject* the prophetic working of the Spirit out of hand. Then again, neither is it wise to *accept* every expression of it in a gullible, uncritical manner. More and more evangelicals, it seems, are becoming aware of the need to eschew the former extreme, while many Pentecostal-charismatics are doing the same with respect to the latter. Like it or not, the Apostle Paul calls for church leaders to become adept at helping their congregants recognize the critical need for *nuance, discernment,* and *balance* with respect to just about everything that goes on in the church, especially its experience of the Spirit. What is not permissible, per the Apostle Paul, is to promote a non-realist pneumatology out of a concern that a realist one will create too much ambiguity in the hearts and minds of the saints.

Embodying the Embrace

Finally, I propose that perhaps the most important thing church leaders can do to encourage the embrace of a pneumatological realism is to exemplify such a commitment themselves. It does no good to talk to others about the need to be led by the Spirit if we are not attempting to take this apostolic exhortation seriously. We radiate a stunning and leadership-stunting lack of authenticity when we teach on the reality and propriety of prophetic capacity, while at the same time rarely, if ever, acting on the devotional, moral, and ministry promptings of the Spirit ourselves. At the end of the day, when it comes to a church's collective embrace of a pneumatological realism, church leaders simply must lead the way!

It's my fervent hope that this chapter has provided the reader with some practical steps toward the cultivation of ecclesial environments which encourage church members to interact with the Holy Spirit in ways that are real, rather than merely theoretical and/or ritualistic. I fully recognize how new and novel this call for a pneumatological realism might seem to those leading churches that are not Pentecostal-charismatic in orientation. I recently came across an online post in which the pastor-blogger concluded his essay—the goal of which was to emphasize the importance of the Holy Spirit to missional ministry—stating:

> In a pre-Missio Alliance gathering, Greg Boyd spoke about the Church's need for a sanctified imagination that can entertain an image of the Spirit at work in us, with us, and among us even if

it [is] not obviously apparent to our eyes trained by a dominating naturalistic worldview. We need an imagination that allows us to listen for the Spirit's voice *as if* the Spirit speaking to us was normal. We need an imagination that makes room for us to be interrupted and directed *as if* the Spirit were the one interrupting and directing us. *When we talk about our responsiveness toward the Spirit with others, we might sound a little nutty.*[28]

Despite the "as if" rhetoric used by Boyd, it appears that what was being discussed at this gathering of missional proponents was the need for a realist understanding and experience of the Holy Spirit.[29]

I cite this anecdote to make the point that I'm not the only missional theologian calling for a greater degree of "responsiveness" to Christ's Spirit. That said, I will (at the risk of sounding "nutty") go even further, reiterating the hope expressed in the introduction of this chapter that the pneumatological perspective put forward here will enable a *Spirit-empowered* engagement in the equipping task alluded to in Ephesians 4:11–13. Given the functional deism currently at work in far too many evangelical churches, it's hard for me to imagine a greater practical ministry move than the recovery of a full-throated doctrine of the Holy Spirit. The cultivation of ecclesial environments earmarked by an eager embrace of a pneumatological realism is simply crucial if the multi-faceted faithfulness God desires and deserves is to be manifested in the lives of those who claim to follow Christ. In sum, there seems to be no question that the need for a Spirit-empowered approach to ministry formation is real. The question is: How real is our understanding and experience of Christ's Spirit? If there was ever a time for local churches to get real about getting real, it's now!

---

28. Grigg, "The Spirit of #TrulyHuman," emphasis original.

29. It's interesting to note that in one of his sermons, Karl Barth contrasts an "as if" approach to the righteousness of God with its "reality," implicitly arguing for a theologically real relationship with God over one that's functionally deistic in the process. See Barth, *Word of God*, 15, 20.

Conclusion

IN HIS BOOK *WHEN* Pride Still Mattered: *A Life of Vince Lombardi,* David
Maraniss reports that as the Green Bay Packers gathered for their training camp in the summer of 1961, their recently acquired head coach was
worried. Though they had yet to win a championship under his leadership,
they had come close the year before, losing the 1960 NFL championship
game to the Philadelphia Eagles by a mere four points. The team's improve-
ment under Lombardi's leadership had been apparent. Thus, he knew that
every other team in the NFL would be gunning for the Packers that season.
Coach Lombardi was concerned about how his team would respond to this
pressure. Maraniss writes:

> Lombardi carried this dread with him to St. Norbert that summer.
> In an effort to overcome it, he took nothing for granted. He began
> a tradition of starting from scratch, assuming that the players were
> blank slates who carried over no knowledge from the year before.
> He reviewed the fundamentals of blocking and tackling, the basic
> plays, how to study the playbook. He began with the most elemen-
> tal statement of all. "Gentlemen," he said, holding a pigskin in his
> right hand, "this is a football."[1]

Lombardi's commitment to the fundamentals is legendary, precisely
because of the effect it had on the Packers franchise. Under Lombardi's
leadership, the team went on to win the NFL championship in 1961, 1962,
1965, 1966, and 1967. They also scored easy victories in the first two Super
Bowls (1966 and 1967). When it comes to football, apparently, *the fundamentals matter!*

The same is true, I want to suggest, when it comes to the spiritual,
moral, and ministry formation of Christ's followers. The message of *Getting
Real* is patently basic: because of the importance of a realist understanding

1. Maraniss, *When Pride Still Mattered,* 274.

and experience of Christ's Spirit to the ability of Christ's followers to render to God the full-orbed faithfulness he desires and deserves, it's crucial that church leaders commit to something very, very basic—the prayerful cultivation of ecclesial environments earmarked by an eager embrace of a pneumatological realism. But just because something is basic, doesn't mean that it's unworthy of attention. Really, just the opposite is true: the fundamentals matter!

Just ask the Swiss theologian Karl Barth, who's as legendary with respect to modern theology as Vince Lombardi is to football. Because of the unflinching, unrelenting christological focus of Barth in his massive, multi-volumed *Church Dogmatics*—i.e., his strong emphasis on Christ as the key to knowing and experiencing the Trinitarian God—it's not uncommon for theologians to accuse Barth of giving short shrift to the Holy Spirit. But in his book, *Reading Karl Barth: New Directions for American Theology*, Kurt Anders Richardson makes the following observation: "This third member of the Trinity is sometimes incorrectly deemed to be in need of defense from Barth's supposed neglect, and yet this is entirely not the case."[2] To support this corrective assertion, Richardson goes on to cite a passage from the *Church Dogmatics* which not only has Barth affirming the importance of the Holy Spirit to the inner life of the Trinity, but to human beings as well. Explaining how it is that imperfect creatures (including theologians) can nevertheless glorify God, Barth says,

> It is as well to realise [sic] at this point that the glory of God is not only the glory of the Father and the Son but the glory of the whole divine Trinity, and therefore the glory of the Holy Spirit as well. But the Holy Spirit is not only the unity of the Father and the Son in the eternal life of the Godhead. He is also, in God's activity in the world, the *divine reality* by which the creature has its heart opened to God and is made able and willing to receive Him. He is, then, the unity between the creature and God, the bond between eternity and time. If God is glorified through the creature, this is only because by the Holy Spirit the creature is baptized, and born again and called and gathered and enlightened and sanctified and kept close to Jesus Christ in true and genuine faith. There is no glorification of God by the creature that does not come about through this work of the Holy Spirit by which the church is founded and maintained. . . . It is the Holy Spirit who begets the new man in Jesus Christ whose existence is thanksgiving. It is in virtue of His

2. Richardson, *Reading Karl Barth*, 159.

glory, which is the glory of the one God, that what this new man does is the glorification of God, and therefore the creature may serve this glorification.[3]

The reader will notice the emphasis I've placed on the way Barth refers to the Holy Spirit as the "divine reality" in which, essentially, we followers of Christ veritably live and move and have our being (cf. Acts 17:28). This is one of many passages from Barth's hand which, I believe, implies a realist, rather than non-realist, understanding of the Holy Spirit. At the very least, it cannot be doubted that Barth considered the work of the Spirit to be crucial to the ability of Christian disciples to live in a manner which glorifies, honors, and is faithful to God. In other words, scattered throughout the *Church Dogmatics* we find references to the Holy Spirit, by means of which Barth, in a Lombardi-like manner, seems to be saying to his readers: "the fundamentals matter!"

The task before us as fully devoted followers of Jesus in our place and day is not to win an athletic championship, but to do our best to encourage our post-Christian peers to take another look at Christ and his church. Ironically, one of the great obstacles toward this goal is the functional deism that, as we've seen, is rife within way too many Christian congregations, even those that are evangelical or Pentevangelical in stripe. I've argued in this work that the presence of this functional deism is both the root and fruit of a discipleship deficit—a failure on the part of the church to fully form its members toward a spiritual, moral, and missional faithfulness. I've also argued throughout this work that a critical key to overcoming this functional deism and the nominal, "almost Christianity" it spawns, is the recovery of an unmitigated, full-throated doctrine of the Spirit. Such a pneumatology, I've insisted, will be realist in nature, rather than non-realist. Moreover, an ecclesial environment earmarked by the pneumatological realism I've advocated for in this work will be filled with church members whose posture toward the Holy Spirit is one of expectation rather than presumption. Without having become super-spiritual as a result, they will have been encouraged by their ecclesial leaders to *expect* that their walk with Christ will occasionally involve interactions with the Spirit of Jesus that are *real*—i.e., personal, phenomenal, and life-story shaping—rather than merely theoretical, conceptual, or ritualistic.

If I've sounded like a broken record throughout this work, recall what both Lombardi and Barth had to say about the fundamentals. So, here's the

3. Barth, *Church Dogmatics*, II/1, 669–70, emphasis added.

bottom line: *We can do this!* With the help of the Holy Spirit we can make this high leverage ministry move that will unleash within our communities of faith a Spirit-empowered engagement in ministry formation. This is not a Pentecostal-charismatic versus a non-Pentecostal-charismatic issue. This is a fully Trinitarian versus a not-fully-Trinitarian issue. John Jefferson Davis was right to issue a call for the evangelical church in the West to unsaddle itself from theological views that "can handcuff the Holy Spirit in the life of the church and blind it to where the Spirit may be working dramatically in the world today."[4] Ironically, the same thing needs to happen in many Pentevangelical churches as well. There's still time for evangelical churches of all stripes to reach an increasingly post-Christian generation for Christ. But to do so, all of us, congregants and leaders alike, will need to make a commitment to *get real* with respect to Christ's Spirit. I can only hope that in some small way, *Getting Real* helps.

> Again Jesus said, "Peace be with you!
> As the Father has sent me, I am sending you."
> And with that he breathed on them and said,
> "Receive the Holy Spirit."
> —JOHN 20:21–22

4. Davis, *Worship and the Reality of God*, 121–25, 197–98.

Appendix

From Sola Scriptura to the Sacramental Sermon: Karl Barth and the Phenomenon of Prophetic Preaching

Gary Tyra, D. Min.
Professor of Biblical and Practical Theology
Vanguard University of Southern California

Presented at the Tyndale Fellowship Christian Doctrine Study Group[1]

June 28, 2017

Introduction

Compared to some other ministry topics, the phenomenon of prophetic preaching has not garnered a lot of attention. Still, it has been discussed. In addition to sermons that focus on the end times, it has been conceived of as a form of preaching that: (1) addresses "secret sins, spiritual immaturity, and unhealed wounds";[2] (2) confronts false doctrine;[3] or (3) challenges the

---

1. Actually, the essay presented here is a slightly revised version that incorporates some of the constructive feedback provided by the international group of scholars to whom it was presented during the summer of 2017 in Cambridge, England.

2. Matt Woodley, "Introduction," in *Prophetic Preaching*, ed. Craig Brian Larson, 1–7 (Peabody, MA: Hendrickson, 2012), 1.

3. Craig Brian Larson, "What All Good Preachers Do," in *Prophetic Preaching*, ed. Craig Brian Larson, 59–66 (Peabody, MA: Hendrickson, 2012), 60.

status quo[4] by inciting hearers to pursue justice[5] and thus change the current social order.[6]

Certainly, these are noble sermonic aims. But what if there were yet another way of understanding the nature of prophetic preaching? In a book titled *Speaking the Truth in Love: Prophetic Preaching in a Broken World*, Philip Wogaman reminds us that

> [t]o be prophetic is not necessarily to be adversarial, or even controversial. The word in its Greek form refers to one who speaks on behalf of another. In Hebrew tradition, a prophet is one who speaks for God. . . . To speak for another is to grasp, first, the mind of the other . . . *genuinely prophetic preaching draws people into the reality of God in such a way that they cannot any longer be content with conventional wisdom and superficial existence.*[7]

This is a very basic conception of prophetic preaching that is, ironically, founded upon a highly nuanced understanding of the prophetic phenomenon.[8] According to this view, prophetic preaching is transformational in its effect precisely because it facilitates an existentially impactful (life-story shaping) encounter with the living God.[9]

4. See Walter Brueggemann, *The Practice of Prophetic Imagination: Preaching an Emancipating Word* (Minneapolis: Fortress Press, 2012), 4, 21.

5. John Ortberg, "Preaching Like a Prophet," in *Prophetic Preaching*, ed. Craig Brian Larson, 47–58 (Peabody, MA: Hendrickson, 2012), 49–58.

6. See Leonora Tubbs Tisdale, *Prophetic Preaching: A Pastoral Approach* (Louisville, KY: Westminster John Knox, 2010), 10.

7. J. Philip Wogaman, *Speaking the Truth in Love: Prophetic Preaching in a Broken World* (Louisville, KY: Westminster John Knox Press, 1998) 3–4, (emphasis added) as cited in Tisdale, *Prophetic Preaching*, 4.

8. See also my own treatments of the prophetic phenomenon in Gary Tyra, *The Holy Spirit in Mission: Prophetic Speech and Action in Christian Witness* (Downers Grove, IL: IVP Academic, 2011), 22n24; and Gary Tyra, *Pursuing Moral Faithfulness: Ethics and Christian Discipleship* (Downers Grove, IL: IVP Academic, 2015), 166–67.

9. From the outset, I wish to make clear that, while my understanding of prophetic preaching presumes a likely engagement on the part of the preacher in a "Spirit hermeneutics" (see Craig S. Keener, *Spirit Hermeneutics: Reading Scripture in Light of Pentecost* [Grand Rapids, MI: Eerdmans, 2017]), and/or the spiritual/theological exegesis practiced by the early church fathers (see Michael Graves, *The Inspiration and Interpretation of Scripture: What the Early Church Can Teach Us* [Grand Rapids, MI: Eerdmans, 2014]; Kevin J. Vanhoozer, "Introduction: What Is Theological Interpretation of the Bible?", in *Theological Interpretation of the Old Testament: A Book-by-Book Survey*, ed. Kevin J. Vanhoozer, 15–28 [Grand Rapids, MI: Baker Academic, 2008]), what I am describing in this paper is more than a public rehearsing of the preacher's Spirit-illuminated interaction

Perhaps another way of referring to the phenomenon of prophetic preaching is to speak of the possibility of a *sacramental sermon*. Those familiar with the work of theologian Hans Boersma will find some tacit support there for what I am proposing here. Our mutual embrace of what I refer to as a "theological realism" (Boersma's "sacramental ontology"[10]) means that we both possess a "sacramental understanding of the Scriptures"[11] that opens the door to the possibility of "sacramental preaching."[12] That said, I will humbly suggest that, while we are ultimately after the same thing—sermons that enable hearers to "enter further into the life of God as revealed in Christ"[13]—the prophetic dynamic I focus on in this essay differentiates my proposal in an important way from the one put forward by Boersma.[14]

With that thought in mind, a description of sacramental preaching that comes a bit closer to capturing the prophetic element I believe is

---

with the text (see Keener, *Spirit Hermeneutics,* 250). Instead, the sermon involves a genuine prophetic prompting that, because it affects not only what the preacher proclaims, but when, how, and to whom he or she does so, results in a greater sense of formational immediacy between the Spirit of Christ and the auditors of the sermon.

10. See Hans Boersma, *Heavenly Participation: The Weaving of a Sacramental Tapestry* (Grand Rapids, MI: Eerdmans, 2011).

11. See Hans Boersma, *Scripture as Real Presence: Sacramental Exegesis in the Early Church* (Grand Rapids, MI: Baker Academic, 2017), xi.

12. See Hans Boersma, *Sacramental Preaching: Sermons on the Hidden Presence of Christ* (Grand Rapids, MI: Baker Academic, 2016), xx.; see also Boersma, *Heavenly Participation,* 138–39; 150–53; Boersma, *Scripture as Real Presence,* 1–2.

13. Ibid., 1–2.

14. To be more specific, Boersma's advocacy is for sermons that "move from the surface level of the text . . . to the deeper, contemplative level"—i.e., preaching that, following the practice of the early church fathers, points hearers to "Christ as the sacramental mystery present in the text" (Boersma, *Sacramental Preaching,* xxii). I will offer that my understanding of the "sacramental sermon" is a bit more pneumatologically explicit, dependent, and immediate. My focus moves beyond the spiritual/theological *exegesis* that's presented to the congregation, to the existentially-impactful *encounter* with the risen Christ that results when the Holy Spirit prompts and enables the preacher to speak to the congregation in a prophetic, biblically-informed, and Christ-honoring manner. In other words, while both Boersma and I agree that there is such a thing as sacramental preaching, I suspect we may disagree somewhat as to whether an engagement in what he refers to as "sacramental exegesis" is, by itself, capable of producing sermons that function sacramentally. It's my contention that an anointing of the Spirit upon the preparation and presentation of the sermon is also required—prophetic prompting and enablement by the Spirit of Christ that the preacher can and must prayerfully cooperate with for the sacramental encounter between congregants and the risen Christ to occur.

crucial to it has been provided by John Frye, a frequent contributor to the *Jesus Creed* blog site. Frye points out that:

> Preaching, in some traditions, is a sacrament or comparable to a sacrament. . . . Preaching is a *holy event* when the preacher and the preached to *encounter the living God together.* The aim of preaching is community-encounter with the living, eyes-blazing Christ Who [*sic*] walks in the community's ordinary, particular midst. Revelation chapters 2-3 are not just about the living Christ showing up a long time ago to seven churches in Asia Minor. The glorified Jesus, as Lord of his church, still walks around in the midst of local gatherings.[15]

Frye then goes on to present his understanding of why and how sacramental sermons can often result in the spiritual transformation of those who hear them. In the process, he asserts:

> To be informed by the Bible about God is not the same as to be encountered by the God of the Bible. We preach to encounter God together, not to create a set of preferred human behaviors. Encounter with God in Christ carries its own energies to shape and direct human lives. We preach for corporate encounter with God, believing that encounter will provoke numerous discussions about how we together can live missionally in light of the encounter. Paul suggested even unbelievers and unconvinced will confess an encounter with God (1 Corinthians 14:25) when the church gathers. . . . Authentic kingdom of God gospel announcement (preaching) evokes startling and diverse questions about how we go about adjusting our lives to Jesus as Lord.[16]

According to Frye, this is a real possibility: preaching which facilitates corporate encounters with the risen Christ that are, ultimately, transformational in their effect! *With this more dynamic understanding of the nature and effect of sacramental preaching I heartily concur.*

And yet, as appreciative as I am of Frye's passionate endorsement, I will offer the observation that an element missing from this mini-essay on the sacramental sermon is an explicit indication of the importance of the

---

15. John Frye, "Preaching as Encounter," http://www.patheos.com/blogs/jesuscreed/2013/05/17/from-the-shepherds-nook-preaching-as-encounter/.

16. Ibid., para. 4.

Holy Spirit to it.[17] Though this was certainly an innocent omission,[18] from my perspective it is an important one. The version of prophetic preaching I have in mind presumes a particular pneumatology—one that is capable of generating a truly remarkable, even vital sense of *holy expectation* each time the preaching event occurs.

To be more precise, in a forthcoming work I put forward the provocative thesis that many evangelical (and Pentevangelical) churches are in need of a more robust, fully Trinitarian, *realist rather than non-realist* doctrine of the Holy Spirit. Put simply, it's my suggestion that a doctrine of the Holy Spirit that is fully Trinitarian and realist in nature is one which acknowledges the Spirit's divine personhood and the crucial role he plays in enabling human beings to not only *know* the Father through the Son, but also to *experience*—live in to—what both are about. In other words, a *pneumatological realism* insists that, rather than conceive of the Holy Spirit as a philosophical concept or impersonal force that is simply presumed to be at work in believers' lives, he can and should be known and interacted with in ways that are personal, phenomenal, and life-story shaping. As a result, a pneumatological realism produces among church members an important sense of *pneumatological expectancy* rather than *presumption* (or even *indifference*).

Some tacit support for this thesis has been provided by Timothy Tennent, president of Asbury Theological Seminary. Commenting on the neglect of the Holy Spirit within some quarters of traditional evangelicalism, Tennent has made the following observation:

> The Reformation's emphasis on the authority of Scripture, ecclesiology, and Christology, as crucial as it was, meant that there was a further delay in a full theological development of the doctrine of the Holy Spirit, and *several vital aspects of his work were neglected* in post-Reformation Protestant theology, which focused on solidifying and organizing the theological developments of the Reformers. Over time, Western theological traditions that

17. In addition to the absence of any general reference to the role the Spirit should be expected to play in the sacramental encounter, also missing from this particular discussion is an acknowledgment of the direct and immediate formational effect the Spirit of Christ can produce in the lives of individual disciples (as well as the congregation as a whole) as a result of an *anointed* (Spirit-prompted and empowered) preaching (see 1 Thess 1:4) of God's inspired, inherently powerful word (see 2 Tim 3:16; Heb 4:12).

18. In his book, *Jesus the Pastor,* Frye not only refers repeatedly to the Holy Spirit, but also devotes two entire chapters to the importance of the Holy Spirit in the task of pastoring (John W. Frye, *Jesus the Pastor* [Grand Rapids, MI: Zondervan, 2002], 65–73; 14–59).

developed *greatly limited the active role of the Holy Spirit in the life of the church.* The result was a *pneumatological deficit* that is only now becoming painfully apparent.[19]

Tennent seems to be suggesting that the "pneumatological deficit" at work in some evangelical theologies and churches can be traced back to the Protestant Reformation. If this is true, it would be highly ironic since the magisterial Reformers had much to say about the importance of the Holy Spirit to the Christian life and faith. In an article titled "The Lively Work of the Spirit in the Reformation," Jane Dempsey Douglass writes:

> Historians all too seldom turn their attention to the Reformers' understanding of the Holy Spirit, yet something profoundly significant happened to the doctrine of the Holy Spirit in the Reformation. Theologians like Luther and Calvin, though quite traditional in their view of the person of the Holy Spirit—because they found the tradition biblical—nonetheless reframed the understanding of the Holy Spirit's work in the church and the world, giving the Spirit *a new immediacy* in the lives of believers.[20]

Now, given the increased importance the Reformers attributed to the Spirit, and the fact that they did so because they believed the move enjoyed biblical support, it would be quite ironic were we to discover that the Reformation theme *sola Scriptura* might have in any way contributed to a neglect of the Spirit in post-Reformation Protestant theology.

Hence, this paper. After briefly exploring the connections that seem to exist between two overly restrictive takes on *sola Scriptura* and a marginalization of the Spirit in contemporary evangelical theology and ministry, the remainder of the paper will focus on the possibility that, over against

19. Timothy Tennent, *Invitation to World Missions: A Trinitarian Missiology for the Twenty-First Century* (Grand Rapids, MI: Kregel Academic, 2010), 94, emphasis added. See also Roger Olson, *The Story of Christian Theology* (Downers Grove, IL: IVP Academic, 1999), 521, 523; Veli-Matti Kärkkäinen, *Pneumatology: The Holy Spirit in Ecumenical, International, and Contextual Perspective* (Grand Rapids, MI: Baker Academic, 2002), 17–18. Moreover, Jürgen Moltmann provides not only a nuanced discussion of the reason for the "reserve in the doctrine of the Holy Spirit" within the established churches in Europe during the modern era, but also an eloquent critique of the tendency among some evangelicals to conflate Word and Spirit, and to conceive of the Spirit only in an intellectual manner. See Jürgen Moltmann, *The Spirit of Life: A Universal Affirmation* (Minneapolis: Fortress, 1992), 2–3.

20. Jane Dempsey Douglas, "The Lively Work of the Spirit in the Reformation," *Word & World* 23:2 (Spring 2003) 121–33, https://wordandworld.luthersem.edu/content/pdfs/23-2_Holy_Spirit/23-2_Douglass.pdf, emphasis added.

this unfortunate Spirit-devaluing dynamic, the pneumatological realism implicit in the Scripture-based Reformed theology of Karl Barth, when combined with his distinctive takes on the nature of revelation and the three-fold form of the word of God, might actually provide some rather impressive theological support for the type of *prophetic preaching* I am advocating for—biblically-grounded, Christ-honoring, Spirit-empowered sermons that are sacramental (encounter-facilitating) in their effect. As well, I'll also provide a concluding, Barth-sensitive reflection on what a pneumatologically real approach to the preaching task entails.

From two evangelical understandings of *sola Scriptura* that have proven to be Spirit-marginalizing in their effect, to an eager engagement in a Spirit-empowered form of prophetic preaching: this is the ironic, important possibility this paper will explore.

Sola Scriptura and the Pneumatological Deficit

Many scholars hold that for Luther, Zwingli, and Calvin, the fundamental meaning of *sola Scriptura* was that the Scriptures alone constitute the ultimate authority for Christian faith and practice, rather than the Scriptures and an ecclesiastical tradition conveyed by either the pope or magisterium.[21] However, I am going to draw attention here to a couple of ways in which a tendency among some evangelicals to go beyond the original intention behind the Reformers' promotion of the concept of *sola Scriptura* has contributed to the marginalization of the Holy Spirit in contemporary Christian theology, and has cultivated within too many contemporary churches an ethos of pneumatological presumption (or even indifference) rather than expectancy.

---

21. For example, see Matthew Barrett, *God's Word Alone: The Authority of Scripture* (Grand Rapids, MI: Zondervan, 2016), 21, 27, 36–37, 42, 45, 49, 52–54, 64, 68–70, 74–75. See also W. Robert Godfrey, "What Do We Mean by Sola Scriptura?", in *Sola Scriptura: The Protestant Position on the Bible* (Sanford, FL: Reformation Trust, 2009), 1; and James R. White, *Scripture Alone* (Minneapolis: Bethany House, 2004), 27–28. It should be noted, however, that an alternative to this view is provided by Keith Mathison, who asserts: "What we observe in the Reformation is not Scripture versus tradition. Instead, it is the inevitable clash between two mutually exclusive concepts of tradition" (see Keith A. Mathison, *The Shape of Sola Scriptura* [Moscow, ID: Canon Press, 2001], 86).

The Connection between Sola Scriptura
and the Doctrine of Cessationism

At the heart of my proposal regarding the need for evangelical churches to cultivate an ecclesial atmosphere marked by the embrace of a pneumatological realism, is the conviction that contemporary Christians can and should *expect* to interact with the Holy Spirit in ways that are both personal and sometimes phenomenal (i.e., immediate and evident to the senses) rather than impersonal and purely theoretical. In other words, contemporary Christians can and should *expect* to experience the Spirit of Christ in essentially the same intimate, interactive manner as did Jesus' first followers.

Moreover, as I have indicated elsewhere, the Bible as a whole seems to evidence a dynamic connection between empowering encounters with the Holy Spirit and the phenomenon of *prophetic activity* (Spirit-prompted and enabled speech and action). Passage after passage in both testaments demonstrate a pattern that is simply too apparent to ignore: when the Spirit of God comes upon a person or persons, a divinely enabled ability to speak and/or act into the lives of others on God's behalf is often the result.[22] Thus, my thesis is that both the Old and New Testaments teach that when the Holy Spirit—the Spirit of mission—comes upon God's people in an empowering manner, something missionally significant occurs: the impartation of prophetic capacity. Put simply, this prophetic capacity involves a Spirit-enabled ability to—like Ananias of Damascus—hear God's voice, receive ministry assignments from him, and speak and act into the lives of people on his behalf, making disciples, and building up Christ's church in the process (see Acts 9:10–22).[23]

Obviously, then, the version of prophetic preaching I have in mind presumes a *continuationist* rather than *cessationist* pneumatological perspective. Now, while a church does not have to self-identify as Pentecostal-charismatic to be continuationist in orientation, it is not at all uncommon to find evangelical scholars basing their fervent rejection of continuationism on an understanding of *sola Scriptura* that is explicitly anti-Pentecostal-charismatic in its application. Consider, for example, this explanation provided by a Reformed theologian as to why the charismatic movement

---

22. For example, see Num 11:25–29; 1 Sam 10:6–11; 19:19–24; 1 Chr 12:18; 2 Chr 24:20; Joel 2:28–29; Luke 1:41–45, 67; 2:25–28; Acts 2:4; 4:8; 8:4–19; 9:17–18 (cf. 1 Cor 14:18); 10:44–46; 13:9; 19:6; Eph 5:18–20.

23. See Tyra, *The Holy Spirit in Mission*, 68, 98, 129.

as a whole should be seen as nothing less than an enemy of the Protestant Reformation:

> [T]he most fundamental element of the Reformation was the cry of "Sola Scriptura" from students of the Bible. The "charismatic movement" does not carry on the Reformation, but rather strikes a damaging blow to its very roots. They would destroy the Protestant foundation of confiding in Scripture alone.[24]

In a pertinent volume titled *Sola Scriptura and the Revelatory Gifts,* Don Codling elaborates at some length upon why some evangelicals insist that *sola Scriptura* and the charismatic movement are inimical to one another. According to Codling, at the heart of the doctrine of cessationism is an understanding of *sola Scriptura* which emphasizes a *closed canon* and the *sufficiency of Scripture.*[25] The presumption on the part of some cessationists seems to be not only that commitments to these two notions are absent in the continuationist perspective, but that many, if not most, Pentecostal-charismatics have explicitly rejected them in favor of the possibility of "new revelation" they consider as authoritative as (or even more so than) the canonical Scriptures.

For instance, in Matthew Barrett's *God's Word Alone: The Authority of Scripture,* a linkage is established between contemporary Pentecostalism and the view of the radical reformers who "believed the Spirit trumped even the Bible." Says Barrett of these radicals: "The internal, personal word or revelation from the Spirit *they* received took priority over what the Bible said."[26] Then, Barrett summarizes the belief of those within contemporary "Pentecostal circles" thusly: "While the Bible is appreciated, even revered, what is of ultimate significance and authority is a *new, additional* revelation from the Spirit, one that goes above and beyond the Bible."[27]

Though to his credit Barrett includes a footnote in which he acknowledges that "many charismatics ... affirm *sola Scriptura* and argue that their view of the gifts is not to be set over or against Scripture,"[28] it's my sense that many non-Pentecostal/charismatic evangelicals are not buying it. For one

24. Walter J. Chantry, *Signs of the Apostles* (Edinburgh, Scotland: Banner of Truth Trust, 1973), 33, as cited in Don Codling, *Sola Scriptura and the Revelatory Gifts: How Should Christians Deal with Present Day Prophecy?* (Rice, WA: Sentinel Press, 2005), 51.

25. Ibid., 51–53.

26. Barrett, *God's Word Alone,* 369, emphasis original.

27. Ibid., 369, emphasis original.

28. Ibid., 369, 119n.

thing, my experience of presenting academic papers at some evangelical conference venues has been that any suggestion that the prophetic phenomenon witnessed to in Scripture might occur today is for many conferees an absolute non-starter. Furthermore, my experience of working with Christian university students who hail from some evangelical churches is that they have been taught to be deeply distrustful of anyone, regardless of academic degree, who speaks too much or too enthusiastically about the Holy Spirit.

Now, because the purpose of this paper is *not* to suggest that prophetic preaching will (or even might) contain new, extra-biblical revelation that should be considered authoritative alongside sacred Scripture, the cessationist argument is not one I feel the need to respond to here.[29] I draw attention to the connection some have made between *sola Scriptura* and the doctrine of cessationism, simply to indicate one of the ways in which the pneumatological deficit referred to by Tennent (and others) can be traced back to the Reformation, and one reason why the ethos or atmosphere of some evangelical communities of faith might not be earmarked by the type of pneumatological expectancy which I believe best accommodates the type of prophetic preaching this paper is about.

The Connection between Sola Scriptura and Pneumatological Heresy

Another contemporary take on the meaning of *sola Scriptura* is pilloried in an essay penned by Lutheran theologian Matthew Block, and is provocatively titled: "Evangelicals, Heresy, and Scripture Alone."[30] In this alarm-sounding piece, Block refers to some LifeWay Research published in 2014 which suggests that increasing numbers of evangelicals "hold views the early church long ago declared heresy."[31] Relevant to the theme of this paper are the following findings: (1) "a majority of Evangelicals deny the personhood of the Holy Spirit, with 56 percent saying he is a 'divine force but not a personal being'";[32] and (2) according to 28 percent of the evangelicals

---

29. For a book-length treatment of the connection between cessationism and *sola Scriptura*, see Codling, *Sola Scriptura*.

30. Matthew Block, "Evangelicals, Heresy, and Scripture Alone," https://www.firstthings.com/blogs/firstthoughts/2016/10/evangelicals-heresy-and-scripture-alone.

31. Ibid., para. 1.

32. Ibid., para. 7.

interviewed, "the Holy Spirit is a divine being, but is not equal with God the Father or Jesus."[33]

So, why are these unorthodox pneumatological perspectives apparently on the rise among contemporary evangelicals? Block is convinced that there is a connection between these substandard takes on the Trinity and a profound misunderstanding of *sola Scriptura*. Instead of the *sola Scriptura* the Reformers had in mind, too many contemporary evangelicals have embraced something which Block refers to as "solo Scriptura" and Matthew Barrett refers to as *nuda Scriptura*.[34] Though their respective aims in drawing attention to this problem differ somewhat, of immediate concern to both Barrett and Block is the surprising number of evangelical Christians who

> seem to think saying *Sola Scriptura* is the ultimate authority somehow means it is my personal "solo" reading of Scripture that is authoritative. They reject the witness of the Church down through the ages in favor of a personal, private understanding of Scripture (which is not at all what the reformers meant by the term "Scripture alone"). Consequently, we see that many Evangelicals deny that the historic Church's creeds and confessions have any relevance today.[35]

Now, straightaway I want to make clear that the "prophetic preaching" I am advocating for, while holding firmly to the concept of *sola Scriptura*, resolutely rejects the notion of "*solo Scriptura*" (or "*nuda Scriptura*") as described above. The sacramental sermon I have in mind is one which is not only based on the canonical Scriptures, but has benefitted from the interpretive assistance provided by the witness of the Church down through the ages.

So why draw attention then to the "solo Scriptura" at work among some evangelicals? I do so for this reason: given the alarming numbers, it's very possible that either of the heretical pneumatological perspectives identified by the LifeWay research might be held *not only* by a rogue church member here or there, but by entire congregations. If so, this is a serious matter. Once again, the phenomenon of prophetic preaching is based on

33. Ibid., para. 7.

34. Barrett, *God's Word Alone*, 23, 54–55, 343–45.

35. Block, "Evangelicals, Heresy, and Scripture Alone." As well, a strident critique of what the author refers to as the "modern Evangelical doctrine of Scripture, or solo Scriptura" can be found in Mathison, *The Shape of Sola Scriptura*, 237–53.

the notion that the Spirit of Christ can be interacted with in ways that are personal, phenomenal, and existentially impactful. It also presumes an ecclesial ethos, defined by a significant sense of *expectancy* based on this belief. Thus, it seems legitimate to ask: what kind of pneumatological expectancy, if any, are we likely to find among groups of Christians sporting a pneumatology which significantly downplays either the personhood or divinity of the Holy Spirit?

Apparently, then, some connections can indeed be made between a couple of controversial takes on the Reformation theme *sola Scriptura* and a tendency in some evangelical theologies and churches to not only deemphasize the work of the Spirit, but to depersonalize him as well. But does it have to be this way?

Karl Barth and the Possibility of Prophetic Preaching

I want to press on now to explore the possibility that the practice of a Spirit-empowered version of prophetic preaching might actually enjoy some impressive theological support, and from a somewhat surprising source: a Reformed theologian who is not only famous for his "biblicism" (i.e., his methodological turn to the Bible[36]), but who has also been accused of having neglected the doctrine of the Holy Spirit despite his focus on the Trinitarian nature of God. As ironic as it may seem, it's my contention that when we combine the pneumatological realism I suspect is inherent in Barth's theology, with his distinctive (encounter-oriented) notions concerning revelation, the word of God, and Christian proclamation, we stumble upon some significant, if tacit, support for this paper's thesis.

Barth's Pneumatological Realism

To be clear, Timothy Tennent's provocative assertion is that it was the Reformation's emphasis on ecclesiology and Christology, as well as Scripture,

---

36. Says Kurt Anders Richardson: "Reading Barth, one is not pressed to see multiple sources of theology constantly at work, as with those who direct constant attention to some quadrilateral (revelation, tradition, reason, and experience—or variations on this theme). The *CD* [*Church Dogmatics*] attends to these, but the source of theology is always singular: the Word of God" (Kurt Anders Richardson, *Reading Karl Barth: New Directions for American Theology* [Grand Rapids, MI: Baker Academic, 2004], 13). See also Francis Watson, "The Bible," in *The Cambridge Companion to Karl Barth*, ed. John Webster, 57–71 (Cambridge: Cambridge University Press, 2000), 58–59, 61–62.

that seems to have contributed to a marginalizing of the Spirit in at least some post-Reformation Protestant theologies. This was especially true, says Tennent, of some theologies emanating from the Reformed tradition. He explains:

> A typical example can be found in Louis Berkhof's *Systematic Theology*, a classic text in Reformed theology that is still in use today. Berkhof discusses the work of the Holy Spirit but *limits it to applying the work of Christ into our lives* (e.g., regeneration) and in personal holiness (e.g., sanctification). In his development of ecclesiology, *Berkhof is silent about the role of the Holy Spirit in empowering the church for witness and mission or in enabling the church as a whole to live out in the present the eschatological realities of the New Creation.* It is not unusual to find Western systematic theologies that do not even develop the person and work of the Holy Spirit as a separate category of study but develop their theology of the Holy Spirit as subsets under the doctrine of God and the doctrine of soteriology.[37]

Some have argued that Barth, as a Reformed theologian, was himself complicit in this Protestant, post-Reformation marginalizing of the Spirit. A version of this argument was put forward by Robert Jenson in an oft-cited journal article titled: "You Wonder Where the Spirit Went."[38] Barth scholar, Eugene Rogers, explains that in this article, Jenson

> crystallizes an unease about successive nineteenth- and twentieth-century trinitarian revivals: whether they have much interesting to say about the Holy Spirit; whether, indeed, they tend (despite themselves) to reduce the Spirit to a function or "power" of the Son. He poses that question by focusing on the greatest and most ambitious of those revivals, that of Karl Barth.[39]

Anyone concerned about impoverished pneumatologies that put forward depersonalized, overly-conceptualized depictions of the Holy Spirit must take Jenson's critique seriously. And yet, while certainly understanding Jenson's concern, my own reading of Barth, informed by the commentary provided by some experts on Barth's pneumatology, has caused me

37. See Tennent, *Invitation to World Missions*, 94, emphasis added.

38. Robert W. Jenson, "You Wonder Where the Spirit Went," in *Pro Ecclesia: A Journal of Catholic and Evangelical Theology* 2 (1993) 296–304.

39. Eugene Rogers, *The Holy Spirit: Classic and Contemporary Readings* (Hoboken, NJ: Wiley-Blackwell, 2009), 9.

to wonder if his work—despite its conspicuous Christocentrism—might actually be considered a "Spirit theology" nevertheless.

Barth and the Theological Tie-In with T. F. Torrance

In a nutshell, what I'm suggesting is that back of Barth's theologizing was a metaphysics of divine reality in which *both* Christ and the Holy Spirit play vital, indispensable roles. Indeed, so crucial is the Holy Spirit to Barth's widely acknowledged theological realism[40] that a pneumatological realism can be inferred as well.

Crucial to my thesis is the observation that we see something very similar in the theology of Scottish theologian T. F. Torrance who, I will suggest, popularized for evangelicals the concept of theological realism. Both Barth and Torrance famously insisted that because of the incarnation of Christ, a real, trustworthy knowledge of our trinitarian God is possible.[41] This mutually held conviction was grounded on the following Christological tenet: "what God is antecedently and eternally in himself he really is toward us in the concrete embodiment of his Truth in Jesus Christ the word made flesh."[42] Obviously, this theological precept possesses huge epistemological significance.[43] Supportive of the notion of a pneumatological realism is the fact that both Torrance and Barth also spoke of the dramatic, critical importance of the *indwelling of the Holy Spirit* to the process

40. For example, see McGrath, *A Scientific Theology: Volume 2: Reality* (Grand Rapids, MI: Eerdmans, 2002), 257–64. See also Sandra Sonderegger, "Barth and Feminism," in *The Cambridge Companion to Karl Barth*, ed. John Webster, 258–73 (Cambridge: Cambridge University Press, 2000), 264; Graham Ward, "Barth, Modernity, and Postmodernity," in *The Cambridge Companion to Karl Barth*, ed. John Webster, 274–95 (Cambridge: Cambridge University Press, 2000), 281; George Hunsinger, *How to Read Karl Barth: The Shape of His Theology* (New York: Oxford University Press, 1991), 4–5. Even though "realism" is the label Hunsinger attaches to one of six Barthian motifs, I will offer that the theological/pneumatological realism I have in mind, and see in Barth's work, comprises elements of all six of the motifs to which Hunsinger refers. See Hunsinger's survey of the motifs in ibid., 27–64.

41. See Thomas F. Torrance, *Reality & Evangelical Theology* (Downers Grove, IL: InterVarsity Press, 1999), 23. A very concise comparison of the ways in which the theological realisms of Barth and Torrance compare can be found in McGrath, *A Scientific Theology: Volume 2: Reality*, 265.

42. Torrance, *Reality & Evangelical Theology*, 141. See also see Karl Barth, *Church Dogmatics* I/1, translated by G. W. Bromiley (Peabody, MA: Hendrickson, 2010), 466.

43. As I argue below, I believe this precept also possesses an existential significance as well.

of divine self-revelation. For instance, in a passage underscoring the need for orthodox understandings of both Christ and the Spirit, Torrance wrote:

> Everything hinges on the *reality* of God's *self*-communication to us in Jesus Christ, in whom there has become incarnate, not some created intermediary between God and the world, but the very Word who eternally inheres in the Being of God and is God, so that for us to know God in Jesus Christ is really to know him as he is in himself. *It is with the same force that attention is directed upon the Holy Spirit*, whom the Father sends through the Son to dwell with us, and who, like the Son, is no mere cosmic power intermediate between God and the world, but is the Spirit of God who eternally dwells in him and in whom God knows himself, so that for us to know God in his Spirit is to know him in the hidden depths of his divine Being.[44]

According to this passage, Torrance held that it's both the *incarnation of Christ* and the *indwelling of his Spirit* that makes a theological realism— a real, trustworthy knowledge of our Trinitarian God—possible. Thus, it's my contention that even though Torrance never used the term "pneumatological realism" in his writings, given the importance of the Spirit to his Christ-centered theological realism,[45] the presence of a pneumatological realism can be inferred. The burden of the next few pages of this essay is to provide some support for the contention that the very same thing can be said of Barth as well.

Barth Himself on the Importance of the Holy Spirit

For instance, here are three initial quotes from the mature Barth which indicate the critical importance he attached to the Holy Spirit for Christian theology:

> It was the Spirit whose existence and action make possible and real (and possible and real up to this very day) the existence of Christianity in the world.[46]

---

44. Torrance, *Reality & Evangelical Theology*, 23, emphasis added.

45. See Tyra, *The Holy Spirit in Mission*, 112–13, 164; Tyra, *A Missional Orthodoxy*, 119–21; 327; Tyra, *Pursuing Moral Faithfulness*, 20–21.

46. Karl Barth, *Evangelical Theology: An Introduction* (Grand Rapids, MI: Eerdmans, 1963), 55, emphasis added.

It is clear that evangelical theology itself can only be pneumatic, spiritual theology. Only in the realm of the power of the Spirit can theology be realized as a humble, free, critical, and happy science of the God of the Gospel.[47]

Only the Spirit himself can rescue theology! He, the Holy One, the Lord, the Giver of Life, waits and waits to be received anew by theology as by the community. He waits to receive from theology his due of adoration and glorification. He expects from theology that it submit itself to the repentance, renewal, and reformation he effects. He waits to vivify and illuminate its affirmations which, however right they may be, are dead without the Spirit.[48]

Still, what do we do with the accusation that Barth's earlier theological work, so very Christ-centered, was guilty of not only neglecting the Holy Spirit but depersonalizing him as well? In the next several pages I will interact with several observations put forward by two prominent Barth scholars who insist that such an accusation is without merit, that Barth's theology was always as much pneumatocentric as it was Christocentric.

Aaron Smith and Barth's Dual-Focused Theology

One of the stated aims of Aaron T. Smith's A Theology of the Third Article: Karl Barth and the Spirit of the Word, is to function as a "summary defense of Barth" against the charge that his Christocentrism had left him "little room for thinking and speaking of the Holy Spirit."[49] In the process, Smith is also pushing back against the notion (promoted by Eberhard Busch) that the famous remark made by Barth late in his career regarding the possibility of a theology of the Third Article, meant that he "was thinking of a theology which, unlike his own, was not written from the dominant perspective of Christology but from pneumatology."[50] For both of these reasons, Smith's work is filled with passages which strongly indicate Barth's pneumatological realism, despite how Christ-centered his theology was. For instance, Smith writes:

47. Ibid., 55.

48. Ibid., 57.

49. Aaron T. Smith, A Theology of the Third Article: Karl Barth and the Spirit of the Word (Minneapolis: Fortress Press, 2014), 2.

50. Ibid., 19, 50–51.

Barth's christocentrism is at once pneumato-logical. His thought trades on the agency of the Spirit at every turn; apart from the event of faith, which is Spirit-inspired and maintained, there is no christocentric point of departure for pastoral or theological thought and speech. And at the same time, apart from the ex-egetical work and Person of Christ, there is no pneumatocentric content upon which one could think and speak of God. . . . Thus, Barth has to be directing us to a pnematocentrisim materially and methodologically consistent with the content and shape of his christocentrism.[51]

In other words, according to Smith, Barth's theology is actually suggestive of what a theology of the third article might look like, his Christocentrism notwithstanding. Again, Smith says of Barth: "there is a substantive pneumatological undercurrent flowing with and even guiding his christological conclusions. One can draw out and build on Barth's own 'pneumatocentric dialectic.'"[52] Then, within a very important footnote devoted to this discussion, Smith articulates the critical relationship between pneumatology and Christology in the theology of Karl Barth thusly: "There is no Christology that is not also Pneumatology. One simply cannot understand the Word, particularly as the center of dogmatic reflection in the light of which Christian thought takes defining shape and substance, apart from the living action and distinct identity of the Spirit."[53]

Philip Rosato and the Dual Importance of the Spirit in Barth's Theology

Another source of support for my thesis that a pneumatological realism is crucial to Barth's theological project is Philip J. Rosato. In his work titled *The Spirit as Lord: The Pneumatology of Karl Barth,* Rosato provides multiple passages which signal not only the profound *epistemological significance* that Barth, like Torrance, attributed to the work of the Holy Spirit, but the *existential significance* Barth associated with the Spirit as well. In other words, the references presented below suggest a truly dynamic,

---

51. Ibid., 52–53

52. Ibid., 18–19.

53. Ibid., 19, 10n. This contention that a biblically-informed pneumatological realism will necessarily be Christ-honoring also finds support in George Hunsinger's essay titled "The Mediator of Communion: Karl Barth's Doctrine of the Holy Spirit" in *The Cambridge Companion to Karl Barth,* ed. John Webster, 177–94 (Cambridge: Cambridge University Press, 2000), 181–82.

two-pronged connection between the Holy Spirit and the realism at work in Barth's theological project.

First, with respect to the *epistemological significance* of the Spirit for Barth, Rosato offers the following assessment:

> Barth grounds his insistence on a single source of man's knowledge about the Trinity on nothing less than the Holy Spirit. . . . Since the doctrine of the Trinity lies at the core of the revealed Word, and since the Word can only be known through the power of the Spirit, Barth links the knowledge of the Trinity to the mystery of the Spirit at work in Christian experience.[54]

Then, as if eager to put an even finer point on the matter, Rosato continues:

> The Holy Spirit, God's own historical self-impartation to man, guarantees a correspondence between God in himself and God as He is known by man. Clearly the solution to the problem concerning knowledge of the immanent Trinity must be for Barth a pneumatological solution. Only the Spirit, as the spiritual power of God's own eternal Word, can create through faith a human knowledge which substantially corresponds to the truth of God himself. That man can know the immanent nature of God as the mystery which coincides with the economic activity of God on man's behalf is the work of the Holy Spirit.[55]

> Just as God the Father knows Himself in His Son through the Spirit, the man of faith can come to know his Father in Jesus Christ though the Spirit. Only a metaphysics rooted in *divine reality* guarantees that man can mediately know God as God immediately knows Himself.[56]

Furthermore, Rosato also has much to say about the *existential significance* of the Spirit for Barth. I have already suggested that a realist understanding of the Spirit entails that he can and should be related to in ways that are real, personal, and life-story-shaping (i.e., existentially impactful). In support of this notion is Rosato's insistence that, for Barth, the work of the Holy Spirit is not only objectively *revelational* in nature, but subjectively *transformational* also. For instance, in a discussion titled "The Father and

54. Philip J. Rosato, *The Spirit as Lord: The Pneumatology of Karl Barth* (Edinburgh, Scotland: T & T Clark, 1981), 55.

55. Ibid., 57.

56. Ibid., 72, emphasis added.

the Son Meeting Man from Within," we find repeated references to *God's reality* and his very real working in human history toward the goal of an existentially-impactful "communion" with humanity through the Holy Spirit.[57] In this important discussion, Rosato asserts that

> it is God the Holy Spirit, God in His third mode of existence, who according to Barth makes the actions of the Father and of the Son become historical realities. . . . The Holy Spirit is God personally manifest to and in men . . . "men who become what by themselves and of themselves they can neither be nor become, men who belong to God, who are in real communion with God, who live before God and with God." Man's being-related to God, being present before him and with him is the distinct work of the Holy Spirit.[58]

Moreover, in another telling passage, Rosato makes the point that, according to Barth, the Holy Spirit lies behind not just the *faith* of the believer but his or her capacity for *faithfulness* as well:

> The obvious, yet mysterious, reality of the conscious faith of the Christian induces Barth to investigate the various observable aspects of this faith before he can adequately explain their possibility. The first of these concrete aspects is that the individual Christian is in fact capable of acting publicly as a man who has heard the Word of God addressed to him and accepted that Word with the trust of a child. The believer discovers that he both is and acts in a way which his own powers could not account for. He has become the recipient of a new capacity. This central fact of Christian existence constitutes for Barth the subjective reality of revelation, the work of the Holy Spirit, God present in man creating in him the freedom to become obedient to the Father through faith. When a man believes, God receives a new son through the power of the Holy

---

57. Ibid., 60–65.

58. Ibid., 60. The citation is from Barth, *Church Dogmatics* I/1, 450. It's worth noting that in the middle of this discussion, Rosato makes the following observation: "Barth reiterates here that his presentation of the Spirit as the sole source of *communion* not only between the Father and the Son from eternity but also between man and God in revelation is intended to be a clear answer to the ambiguities of either an *overly philosophical, overly-institutional* or *overly-personal* [i.e., anthropocentric] understanding of the Holy Spirit" (Rosato, *The Spirit as Lord*, 63, emphasis added). Apparently, Barth himself felt the need to argue for a pneumatological realism over against extant understandings of the Spirit!

Spirit who alone makes it possible first that a man is a child of God and thus that he can subsequently become so.[59]

I'm suggesting that, without doing so explicitly, Rosato is ascribing to Barth the type of pneumatological realism described in this essay. Then again, perhaps the question should be asked, to what degree can we trust Rosato's observations regarding Barth's theology? Presented below is a quote from Barth himself, which seems to underwrite not only Rosato's commentary, but this paper's thesis as well. Barth speaks here of a *freedom* the Spirit imparts to Christian disciples that has implications for just about every aspect of the Christian life:

> To receive the Spirit, to have the Spirit, to live in the Spirit means being set free and being permitted to live in freedom. . . . To have inner ears for the Word of Christ, to become thankful for His work and at the same time responsible for the message about Him and, lastly, to take confidence in men for Christ's sake—that is the freedom which we obtain, when Christ breathes on us, when He sends us His Holy Spirit. If He no longer lives in a historical or heavenly, a theological or ecclesiastical remoteness from me, if He approaches me and takes possession of me, the result will be that I hear, that I am thankful and responsible and that finally I may hope for myself and for all others; in other words, that I may live in a Christian way. It is a tremendously big thing and by no means a matter of course, to obtain this freedom. We must therefore every day and every hour pray *Veni Creator Spiritus* [Come, Creator Spirit] in listening to the word of Christ and in thankfulness. That is a closed circle. We do not "have" this freedom; it is again and again given to us by God.[60]

This is one of many passages from Barth's hand which, I believe, implies a realist, rather than a non-realist, understanding of the Holy Spirit—a pneumatology which possesses both an *epistemological* and *existential* significance. It's difficult for me to read Barth (and those more familiar with his theology than I) and not be convinced that his theological project was and is, as it were, "pregnant" with the sense of pneumatological expectancy I associate with a pneumatological realism.

At the same time, I readily acknowledge that some evidence for the importance Barth placed on the Holy Spirit does not by itself constitute

59. Rosato, *The Spirit as Lord*, 71.

60. Karl Barth, *Dogmatics in Outline* (New York: Harper & Row, 1959), 138–39, emphasis added.

compelling support for the phenomenon of prophetic preaching. To be clear, my thesis holds that such support is discerned when we go on to add to Barth's realist understanding of the Spirit the emphasis on *encounter*, which earmarked his doctrines of revelation, word of God, and Christian preaching.

Barth's Encounter-Oriented Takes on Revelation and Proclamation

Assuming some familiarity on the part of the reader with respect to Barth's provocative takes on revelation as event and the threefold form of the word of God will allow me to treat these topics in light of the overarching question: How did Barth's concept of proclamation as the word of God impact his conception of the preaching task?[61]

Perhaps the best way to introduce this discussion, then, is by making use of this summative observation made by Barth scholar Kurt Anders Richardson: "Barth wanted his readers to focus on the active revelation of God's Word, which God is constantly accomplishing through Scripture, and the preaching of Scripture by the power of the Holy Spirit."[62] There's a sense in which this statement succinctly summarizes the theme of not only this section, but the paper as a whole: the way Barth viewed revelation as encounter, proclamation as the word of God, and the crucial role the Spirit plays in this proclamation, combine in such a way as to suggest the possibility of prophetic preaching that is *incarnational, sacramental* (encounter-facilitating), and therefore *transformational* in nature. In order to better understand this equation, we must drill a bit more deeply into several of its components.

61. A summary discussion of these topics which aims to be accessible to those only beginning their study of Barth can be found in John R. Franke, *Barth for Armchair Theologians* (Louisville, KY: Westminster John Knox Press), 115–23. A quite brief, though somewhat pedantic, summary of Barth's takes on these topics is available in Geoffrey W. Bromiley, *Introduction to the Theology of Karl Barth* (Grand Rapids, MI: Eerdmans, 1979), 6–8. For a more nuanced discussion of Barth's perspective on revelation in general, see Roland Chia, *Revelation and Theology: The Knowledge of God in Balthasar and Barth* (New York: Peter Lang, 1999), 129–60. For a nuanced discussion of Barth's concept of revelation as event/encounter in particular, see Trevor Hart, "Revelation," in *The Cambridge Companion to Karl Barth*, ed. John Webster, 37–56 (Cambridge: Cambridge University Press, 2000), 45–55.

62. Richardson, *Reading Karl Barth*, 106.

APPENDIX

Barth's "Prophetic" Understanding of True Proclamation

Well-known is the fact that it was due to a crisis in his preaching as a pastor that Barth was led to abandon his liberal theological training and move in a new direction in his theology.[63] To be more specific, Bernard Ramm insists that, to fully understand Barth, it's necessary to see him reacting to a particular approach to preaching that he eventually came to regard as unsatisfactory. Ramm explains:

> The Enlightenment and liberal Christianity *reduced preaching to a purely human performance.* The sermon may be passionate or learned, clever, textual, prophetic [i.e., confrontational], instructive, or inspirational, and may include fine remarks about Jesus. Nevertheless, its theological presuppositions *prevent it from rising above the level of human discourse.*[64]

Barth himself boldly asserted that both Modernism and Roman Catholicism could be faulted for not taking the task of preaching seriously enough. Both systems erred fundamentally in their low estimation of what constituted true proclamation. Barth made a huge distinction between the churchly tasks of social work, Christian education of youth, and even theology, and the task of proclamation rightly understood.[65]

Of course, such a critique begs the question: What, then, is true proclamation?

With what appears to be some willful, careful precision, Barth articulated a formal definition that is highly evocative of the prophetic dynamic:

> Proclamation is human speech in and by which God Himself speaks like a king through the mouth of his herald, and which is meant to be heard and accepted as speech in and by which God Himself speaks, and therefore heard and accepted in faith as divine decision concerning life and death, as divine judgment and pardon, eternal Law and eternal Gospel both together.[66]

63. See Eberhard Busch, *Karl Barth: His Life from Letters and Autobiographical Texts,* trans. John Bowden (Philadelphia: Fortress Press, 1976), 61. See also John Webster, "Introducing Barth," in *The Cambridge Companion to Karl Barth,* ed. John Webster, 1–16, (Cambridge: Cambridge University Press, 2000), 3; Gregory G. Bolich, *Karl Barth & Evangelicalism* (Downers Grove, IL: InterVarsity Press, 1980), 108.

64. Bernard Ramm, *After Fundamentalism: The Future of Evangelical Theology* (San Francisco: Harper & Row, 1983), 51, emphasis added.

65. Barth, *Church Dogmatics,* I/1, 50–51.

66. Ibid., 52.

That Barth had the prophetic phenomenon in mind is indicated by the language he used when issuing the following clarification and concomitant call for homiletical humility:

> It is a decisive part of the insight of all true *prophecy* that man as such has no possibility of uttering the Word of God. What human utterance concerning God aims to be when it is intended as proclamation is not grace, but service of grace or means of grace. If the will in question were man's will to reach out beyond himself, to put himself with his word about God in the place of God, it would be blasphemous rebellion.[67]

There's no question that Barth sought to make it crystal clear that the preacher cannot, in himself or herself, conjure the reality of God or effect revelation.[68] Still, Barth certainly seemed to suggest that preaching does indeed possess a prophetic quality when it involves true proclamation.

Barth's "Theologically Real" Understanding of the Word of God

To be more specific, according to Barth, the decisive criterion for true proclamation is the word of God. The key to understanding this caveat, however, is to bear in mind that Barth did not understand the word of God in a nominal, static, merely propositional sense. For Barth, the word of God is event—i.e., God's speaking. Says Barth: "Church proclamation is talk, speech. So is Holy Scripture. So is even revelation in itself as such. . . . God's Word means that God speaks."[69] Furthermore, Barth saw this revelatory event as taking place in three forms: the Word of God *revealed* (Jesus Christ); the word of God *written* (the Scriptures); and the word of God *proclaimed* (Proclamation).[70] Barth maintained that there is an order of priority within this threefold expression of the word of God. The word of God proclaimed is contingent upon the word of God written, which is contingent upon the word of God revealed. This explains Barth's insistence that true proclamation is contingent upon the word of God.

---

67. Ibid., 52–53, emphasis added.

68. Karl Barth, *Homiletics* (Louisville, KY: Westminster John Knox Press, 1991), 48–49.

69. Barth, *Church Dogmatics*, I/1, 132.

70. Ibid., 88–124.

APPENDIX

Or does it, fully? My contention is that one further degree of nuance is needed. While, *immediately*, true proclamation is contingent upon both the word of God written (the Scriptures) and Word of God revealed (Christ), *ultimately*, it is contingent upon the theologically real dynamic of "God's speaking." In other words, for Barth, real proclamation is not only biblical and Christ-centered, but prophetic as well. Real proclamation sees itself as a possibility, precisely because of the reality of the word of God—God's speaking—and humanity's Spirit-endowed ability to hear/receive it.[71]

Barth's "Incarnational" Understanding of Christian Proclamation

Another distinctive of true proclamation for Barth is the encounter with God's speaking it facilitates, the humanity of the preacher and sermon notwithstanding.[72]

Barth was never reticent in his insistence that true proclamation is a miracle. However, he was also very careful to specify that the miraculous is not merely the divinization of human utterance, nor the humanization of the divine. Instead, true proclamation involves the phenomenon of incarnation.[73] Barth's reasoning was thus: just as the Word of God revealed (Christ) involved the assumption of human flesh, and just as the word of God written (the Scriptures) involved the pen and intellect of human authors, even so, the word of God proclaimed (Proclamation) involves the full involvement of fallible, imperfect human heralds.

The incarnational aspect of true proclamation is a concept Aaron Smith really leans into in his book *A Theology of the Third Article*. Throughout this work, he (following Barth) refers to the Spirit as "God a third time,"[74] and keeps referring to a dynamic he calls "inverberation."[75] Says Smith:

> I argue that the Spirit of God is God a third time, subsisting in ontological unity with the Father and Son, yet distinctly his own Person in that he is the contemporaneity of the revelation event in which God has his existence. The Spirit self-determinatively

71. Ibid., 89. For more on this, see Tyra, *Pursuing Moral Faithfulness*, 20; Tyra, *A Missional Orthodoxy*, 119–21.

72. Barth, *Church Dogmatics*, I/1, 93–94.

73. Ibid., 94.

74. Smith, *A Theology of the Third Article*, 2, 7, 194, 241, 249.

75. Ibid., 7, 12, 20, 22, 35, 44, 58, 60, 82, 83, 92, 108, 110, 114, 120, 121, 127, 156, 169, 189, 200, 253.

repeats the (ontologically decisive) will of God to be God-with-us by reiterating the life-act in which God is in fact with us. The Spirit is contemporary instantiation of the Incarnation, or, the parallel life-act of *Inverberation*.[76]

Why coin and then make so much use of the term *inverberation*? In doing so, Smith means to connote three ideas: *incarnation, verba* (words), and the dynamic of *verberation* (resounding). According to Smith, the concept of inverberation best describes the contemporaneous, ongoing manner in which the Holy Spirit, himself incarnate in the reading and preaching of sacred Scripture, functions as a fresh, contemporaneous incarnation of the prophetic and apostolic witness to Christ. Says Smith:

> When I say that in and as the Spirit God is inverberate I mean that he continues to generate a real object for ocular and auditory ingestion by placing himself before us in the reading and proclaiming of Scripture. As these human words throttle space-time, the Spirit mediates correspondence between them and the eternal Word.[77]

Hopefully, the significance of the notion of *inverberation* for the type of prophetic preaching I have advocated for in this paper is apparent. According to Smith:

> The Holy Spirit is *Spirit of the Word*. He is not a free-floating second revelation of God alongside or at variance with Christ, but the ongoing reality of God in historical revelation as that revelation takes place in the idiomatic thoughts and words (verba) of Christ's proclamation today. . . . He is God in active generation and assumption of ongoing, contextualized human words bearing witness to the revelation event of the Word's enfleshing. . . . The Spirit is Spirit, then, in the event of the *church*—the where and when of gospel proclamation—in a manner parallel to the way that the Word is Word in the specific flesh of Jesus of Nazareth (and not

---

76. Ibid., 7.

77. Ibid., 7. Likewise, Thomas Christian Currie implies that an incarnational dynamic is at work in Christian preaching when he asserts that, for Barth, "the Holy Spirit is the bond of union between the divine voice and the human voice in the event of the Word of God" (Thomas Christian Currie, *The Only Sacrament Left to Us: The Threefold Word of God in the Theology and Ecclesiology of Karl Barth* [Eugene, OR: Pickwick Publications, 2015], 31).

flesh or humanity in general). The Word assumed *this* flesh, and the Spirit assumes witness to *this* logically prior assumption.[78]

Though I'm concerned that Smith's language here and there can seem to *conflate* the Spirit with Christian proclamation—as if it is only through the act of preaching that the Spirit is present and active—still, in this notion of *inverberation* I find some tacit support for the possibility of biblically-grounded, Christ-honoring sermons that are incarnational in the sense that the Holy Spirit is not only using human words to convey to the congregation some general sense of divine reality, but (more specifically) some genuine ad hoc mentoring from the risen Jesus (see John 16:12–15). Therefore, to the degree Smith is justified in attributing the inverberation dynamic to Barth, I feel justified in suggesting that Barth's pneumatocentric, as well as Christocentric, theology provides some implicit support for the phenomenon of prophetic preaching.

Barth's "Sacramental" (Encounter-Facilitating) Understanding of Preaching

In his book *Scripture as Real Presence: Sacramental Exegesis in the Early Church*, Hans Boersma acknowledges the significant influence of Barth on what he refers to as "a remarkable and growing interest in theological interpretation of Scripture."[79] As has been noted already, for Boersma, a theological interpretation of Scripture makes possible not only a sacramental reading of God's Word,[80] but a sacramental preaching of it as well.[81] Thus, if only indirectly, Boersma is suggesting that Barth's work was a major cause of the recent upsurge of interest in the notion of sacramental preaching.

Some substantiation for the credit Boersma attributes to Barth for this theological/ministry development may be evidenced in the way Aaron Smith, who has already emphasized Barth's incarnational understanding of Christian proclamation, presses on to note a sacramental conception as well. According to Smith:

> Barth construes God's revelation in the terms of Reformation sacramentology: God is present *consubstantially*. . . . That is, we

78. Smith, *A Theology of the Third Article*, 8, emphasis original.

79. Boersma, *Scripture as Real Presence*, xi.

80. Ibid., 2.

81. Boersma, *Sacramental Preaching*, xvii–xxiii.

encounter God in the dialectic of coming to humanity without sacrificing his being to the media of human thought and speech. He remains Lord over those media by being their source and conception just as the Word was the source and conception of Jesus' flesh, and the enfleshed Word was the source and conception of the prophetic and apostolic words. The Word, God's all-determinative exegesis occurs today precisely as it did in 1–30 CE: *indirectly* identical with the medium of revelation.[82]

To provide support for his commentary, Smith proceeds to quote Barth directly. Early in his career, Barth had opined that "The best preaching is as such an equivalent to the kerygma that the Roman Catholic church offers every day in the form of the sacrament of the altar."[83] Smith then clarifies Barth's meaning thusly: "Whereas for Rome, the presence of God is mediated in the Eucharist, *that presence is encountered in Reformation theology in the event of the sermon*."[84]

A book-length treatment of this topic is provided by Thomas Christian Currie in *The Only Sacrament Left to Us: The Threefold Word of God in the Theology and Ecclesiology of Karl Barth*. The manner in which Currie introduces Barth's understanding of the sacramental nature of Christian proclamation emphasizes the crucial role the Holy Spirit plays in it. He writes:

> Barth describes this proclamation event in terms of mediation, in terms of divine sign-giving, in terms of secondary objectivity, and in sacramental language. Any reference to sacrament does not begin with the Lord's supper or baptism, Barth maintains, but begins with *Jesus Christ and his ongoing presence in the life of the Christian community through the work of the Spirit*. This broader view of sacramental presence, not only includes Scripture and preaching, but renders baptism and the Lord's Supper dependent on the gospel, on the proclaimed and heard Word of God. This sacramental understanding of Scripture and preaching in the church's life is why Barth maintains that *preaching grounded on the witness of Scripture*, "is the only sacrament left to us."[85]

82. Smith, *A Theology of the Third Article*, 85, emphasis added.

83. Karl Barth, *Gottingen Dogmatics: Instruction in the Christian Religion, ed. Hannelotte Reifen*, trans. Geoffrey W. Bromiley (Grand Rapids: Eerdmans, 1990), 31, as cited in Smith, *A Theology of the Third Article*, 85.

84. Smith, *A Theology of the Third Article*, 85, emphasis added. See also Richardson, *Reading Karl Barth*, 114–15.

85. Currie, *The Only Sacrament Left to Us*, 20. Quotation is from Karl Barth, "The

To be sure, we must take into account the manner in which Barth's understanding of this topic evolved over time. To their credit, both Smith and Currie take this into account.[86] Thus, my contention is that between the commentaries provided us by both Smith and Currie we find some not-so-implicit support for my thesis that Barth's theological project has room in it for the possibility of prophetic, sacramental sermons that are encounter-facilitating in their effect.

Barth's "Transformational" Understanding of the Sacramental Sermon's Impact

The fact that not all sermons end up functioning in a sacramental manner prompts some questions: What is the sign of prophetic preaching? How will we as preachers know that it has occurred, or is occurring? My response to this important query is to offer that, in addition to the startling degree of serendipity that earmarks the collection of resources for some sermons, and the somewhat surreal experience we preachers sometimes have of the Holy Spirit seeming to "speak through us" during the preaching event (articulating sermonic content we hadn't intended to deliver), the dead giveaway that something prophetic is occurring in the preaching moment is that the Spirit goes on to impress this especially profound sermonic content upon the hearts of at least some of those listening in an especially powerful manner.[87] In other words, *genuine transformation occurs.*

Barth was famous for his assertion that the ultimate test of true proclamation—a true representation of God's speaking—is its effect. Proclamation is true, said Barth, when it is "talk which has to be listened to and which rightly demands obedience."[88] Barth's assumption seems to have been that, when God speaks, you know it (cf. Jer 23:29; Isa 55:10–11).[89] Put differently, Barth seems to have had in mind the possibility of encounter-facilitating preaching that leaves a mark.

Need and Promise of Christian Preaching," in *The Word of God and the Word of Man,* (New York: Harper & Row, 1957), 114, emphasis added.

86. For example, see the chapter titled "What Happens to the Threefold Word of God: Revision or Rejection" in ibid., 89–137.

87. For more on my take on "prophetic preaching," see Tyra, *The Holy Spirit in Mission,* 156–57.

88. Barth, *Church Dogmatics,* I/1, 93.

89. Ibid., 92–93.

This notion of an existentially-impactful, paradigm-shifting, faith-fulness-producing encounter with a holy God is implicit in the manner in which Aaron Smith presents Barth's high view of the Sunday sermon. Citing Barth in the process, Smith writes:

> The sermon is instructive for Barth because of its existential poignancy. "On Sunday morning when the bells ring to call the congregation and minister to church, there is in the air an *expectancy* that something great, crucial, and even momentous is to *happen*." It is not, of course, that everyone feels or is equally conscious of this anticipation, but that does not alter the fact that "*expectancy* is inherent in the whole situation."
>
> The sermon is wreathed in readiness. For what? Not merely for edification, entertainment, or instruction, Barth says, but to hear and confess that "God *is* present. The whole situation witnesses, cries, simply shouts of it, even when in minister or people there arises questioning, wretchedness, or despair." It is to hear and interrogate the biblical claim that God is in fact present even in the midst of doubting and wretched humanity that people come to church and the minister climbs the pulpit.[90]

Barth seems to be suggesting that, given the human longing for transcendence, it's a sermon-enabled experience of the divine presence that's to take place each Sunday—an existentially poignant audience with God that cannot help but be existentially impactful as well. Indeed, when I think of the ecclesial encounter Barth alludes to in this passage, I cannot help but think of the antecedent archetype depicted in Isaiah 6:1–8. And, if Isaiah's experience in the temple is any indication, the only appropriate response to the manifest presence of God in the worship space is a sincere turning away from sin toward an eager engagement in the *missio Dei*. Some support for this association and the importance Barth placed on the prophetic, theologically real, incarnational, sacramental, and transformational nature of Christian preaching, is provided by Thomas Currie when he writes:

> It is in the church's attempt to proclaim and hear the gospel, that the risen Christ comes and comes again, speaking the Word of God through broken human words, *freeing* the Christian community to *get up and follow in discipleship*, and *sending* the Christian

90. Smith, *A Theology of the Third Article*, 39. The quotations are from Barth, "The Need and Promise of Christian Preaching," 104, emphasis original.

community to *engage the world* in correspondence to the life and activity of Jesus Christ at work in their midst.[91]

For sure, the Holy Spirit is at work in prophetic preaching to awaken and strengthen faith in the risen Jesus. But he is also doing more. He is graciously drawing those who have ears to hear deeper and deeper into the reality of an intimate, interactive, existentially-impactful relationship with the living God. Indeed, it has been my experience that, at times, he may even provide—for some specific disciples, or the community as a whole—some spiritual, moral, or ministry guidance that is amazingly timely and specific!

I have endeavored in this section of my paper to identify and briefly expound upon several Barthian constructs which, taken together, might suggest that it is indeed possible to find in his theologizing some implicit support for the phenomenon of prophetic preaching. What would happen, I wonder, if more evangelical preachers, taking both *sola Scriptura* and the need for a pneumatological realism seriously, were to approach the preaching moment with this type of expectation in mind? Moreover, what would such an approach entail? In the final section of the paper, I will do my best to address the latter of these two questions.

What a Pneumatologically Real Approach to the Preaching Task Entails

Because Karl Barth placed so much importance on the preaching endeavor, he had much to say about how preachers should engage in it. In addition, I will humbly suggest that some of us who have been inspired by Barth's high view of preaching as *encounter*, and enabled by the Holy Spirit to recognize when and how the phenomenon of prophetic preaching has occurred within our own pulpit ministries, might also have some wisdom to share with respect to the preparation and presentation of sermons that prove to be sacramental in their effect.

Because of what has been previously discussed, we are already aware of the need to, like Barth, possess a high view of the preaching endeavor. In addition, I will simply suggest three other earmarks of a pneumatologically real approach to the preaching task.

---

91. Currie, *The Only Sacrament Left to Us,* xiii, emphasis added.

The "Proper Attitude" of Preachers: Holy Expectation

As we've seen, Barth was convinced that it's only normal for a profound sense of expectancy to animate the congregation each Sunday morning. In the foreword he provided for Barth's published lectures on homiletics, David Buttrick indicates Barth's contention that if this corporate sense of expectancy is to occur, it needs to begin with the preacher. Buttrick explains:

> Those who preach the scriptures will not be pontificating clerics or detached visionaries or merely dull. For, again and again, the scriptures will speak God's *new* word. "The proper attitude of preachers," Barth says, "does not depend on whether they hold on to the doctrine of inspiration but on whether or not they expect God to speak to them...." Barth calls ministers to "active expectation" and "ongoing submission" in their study of the Bible.[92]

Barth was adamant, it seems, that, given the prophetic potential inherent in the preaching moment, it is imperative that preachers approach it with a sense of holy expectation and reverent submission. In other words, a pneumatologically real approach to the preaching task will be neither perfunctory nor presumptive. Instead, it will be earmarked by a tremendous degree of anticipation and sense of responsibility born of the realization that, when empowered by the Spirit, something prophetic might occur.[93]

It's hard to overstate how important this first earmark is. In fact, there's a sense in which the other two entailments of a pneumatologically real approach to preaching are related to it. One is the *root* of the preacher's elevated sense of expectancy; the other is its *fruit*—a set of behaviors that flow from it.

---

92. David G. Buttrick, "Foreword" in Karl Barth, *Homiletics*, 9.

93. Indeed, speaking specifically of the prophetic aspect of preaching, Barth offers preachers an important clarification, some encouragement, and then a warning when he states: "Our preaching today differs from that of the prophets and apostles who saw and touched Christ. To be sure, it does not differ qualitatively, but it differs inasmuch as it is done in a different place. If, however, God speaks through our word, then the prophets and apostles are actually there even though it be a simple pastor that speaks. Yet we should not be self-conscious about this, nor listen for our own prophetic booming, for even though Christ be present, it is by God's own action. Preachers are under a constraint, and *anankē* (1 Cor. 9:16) that strips them of all their own proposals and programs" (Karl Barth, *Homiletics*, 48–49).

The Root of Holy Expectation: The Preacher's Own
Encounter with the Risen Christ

Because the attitude of *holy expectancy* Barth insists upon seems akin to the posture of *pneumatological expectancy* I associate with a realist understanding of the Holy Spirit, I will suggest that another requirement for prophetic preaching is a personal commitment to the pneumatological realism implicit in Barth's theology. Some tacit support for this deduction might be discerned in the way Barth insisted that those who would function as prophetic witnesses for Christ need to have had their own revelatory, existentially-impactful encounter with him. Elaborating on the manner in which Barth considered John the Baptist the paradigm for prophetic witness to Christ, Aaron Smith writes:

> Prophetic testimony derives from its object, not from the subject of the prophet; witness to God in Christ derives from the reality of Christ and not from the compromised reality of the human speaker. Witnesses are only witnesses, only persons whose thought and speech actually, truly reflect the divine reality, *insofar as they have been encountered by that reality*, found by it such that they may, in turn, find their entire reason for being in it.[94]
>
> The Baptist and all witnesses are subordinate to the content of their collective witness because they, like all things, exist only through the Word to which they testify. . . . One can only be a prophet by *first being encountered* by the Word made flesh, by finding oneself in subordination to this event even as a participant in it.[95]

Because of the way Smith, following Barth, refers to the Spirit as the "contemporaneity of Christ"—the means by which all disciples in any era encounter Christ[96]—I find in these words a very important principle: before we can hope to preach sermons that may be used by the Holy Spirit to facilitate a spiritual encounter with the risen Jesus—we need to have had such a Spirit-enabled encounter ourselves!

Moreover, I will press on to suggest that this encounter needs to go beyond the one that led to our personal discipleship, and even the one that produced within us a sense of call to the preaching ministry. Speaking

94. Smith, *A Theology of the Third Article*, 207, emphasis added. See also Currie, *The Only Sacrament Left to Us*, 30, 37, 71, 100, 136, 144.

95. Smith, *A Theology of the Third Article*, 208, emphasis added.

96. E.g., see ibid., 7, 60, 100, 103, 108, 123, 146, 151–52, 169, 186, 194.

personally now, I have found that an important indication that I might end up functioning in a prophetic manner during this or that preaching event is my own sense of encounter with Christ as I prepared for it. For instance, I'm referring here to the occasional experience of feeling the need to put down a sermon resource, or to lean away from my computer so that I might worship the one I'm hoping to help others encounter. I will have a bit more to say about this experience below, but here I will hasten to offer the bold suggestion that, to function as prophetic (John-the-Baptist-like) witnesses to Christ in our contemporary era, we preachers must do more than merely nod our assent to the notions of a theological and pneumatological realism; we must do more than simply affirm the theoretical possibility of a personal, intimate, interactive, existentially-impactful relationship with Christ through his Spirit; we must be living into this reality ourselves, and doing so on an everyday basis! This is how that all-important attitude of holy expectation becomes in the preacher an ongoing, rather than occasional, attribute!

The Fruit of Holy Expectation: Pneumatologically Real Prayer

Thus far, I have identified as earmarks of a pneumatologically real approach to the preaching task: (1) the "proper attitude" required, and (2) the personal experience that feeds it. What we have yet to discuss are any *specific behaviors* that are likewise essential—practices that, when engaged in, increase the possibility that the Spirit of Christ might choose to speak prophetically through us during the preaching event.

Actually, there is only one practice I will focus on here—a single spiritual/ministry discipline that takes several forms as the preacher prepares and presents his or her sermon. The critical importance of this third earmark is indicated by the pronounced emphasis Barth placed on "the free and dynamic movement of God that can never be bound to or imprisoned by the proclaimed Word," and his insistence that "it is never in humanity's power 'that our human word should be God's Word.'"[97] This emphasis on the freedom of God would suggest that, while a sacramental effect is possible in Christian preaching, it should never be considered inevitable. Instead, it is the product of some serious *prayer*,[98] for, according to Barth, "it is prayer

97. Currie, *The Only Sacrament Left to Us,* 24. Quotation is from Barth, *Homiletics,* 90.

98. Currie, *The Only Sacrament Left to Us,* 24–25, 40, 43–44, 120. Worthy of note is

that puts us in rapport with God and permits us to collaborate with him."[99] Thus, while not suggesting that Barth would endorse everything I have to say on the subject, I will offer that at the heart of a pneumatologically real approach to the preaching task is a certain kind of praying.

To be more specific, it has been my experience that the likelihood that I will experience something prophetic occurring while I am preaching (or lecturing for that matter) correlates with some serious time spent engaging in prayer that is: (1) theologically real; (2) missionally discerning; (3) in the Spirit; (4) in the moment; and (5) deferentially and enduringly hopeful. Presented below is a very brief description of these five forms of *pneumatologically real prayer* and the role I contend each plays in the phenomenon of prophetic preaching.

Praying in a Theologically Real Manner

As I have already indicated, a realist understanding of God maintains that he is much more than a philosophical concept or impersonal spiritual force. The God revealed to us in Jesus Christ is a personal, relational, and responsive "heavenly Father" with whom, because of grace, it is possible for humans to interact in ways that are personal, relational, and responsive. At the risk of greatly oversimplifying things, I contend that this basic understanding of the reality, relationality, and responsiveness of God suggests at least three prayer principles. First, there is a huge difference between *praying to God* and *praying toward the idea of God*. Second, the goal of prayer should *not* be to simply get something from God, but to discern and align ourselves with his benevolent purposes. Third, we can and should develop the habit of prayerfully waiting upon God, actually anticipating a response (e.g., Acts 13:1–3). Putting these three principles together, I want to suggest that one of the most fundamental and always-appropriate theologically real prayers any Christian can utter is this: *Father, what are you up to in this situation, and how can I cooperate with you in it?* I trust the implication of this suggestion for our current discussion is apparent. It's my contention that praying in this relational, responsive, theologically real manner puts us in a position to, in one way or another, "hear" God's voice. As I have

---

Currie's suggestion that the importance Barth placed on prayer in the life of the church increased over the course of his academic career. For example, see ibid., 107, 112, 135.

99. Karl Barth, *Prayer* (Louisville: Westminster John Knox Press, 2002), 20, as cited in Currie, *The Only Sacrament Left to Us*, 113.

already indicated, hearing God's voice is a dynamic that lies at the heart of the prophetic phenomenon.

Praying in a Missionally Discerning Manner

Building on the foundation of theologically real prayer just presented, I will press on to offer that because the Holy Spirit is *"the missionary Spirit sent by the missionary Father and the missionary Son, breathing life and power into God's missionary Church,"*[100] another prayer that should often be on the lips of devoted disciples of Jesus is this: *Spirit of mission, what are you up to in this ministry context, and how can I cooperate with you in it?*

As I have indicated elsewhere, at the heart of the ministry contextualization dynamic is the need for this type of mission-discerning praying that makes no sense unless we genuinely expect that, in one way or another, the Holy Spirit might actually respond.[101] Applying this logic to the topic at hand, is it too much of a stretch to think that a similar form of missionally discerning prayer would also earmark a pneumatologically real approach to Christian preaching? I am dead serious when I suggest that, as we evangelicals approach the preaching task, we can and should pray, seeking discernment regarding:

- what the Holy Spirit is currently up to in the life of this congregation;

- the biblical text the Holy Spirit seems to be encouraging us to have the congregation focus on at this particular time;

- what the Holy Spirit *was* up to in this biblical text (i.e., assuming some inspirational immediacy, what message was the Spirit inspiring the original author to communicate to his original ministry context?);[102]

100. Lausanne Movement, "Cape Town Commitment," Part 1, §5, http://www.lausanne.org/ctcommitment, emphasis original.

101. See Tyra, *A Missional Orthodoxy,* 220. For a more elaborate discussion of the role the Holy Spirit plays in the ministry contextualization endeavor, see Tyra, *The Holy Spirit in Mission,* 133–44.

102. See the discussion of how Pentecostals approach authorial intention in Keener, *Spirit Hermeneutics,* 138–39. For his part, while Boersma can seem to provide some justification for grounding authorial intent in the Holy Spirit (see Boersma, *Scripture as Real Presence,* 16), I will suggest here that his stance on the importance of authorial intention to the sacramental sermon needs to be nuanced. Though he asserts that "the proponents of genuine spiritual interpretation will take the literal sense seriously, since it is the starting point (*sacramentum*) of a search for the greater, more christological reality (*res*)

- what the Spirit *is* up to in this text (i.e., what message, keeping the original meaning ever in view, might the Spirit be encouraging us to communicate to our ministry context?);[103]

---

of the gospel" (see Boersma, *Heavenly Participation,* 152), he also states rather bluntly and with evident approval that "the [early church] fathers would consider the modern preoccupation with history and authorial intent as insufficiently attuned to the divine purpose of the text" (see Boersma, *Scripture as Real Presence,* 252). Moreover, Boersma is forthcoming with respect to: (1) his Gadamer-influenced skepticism regarding the interpreter's ability to discern the biblical author's intention, and, therefore, (2) his conviction regarding the need to take seriously how the *wirkungsgeschichte* (history of the influence of the text) can and should influence our biblical exegesis (see ibid., 231–36). For what it's worth, I tend to struggle some with the way Boersma's approach to sacramental exegesis seems to, despite some assertions to the contrary, overly relativize the importance of authorial intention. Moreover, missing from this incredibly important discussion is any explicit reference to the role the Holy Spirit plays in the contemporary interpretive exercise. Instead, the major, if not sole, focus seems to be on the impact of the Great Tradition/liturgy on one's hermeneutical horizon. That said, I will quickly add that there's reason to believe that, for Boersma, the Spirit's illuminating activity is simply assumed. I have in mind here the way he references with overall approval the manner in which Yves Congar, presuming a commensurate influence of the Spirit in both, essentially conflates Scripture and the interpretive tradition (Boersma, *Heavenly Participation,* 63, 130–36).

103. See the discussions of divine illumination and the application of biblical texts in Keener, *Spirit Hermeneutics,* 12–13 and 31, 77–78, 149–51, 237–38, 249–50; 257–58 respectively. Note also how that Hans Boersma provides a helpful discussion of the reason why the church fathers were open to finding multiple meanings in biblical texts. According to Boersma: "what we have here is really a form of contemplation—*theoria*—in which the plain sense of the text becomes the basis on which to reflect on God's providential dealings with believers in Christ" (Boersma, *Scripture as Real Presence,* 255). Boersma goes on to explain how important one's growth in virtue was to the fathers, and then, using Gregory Nyssen as his example, asserts that "Gregory will let pretty much any interpretation stand, as long as it leads to virtue" (ibid., 257). Moreover, having indicated the distinction Stephen Fowl makes between "virtue-through-interpretation" and "virtue-in-interpretation," Boersma states: "I am interested here especially in virtue-through-interpretation, interpretation *leading* to virtue" (ibid., 263). He then explains: "Virtue, for the fathers, is the *aim* of interpretation. Any interpretation that does not lead to growth in virtuous habits is, according to patristic exegesis, not interpretation that is worthy of God. If the Christian life is a journey into ever-deeper communion with God, then the Scripture is the guide on this journey" (ibid., 263). Then, citing Fowl in the process, Boersma continues, "'Scripture plays a dual role. It articulates the shape and nature of the virtues. Further, as Christians interpret and embody their interpretations of Scripture, Scripture becomes a vehicle to help in the formation of virtues, so that Christians are moved ever closer to their true end.' Scripture, for the fathers, is an aid—a means of grace (or a sacrament)—that assists in the development of virtue. If Scripture really has this function, it becomes imperative to approach the text with the question in mind of *how* it might assist in the development of virtue" (ibid., 263–64. The quotation is from Stephen Fowl, "Virtue," in *Dictionary of Theological Interpretation of the Bible,* ed. Kevin

- the best way (homiletically speaking) to communicate this message to our ministry context (i.e., we can and should pray for wisdom and supernatural assistance in putting the sermon together, keeping the contextualization endeavor and prophetic aims referred to in 1 Corinthians 14:3 in mind);[104] and

- how we might encourage congregation members to enter into their own pneumatologically real dialogue with the Spirit regarding the existential significance of this text/message for their lives.[105]

For what it's worth, I'm convinced that, were evangelical preachers to develop the habit of praying each week in a missionally discerning manner (actually expecting a response), this would, by itself, add a prophetic element to their Sunday endeavors. And yet, I would be remiss if I did not go on to address three additional forms of pneumatologically real prayer that I believe will only enhance the prophetic experience.

Vanhoozer, 837–39 [Grand Rapids, MI: Baker Academic, 2005], 838). In sum, according to Boersma, it is because sacramental preaching aims at the cultivation of virtue (cf. 2 Tim 3:16) that it is legitimate for preachers to consider the possibility that a biblical text is capable of a spiritual as well as a historical meaning. My contention is that prophetic preaching occurs when preachers are careful before and during the preaching event to pray in a theologically real manner about how the Spirit of Christ would have them, on the basis of the sermon's text(s), encourage and exhort the congregation toward a greater spiritual, moral, and missional faithfulness.

104. For more on what a missionally orthodox approach to gospel contextualization involves, see Tyra, *A Missional Orthodoxy*, 64–86. Some additional, quite specific, homiletical suggestions toward effective sacramental sermons are proffered by Boersma in his work *Sacramental Preaching: Sermons on the Hidden Presence of Christ*. However, I must confide that I am somewhat amazed by the scarcity of references to the work of the Spirit in Boersma's treatment of this homiletical endeavor. Though this volume of sermons refers to the Spirit dozens of times, the principal reason for this seems to be that the biblical passages treated in the sermons do so. It's my sense that Boersma simply presumes the working of the Holy Spirit in the sermon-building task since, according to him, the goal of the sacramental sermon is ever and always to point the hearer to Christ as the ultimate telos of all biblical texts, and because he seems to concur with Gregory Nyssen's doctrine that "the external activities of the Trinity are indivisible" (Boersma, *Heavenly Participation*, 49). In other words, I wonder if Boersma does not simply presume the Spirit's agency/activity any time he refers to the presence or influence of Christ.

105. For more on the communal, dialogical, confessional manner in which congregation members can be enabled to become doers of the word rather than hearers only (Jas 1:22–25), see Tyra, *Defeating Pharisaism*, 220–32.

Appendix

Praying in the Spirit

One of the most significant theological statements presented in Scripture is found in Romans 8:28, which reads: "And we know that in all things God works for the good of those who love him, who have been called according to his purpose" (Rom 8:28). We must keep in mind that this stunning word of assurance is preceded by an equally stunning pneumatological promise:

> In the same way, the Spirit helps us in our weakness. We do not know what we ought to pray for, but the Spirit himself intercedes for us through wordless groans. And he who searches our hearts knows the mind of the Spirit, because the Spirit intercedes for God's people in accordance with the will of God. (Rom 8:26–27)

Scholars are divided on whether Paul had in mind a literal groaning before God, or the dynamic of glossolalic prayer (i.e., the praying in tongues referred to in 1 Corinthians 14:13–15).[106] Regardless, I will humbly offer here a studied observation: my experience over four decades of preaching and teaching has been that there is a discernible correlation between my spending some time intentionally praying in the Spirit prior to a preaching/teaching event, and the likelihood that something prophetic will occur during it. Because I know this personal observation may prove provocative to some, I do not want to belabor it. Still, it is hard for me to overstate how important this connection has proved to be in my preaching and teaching ministries. Thus, whether our praying in the Spirit before we preach is glossolalic in form or literally involves our crying out to him with wordless groans, I very much want to encourage those who wish to experience the prophetic phenomenon in their preaching to at least experiment with this prayer discipline on their own.

---

106. Eminent evangelical scholars F. F. Bruce and C. K. Barrett both acknowledge the *possibility* that Paul may have had *glossolalia* in mind in Romans 8:26 (see F. F. Bruce, *Romans* [Downers Grove, IL: InterVarsity, 1985], 165; and C. K. Barrett, *The Epistle to the Romans* [New York: Harper & Row, 1957], 168). For his part, Gordon Fee is a bit more confident that this is the case (see Gordon Fee, *God's Empowering Presence: The Holy Spirit in the Letters of Paul* [Peabody, MA: Hendrickson, 1994], 580). Moreover, according to Fee, Ernst Käsemann also sees a reference to prayer in tongues at work in this passage (see Ernst Käsemann, *Perspectives on Paul*, trans. Margaret Kohl [London: SCM, 1971], 135). Regardless of whether Paul had *glossolalia* in mind or not, it appears that he meant to suggest that the Spirit can and will pray *through* the believer, offering effective intercession on his or her behalf. It's my contention that only a realist understanding of the Spirit makes sense of this provocative passage.

APPENDIX

Praying in the Moment

Not only do I consider it very important to pray for the Spirit's wisdom and anointing before the preaching/teaching event, I will sometimes do so during the event—inwardly, silently, beseeching, inviting, counting on the empowering presence of Christ. I would like to think that such praying has resulted in something prophetic occurring: the Spirit prompting speech that caused the sermon (or lecture) to impact hearers in a way that was especially compelling. I am convinced this really can happen. The Holy Spirit really does at times enable prophetic speech (see Matt 10:19–20; Lk 12:11–12; cf. Matt 7:28–29; Jn 7:45–46; Acts 4:31; 6:8–10).

Praying Deferentially and Enduringly in Hope

Interestingly, Donald Bloesch's take is that, though Barth affirmed that the "Spirit is presumably at work as the pastor preaches," it is "not so much in and through the words of the sermon as with, over, and against these words."[107] If this read of Barth is correct, it could mean that he did not consider the actual words of the preacher to be all that important. While this observation *might* serve to suggest that Barth would not have felt the need for the "in the moment" praying I just advocated for, it also reminds us that the convicting/convincing work of the Holy Spirit (John 16:7–8) is not ultimately dependent on the preacher's performance. Thus, thesis-countering or not, I will assert that this reminder is sorely needed.

It's for this reason that I continually encourage my ministry-bound students to do their best in their witness to Christ, and then to be careful to pray deferentially and enduringly in hope. To pray deferentially is to entrust to the Holy Spirit the person or persons being ministered to rather than assuming responsibility for the ministry outcome ourselves. To pray enduringly in hope is, obviously, to engage in this entrusting dynamic in an enduringly hopeful manner rather than allow some initial resistance to cause us to conclude that God's working through us has necessarily failed. Immediately after reminding his disciples that not everyone would be "ready" for their ministry into their lives (Matt 7:6), Jesus spoke of the importance of persisting in prayer (Matt 7:8–11), and engaging in ongoing

---

107. Donald Bloesch, *Jesus is Victor! Karl Barth's Doctrine of Salvation* (Eugene, OR: Wipf and Stock, 2001), 130, as cited in Currie, *The Only Sacrament Left to Us*, 130.

prophetic *action* (Matt 7:12).[108] Simply put, what I'm suggesting is that, because a pneumatologically real approach to the preaching task takes very seriously the role of the Holy Spirit in the ministry endeavor, it is earmarked by some serious theologically real prayer before, during, and even after the preaching moment.

Conclusion

I have argued in this paper *against* the idea that the Reformation theme *sola Scriptura* must necessarily produce in evangelical churches a pneumatological deficit. I have contended instead that in Karl Barth's theologizing we might find some ironic, though implicit, support for the phenomenon of prophetic preaching. As well, I've suggested that the key to sermons that are sacramental (encounter-facilitating) in their effect is a pneumatologically real approach to the preaching task that is earmarked by a "proper attitude" (holy expectation) which is born of a personal encounter/commitment and engenders a certain kind of pneumatologically real praying before, during, and after the preaching moment. What I have yet to do is indicate why I believe we evangelicals simply must take this notion of prophetic preaching seriously.

As we've seen, a growing number of evangelical scholars are acknowledging the pneumatological deficit at work in some post-Reformation Protestant theologies. Just to be clear, behind Timothy Tennent's boldly stated concern is his desire for contemporary evangelical churches to "understand better the role of the Holy Spirit in the *missio dei*.[109]

Because I share this concern, I'll conclude this paper with a very important reminder. We've already noted how Isaiah's encounter with God in the temple led to his engagement in *mission* (Isa 1:8). Moreover, the Apostle Paul, having already clarified that the purpose of genuine prophetic utterance in the worship gathering is to speak to congregation members "for their strengthening, encouragement and comfort" (1 Cor 14:3), goes on in that same discussion to refer to the dramatic, *missional* impact a prophetic—and therefore encounter-rich—ecclesial environment can have even upon those who are not yet disciples (1 Cor 14:24–25)! What I am insinuating here is the huge missional import of biblically-grounded,

108. For more on this, see Gary Tyra, *Defeating Pharisaism: Recovering Jesus' Disciple-Making Method* (Downers Grove, IL; IVP Books, 2009), 168–78.

109. Tennent, *Invitation to World Missions*, 94.

Christ-centered, Spirit-empowered sermons that, precisely because they are prophetic in nature, are sacramental (encounter-facilitating) in their effect. My experience of working with thousands of members of the emerging generations has been that while increasing numbers are becoming post-Christian/post-religious in orientation, they still crave the experience of something transcendent. So, just think of it: sacramental sermons that not only empower a missional faithfulness among congregants, but can be used by the Holy Spirit to awaken Christian faith in uninitiated seekers! Surely any evangelical truly committed to *sola Scriptura,* the *missio Dei,* and a fully Trinitarian doctrine of the Holy Spirit will be inclined to at least give such a possibility some serious consideration. It's my sincere hope that this paper will encourage those who have been called to a preaching ministry to do just that.

> If anyone speaks, he should do it as one
> speaking the very words of God.
>
> —1 PET 4:11

> The lion has roared—who will not fear?
> The Sovereign LORD has spoken—who can but prophesy?
>
> —AMOS 3:8

Bibliography

Adler, Jerry. "In Search of the Spiritual." *Newsweek*. http://www.newsweek.com/id/147035.

Anderson, Allan. *An Introduction to Pentecostalism*. New York: Cambridge University Press, 2004.

Bainton, Roland H. *Christianity*. Boston: Houghton Mifflin, 1964.

Barna Group. "Six Reasons Young Christians Leave Church." https://www.barna.com/research/six-reasons-young-christians-leave-church/.

———. "Twentysomethings Struggle to Find Their Place in Christian Churches." https://www.barna.com/research/twentysomethings-struggle-to-find-their-place-in-christian-churches/#.

Barrett, C. K. *The Epistle to the Romans*. Harper's New Testament Commentaries. New York: Harper & Row, 1957.

Barrett, Matthew. *God's Word Alone: The Authority of Scripture*. Grand Rapids, MI: Zondervan, 2016.

Barth, Karl. *Church Dogmatics*. I/1: *The Doctrine of the Word of God*. Translated by G. W. Bromiley. Peabody, MA: Hendrickson, 2010.

———. *Church Dogmatics*. II/1: *The Doctrine of God*. Translated by G. W. Bromiley. Peabody, MA: Hendrickson, 2010.

———. *Dogmatics in Outline*. New York: Harper & Row, 1959.

———. *Evangelical Theology: An Introduction*. Grand Rapids, MI: Eerdmans, 1963.

———. *Gottingen Dogmatics: Instruction in the Christian Religion*. Edited by Hannelotte Reifen, translated by Geoffrey W. Bromiley. Grand Rapids, MI: Eerdmans, 1990.

———. *Homiletics*. Louisville, KY: Westminster John Knox, 1991.

———. "The Need and Promise of Christian Preaching." In *The Word of God and the Word of Man*. New York: Harper & Row, 1957.

———. *The Word of God and the Word of Man*. New York: Harper & Row, 1957.

Barth, Karl, and Heinrich Barth. *Zur Lehre vom Heilegen Geist*. Munich: Chr. Kaiser Verlag, 1930.

Bavinck, J. H. *An Introduction to the Science of Missions*. Translated by David Hugh Freeman. Phillipsburg, NJ: P&R, 1992.

Bhaskar, Roy. *A Realist Theory of Science*. New York: Routledge, 2008.

Biggar, Nigel. "Barth's Trinitarian Ethic." In *The Cambridge Companion to Karl Barth*, edited by John Webster, 212-27. Cambridge: Cambridge University Press, 2000.

Bilezikian, Gilbert. *Christianity 101: Your Guide to Eight Basic Christian Beliefs*. Grand Rapids, MI: Zondervan, 1993.

Bird, Michael F. *Evangelical Theology: A Biblical and Systematic Introduction*. Grand Rapids, MI: Zondervan, 2013.

Block, Matthew. "Evangelicals, Heresy, and Scripture Alone." https://www.firstthings. com/blogs/firstthoughts/2016/10/evangelicals-heresy-and-scripture-alone.

Bloesch, Donald. *Freedom for Obedience: Evangelical Ethics for Contemporary Times*. San Francisco: Harper & Row, 1987.

Bolich, Gregory G. *Karl Barth & Evangelicalism*. Downers Grove, IL: InterVarsity, 1980.

Boersma, Hans. *Heavenly Participation: The Weaving of a Sacramental Tapestry*. Grand Rapids, MI: Eerdmans, 2011.

———. *Sacramental Preaching: Sermons on the Hidden Presence of Christ*. Grand Rapids, MI: Baker Academic, 2016.

———. *Scripture as Real Presence: Sacramental Exegesis in the Early Church*. Grand Rapids, MI: Baker Academic, 2017.

Braaten, Carl E., and Robert W. Jenson, eds. *Christian Dogmatics*. Vol. 1. Minneapolis: Fortress, 1984.

Bromiley, Geoffrey W. *Introduction to the Theology of Karl Barth*. Grand Rapids, MI: Eerdmans, 1979.

Bruce, F. F. *The Epistle to the Galatians*. New International Greek Testament Commentary. Grand Rapids, MI: Eerdmans, 1982.

———. *The Gospel of John: Introduction, Exposition, Notes*. Grand Rapids, MI: Eerdmans, 1994.

———. *Romans*. Tyndale New Testament Commentaries. Downers Grove, IL: InterVarsity, 1985.

Brueggemann, Walter. *The Practice of Prophetic Imagination: Preaching an Emancipating Word*. Minneapolis: Fortress, 2012.

———. *The Prophetic Imagination*. 2nd ed. Minneapolis: Fortress, 2001.

Bruner, Dale Frederick. *The Gospel of John: A Commentary*. Grand Rapids, MI: Eerdmans, 2012.

Burge, Gary M. *John*. NIV Application Commentary. Grand Rapids, MI: Zondervan, 2000.

Busch, Eberhard. *The Great Passion: An Introduction to Karl Barth's Theology*. Grand Rapids, MI: Eerdmans, 2004.

———. *Karl Barth: His Life from Letters and Autobiographical Texts*. Translated by John Bowden. Philadelphia: Fortress Press, 1976.

Cairns, Earle E. *Christianity Through the Centuries: A History of the Christian Church*. 3rd ed. Grand Rapids, MI: Zondervan, 1996.

Chan, Simon. *Grassroots Asian Theology: Thinking the Faith from the Ground Up*. Downers Grove, IL: IVP Academic, 2014.

Chantry, Walter J. *Signs of the Apostles*. Edinburgh, Scotland: Banner of Truth Trust, 1973.

Chia, Roland. *Revelation and Theology: The Knowledge of God in Balthasar and Barth*. New York: Peter Lang, 1999.

Codling, Don. *Sola Scriptura and the Revelatory Gifts: How Should Christians Deal with Present Day Prophecy?* Rice, WA: Sentinel, 2005.

Coe, John. "Resisting the Temptation of *Moral* Formation: Opening to *Spiritual* Formation in the Cross and the Spirit." *Journal of Spiritual Formation & Soul Care* 1 (2008) 54–78.

Colyer, Elmer. *How to Read T. F. Torrance: Understanding His Trinitarian and Scientific Theology*. Downers Grove, IL: InterVarsity, 2001.

Cooper, John W. *Panentheism: The Other God of the Philosophers—from Plato to the Present*. Grand Rapids, MI: Baker Academic, 2006.

Currie, Thomas Christian. *The Only Sacrament Left to Us: The Threefold Word of God in the Theology and Ecclesiology of Karl Barth*. Eugene, OR: Pickwick, 2015.

Davis, John Jefferson. *Worship and the Reality of God*. Downers Grove, IL: IVP Academic, 2010.

Dean, Kenda Creasy. *Almost Christian: What the Faith of Our Teenagers Is Telling the American Church*. New York: Oxford University Press, 2010.

Douglass, Jane Dempsey. "The Lively Work of the Spirit in the Reformation." *Word & World* 23:2 (Spring 2003) 121–33. https://wordandworld.luthersem.edu/content/pdfs/23-2_Holy_Spirit/23-2_Douglass.pdf.

Dunn, James D. G. *Baptism in the Holy Spirit: A Re-examination of the New Testament Teaching on the Gift of the Spirit in Relation to Pentecostalism Today*. Philadelphia: Westminster John Knox, 1977.

Dunn, Richard R., and Jana L. Sundene. *Shaping the Journey of Emerging Adults: Life-Giving Rhythms for Spiritual Transformation*. Downers Grove, IL: IVP, 2012.

Dyck, Drew. "The Leavers: Young Doubters Exit the Church." *Christianity Today*. http://www.christianitytoday.com/ct/2010/november/27.40.html.

Fee, Gordon. *God's Empowering Presence: The Holy Spirit in the Letters of Paul*. Peabody, MA: Hendrickson, 1994.

Foulkes, Francis. *Ephesians*. 2nd ed. Tyndale New Testament Commentaries. Downers Grove, IL: InterVarsity, 1983.

Fowl, Stephen. "Virtue." In *Dictionary of Theological Interpretation of the Bible*, edited by Kevin Vanhoozer, 837–39. Grand Rapids, MI: Baker Academic, 2005.

France, R. T. *The Gospel of Matthew*. New International Commentary on the New Testament. Grand Rapids, MI: Eerdmans, 2007.

Franke, John R. *Barth for Armchair Theologians*. Louisville: Westminster John Knox, 2006.

Frye, John. W. *Jesus the Pastor*. Grand Rapids, MI: Zondervan, 2002.

———. "Preaching as Encounter." http://www.patheos.com/blogs/jesuscreed/2013/05/17/from-the-shepherds-nook-preaching-as-encounter/.

Fung, Ronald Y. K. *The Epistle to the Galatians*. New International Commentary on the New Testament. Grand Rapids, MI: Eerdmans, 1988.

Godfrey, W. Robert. "What Do We Mean by *Sola Scriptura?*" In *Sola Scriptura: The Protestant Position on the Bible*, 1–16. Sanford, FL: Reformation Trust, 2009.

González, Justo L. *A History of Christian Thought*. Vol. 3. Nashville: Abingdon, 1975.

Graves, Michael. *The Inspiration and Interpretation of Scripture: What the Early Church Can Teach Us*. Grand Rapids: Eerdmans, 2014.

Grenz, Stanley. "Wolfhart Pannenberg's Quest for Ultimate Truth." *Religion Online*. http://www.religion-online.org/article/wolfhart-pannenbergs-quest-for-ultimate-truth/.

Grigg, Ty. "The Spirit of #TrulyHuman: Jesus Was No Jesus without Help." *Missio Alliance*, http://www.missioalliance.org/the-spirit-of-trulyhuman-jesus-was-no-jesus-without-help/?utm_content=buffer31fbe&utm_medium=social&utm_source=plus.google.com&utm_campaign=buffer.

Grossman, Cathy Lynn. "Young Adults Aren't Sticking with Church." *USA Today*. http://usatoday30.usatoday.com/news/religion/2007-08-06-Church-dropouts_N.htm.

Guder, Darrell, ed. *Missional Church: A Vision for the Sending of the Church in North America*. Grand Rapids, MI: Eerdmans, 1998.

Gunton, Colin. "Salvation." In *The Cambridge Companion to Karl Barth*, edited by John Webster, 143–58. Cambridge: Cambridge University Press, 2000.

Hart, Trevor. "Revelation." In *The Cambridge Companion to Karl Barth*, edited by John Webster, 37–56. Cambridge: Cambridge University Press, 2000.

Holmes, Arthur. *Ethics: Approaching Moral Decisions*. Downers Grove, IL: InterVarsity, 1984.

Hunsinger, George. *How to Read Karl Barth: The Shape of His Theology*. New York: Oxford University Press, 1991.

———. "Karl Barth's Christology." In *The Cambridge Companion to Karl Barth*, edited by John Webster, 127–42. Cambridge: Cambridge University Press, 2000.

———. "The Mediator of Communion: Karl Barth's Doctrine of the Holy Spirit." In *The Cambridge Companion to Karl Barth*, edited by John Webster, 177–94. Cambridge: Cambridge University Press, 2000.

Jenson, Robert W. "You Wonder Where the Spirit Went." *Pro Ecclesia: A Journal of Catholic and Evangelical Theology* 2 (1993) 296–304.

Kärkkäinen, Veli-Matti. "How to Speak of the Spirit Among Religions: Trinitarian 'Rules' for a Pneumatological Theology of Religions." *International Bulletin of Mission Research* 30 (2006) 121–27. http://www.internationalbulletin.org/issues/2006-03/2006-03-121-karkkainen.pdf.

———. *Pneumatology: The Holy Spirit in Ecumenical, International, and Contextual Perspective*. Grand Rapids, MI: Baker Academic, 2002.

Käsemann, Ernst. *Perspectives on Paul*. Translated by Margaret Kohl. London: SCM, 1971.

Keener, Craig S. *The IVP Bible Background Commentary: New Testament*. Downers Grove, IL: InterVarsity, 1993.

———. *Spirit Hermeneutics: Reading Scripture in Light of Pentecost*. Grand Rapids, MI: Eerdmans, 2017.

Kimball, Dan. *They Like Jesus but Not the Church: Insights from Emerging Generations*. Grand Rapids, MI: Zondervan, 2007.

Kinnaman, David. *You Lost Me: Why Young Christians Are Leaving the Church . . . and Rethinking Faith*. Grand Rapids, MI: Baker, 2011.

Kinnaman, David, and Gabe Lyons. *unchristian: What a New Generation Really Thinks about Christianity—and Why It Matters*. Grand Rapids, MI: Baker, 2007.

Larson, Craig Brian. "What All Good Preachers Do." In *Prophetic Preaching*, edited by Craig Brian Larson, 59–66. Peabody, MA: Hendrickson, 2012.

Latourette, Kenneth Scott. *A History of Christianity*. Rev. ed. Vol. 2. New York: Harper & Row, 1975.

The Lausanne Movement. "The Cape Town Commitment." http://www.lausanne.org/ctcommitment.

Lovin, Robin. *Christian Ethics: An Essential Guide*. Nashville, Abingdon, 2000.

———. *An Introduction to Christian Ethics*. Nashville: Abingdon, 2011.

Loyer, Kenneth. *God's Love through the Spirit: The Holy Spirit in Thomas Aquinas and John Wesley*. Washington, DC: Catholic University of America Press, 2014.

Macchia, Frank. *Baptized in the Spirit: A Global Pentecostal Theology*. Grand Rapids, MI: Zondervan, 2006.

———. *Justified in the Spirit: Creation, Redemption, and the Triune God*. Grand Rapids, MI: Eerdmans, 2010.

Mangina, Joseph L. *Karl Barth: Theologian of Christian Witness*. Louisville: Westminster John Knox, 2004.

Maraniss, David. *When Pride Still Mattered: A Life of Vince Lombardi.* New York: Simon & Schuster, 1999.

Marshall, I. Howard. *Acts.* Tyndale New Testament Commentaries. Grand Rapids, MI: Eerdmans, 1986.

———. *The Epistles of John.* New International Commentary on the New Testament. Grand Rapids, MI: Eerdmans, 1978.

Mathison, Keith A. *The Shape of Sola Scriptura.* Moscow, ID: Canon, 2001.

Maston, T. B. *Biblical Ethics: A Guide to the Ethical Message of the Scriptures from Genesis to Revelation.* Macon, GA: Mercer University Press, 1997.

McClung, Grant. "Truth on Fire: Pentecostals and an Urgent Missiology." In *Azusa Street and Beyond: 100 Years of Commentary on the Global Pentecostal/Charismatic Movement,* edited by Grant McClung, 77–88. Gainesville, FL: Bridge-Logos, 2006.

McCormack, Bruce. "Grace and Being: The Role of God's Gracious Election in Karl Barth's Theological Ontology." In *The Cambridge Companion to Karl Barth,* edited by John Webster, 92–110. Cambridge: Cambridge University Press, 2000.

———. *Karl Barth's Critically Realistic Dialectical Theology: Its Genesis and Development 1909–1936.* New York: Oxford University Press, 1995.

McGrath, Alister E. *A Scientific Theology: Volume 2: Reality.* Grand Rapids, MI: Eerdmans, 2002.

Miles, Todd. *A God of Many Understandings? The Gospel and a Theology of Religions.* Nashville: B&H Publishing, 2010.

Moltmann, Jürgen. *God in Creation: A New Theology of Creation and the Spirit of God.* Translated by Margaret Kohl. New York: Harper & Row, 1985.

———. *The Spirit of Life: A Universal Affirmation.* Translated by Margaret Kohl. Minneapolis: Fortress, 1992.

Morris, Leon. *The Gospel According to John.* New International Commentary on the New Testament. Grand Rapids, MI: Eerdmans, 1971.

Murphy, Roland. *The Tree of Life: An Exploration of Biblical Wisdom Literature.* 3rd ed. Grand Rapids, MI: Eerdmans, 1990.

Newbigin, Lesslie. *The Gospel in a Pluralist Society.* Grand Rapids, MI: Eerdmans, 1989.

Nullens, Patrick, and Ronald T. Michener. *The Matrix of Christian Ethics: Integrating Philosophy and Moral Theology in a Postmodern Context.* Downers Grove, IL: IVP, 2010.

Olson, Roger, E. *Counterfeit Christianity: The Persistence of Errors in the Church.* Nashville: Abingdon, 2015.

———. *The Mosaic of Christian Belief.* Downers Grove, IL: IVP Academic, 2002.

———. *The Story of Christian Theology.* Downers Grove, IL: IVP Academic, 1999.

Ortberg, John. "Preaching Like a Prophet." In *Prophetic Preaching,* edited by Craig Brian Larson, 47–58. Peabody, MA: Hendrickson, 2012.

Pannenberg, Wolfhart. *Systematic Theology.* Translated by Geoffrey W. Bromiley. Vol. 3. Grand Rapids, MI: Eerdmans, 1997.

Patton, C. Michael. "Why I Don't Think Much of the Spiritual Formation Movement." *Credo House.* http://www.reclaimingthemind.org/blog/2012/01/why-i-dont-think-much-about-the-spiritual-formation-movement/.

Peterson, Derrick. "*Scientia Dei*: A Comparison of the Works of T. F. Torrance and Wolfhart Pannenberg on the Concept of Theology as a Science." *Academia.edu.* https://www.academia.edu/8121208/Scientia_Dei_A_Comparison_of_T.F._Torrance_and_Wolfhart_Pannenberg_on_Theology_as_a_Science.

Pinnock, C. H. *A Wideness in God's Mercy: The Finality of Jesus Christ in a World of Religions*. Grand Rapids, MI: Zondervan, 1992.

Piper, John. "Learning to Pray in the Spirit and the Word, Part 2." *desiringGod.org*. http://www.desiringgod.org/messages/learning-to-pray-in-the-spirit-and-the-word-part-2.

Powell, Kara, and Chap Clark. *Sticky Faith: Everyday Ideas to Build Lasting Faith in Your Kids*. Grand Rapids, MI: Zondervan, 2011.

Powell, Kara, et al. *Growing Young: Six Essential Strategies to Help Young People Discover and Love Your Church*. Grand Rapids, MI: Baker, 2016.

Pomerville, Paul A. *Introduction to Missions: An Independent-Study Textbook*. Irving, TX: ICI University Press, 1987.

Rae, Scott. *Moral Choices: An Introduction to Ethics*. 3rd ed. Grand Rapids, MI: Zondervan, 2009.

Ramm, Bernard. *After Fundamentalism: The Future of Evangelical Theology*. San Francisco: Harper & Row, 1983.

Richardson, Kurt Anders. "Foreword: Introducing Torrance—Wonder over the Intelligibility of God." In *Reality & Evangelical Theology: The Realism of Christian Revelation*, ix–xxi. Downers Grove, IL: InterVarsity, 1999.

———. *Reading Karl Barth: New Directions for American Theology*. Grand Rapids, MI: Baker Academic, 2004.

Ridderbos, Herman. *The Gospel of John: A Theological Commentary*. Grand Rapids, MI: Eerdmans, 1997.

Robeck, Cecil M. "Taking Stock of Pentecostalism." *Pneuma* 15 (1993) 35–60.

Rogers, Eugene. *The Holy Spirit: Classic and Contemporary Readings*. Hoboken, NJ: Wiley-Blackwell, 2009.

Rosato, Philip J. *The Spirit as Lord: The Pneumatology of Karl Barth*. Edinburgh: T & T Clark, 1981.

Roxburgh, Alan J., and M. Scott Boren. *Introducing the Missional Church: What It Is, Why It Matters, How to Become One*. Grand Rapids, MI: Baker, 2009.

Schaeffer, Francis. *True Spirituality: How to Live for Jesus Moment by Moment*. Carol Stream, IL: Tyndale House, 2001.

Sexton, Jason S. *The Trinitarian Theology of Stanley J. Grenz*. New York: Bloomsbury T. & T. Clark, 2015.

Shults, F. LeRon. *The Postfoundationalist Task of Theology: Wolfhart Pannenberg and the New Theological Rationality*. Grand Rapids, MI: Eerdmans, 1999.

Smith, Aaron T. *A Theology of the Third Article: Karl Barth and the Spirit of the Word*. Minneapolis: Fortress Press, 2014.

Smith, Christian, and Melinda Lundquist Denton. *Soul Searching: The Religious and Spiritual Lives of American Teenagers*. New York: Oxford University Press, 2005.

Smith, Christian, and Patricia Smith. *Souls in Transition: The Religious and Spiritual Lives of Emerging Adults*. New York: Oxford University Press, 2009.

Smith, Christian, et al. *Lost in Transition: The Dark Side of Emerging Adulthood*. New York: Oxford University Press, 2011.

Sonderegger, Sandra. "Barth and Feminism." In *The Cambridge Companion to Karl Barth*, edited by John Webster, 258–73. Cambridge: Cambridge University Press, 2000.

Stassen, Glen H., and David P. Gushee. *Kingdom Ethics: Following Jesus in Contemporary Context*. Downers Grove, IL: InterVarsity, 2003.

Stephenson, Christopher A. *Types of Pentecostal Theology: Method, System, Spirit.* New York: Oxford University Press, 2012.

Stott, John R. W. *The Message of Romans.* Downers Grove, IL: IVP Academic, 2001.

Stronstad, Roger. *The Charismatic Theology of St. Luke.* Peabody, MA: Hendrickson, 1984.

Synan, Vinson. *The Holiness-Pentecostal Tradition: Charismatic Movements in the Twentieth Century.* Grand Rapids, MI: Eerdmans, 1997.

Tennent, Timothy C. *Invitation to World Missions: A Trinitarian Missiology for the Twenty-First Century.* Grand Rapids, MI: Kregel Academic, 2010.

Tisdale, Leonora Tubbs. *Prophetic Preaching: A Pastoral Approach.* Louisville, KY: Westminster John Knox, 2010.

Thompson, John. *The Holy Spirit in the Theology of Karl Barth.* Allison Park, PA: Pickwick Publications, 1991.

Torrance, Alan. "The Trinity." In *The Cambridge Companion to Karl Barth*, edited by John Webster, 72–91. Cambridge: Cambridge University Press, 2000.

Torrance, Thomas F. "The Place of Michael Polanyi in the Modern Philosophy of Science." *Ethics in Science and Medicine* 7 (1980) 57–95.

———. *Reality & Evangelical Theology: The Realism of Christian Revelation.* Downers Grove, IL: InterVarsity, 1999.

———. *Reality and Scientific Theology.* Edinburgh, Scotland: Scottish Academic Press, 1985.

———. *Transformation and Convergence in the Frame of Knowledge: Explorations in the Interrelations of Scientific and Theological Enterprise.* Grand Rapids, MI: Eerdmans, 1984.

Tyra, Gary. *Christ's Empowering Presence: The Pursuit of God through the Ages.* Downers Grove, IL: IVP, 2011.

———. *Defeating Pharisaism: Recovering Jesus' Disciple-Making Method.* Downers Grove, IL: IVP, 2009.

———. *The Holy Spirit in Mission: Prophetic Speech and Action in Christian Witness.* Downers Grove, IL: IVP Academic, 2011.

———. *A Missional Orthodoxy: Theology and Mission in a Post-Christian Context.* Downers Grove, IL: IVP Academic, 2013.

———. "Proclaiming Christ's Victory of Sinful, Personal Desires." *Enrichment Journal.* http://enrichmentjournal.ag.org/201303/201303_072_personal_victory.cfm. *Pursuing Moral Faithfulness: Ethics and Christian Discipleship.* Downers Grove, IL: IVP Academic, 2015.

———. *Pursuing Moral Faithfulness: Ethics and Christian Discipleship.* Downers Grove, IL: IVP Academic, 2015.

Vanhoozer, Kevin J. *The Drama of Doctrine: A Canonical Linguistic Approach to Christian Theology.* Louisville: Westminster John Knox, 2005.

———. "Introduction: What Is Theological Interpretation of the Bible?" In *Theological Interpretation of the Old Testament: A Book-by-Book Survey*, edited by Kevin J. Vanhoozer, 15–28. Grand Rapids, Baker Academic, 2008.

———. "Pilgrim's Digress: Christian Thinking On and About the Post/Modern Way." In *Christianity and the Postmodern Turn: Six Views*, edited by Myron B. Penner, 71–103. Grand Rapids, MI: Brazos, 2005.

Ward, Graham. "Barth, Modernity, and Postmodernity." In *The Cambridge Companion to Karl Barth*, edited by John Webster, 274–95. Cambridge: Cambridge University Press, 2000.

Ware, Kallistos. "The Eastern Tradition from the Tenth to the Twentieth Century: [Part] A, Greek." In *The Study of Spirituality*, edited by Cheslyn Jones et al., 235–58. New York: Oxford University Press, 1986.

Watson, Francis. "The Bible." In *The Cambridge Companion to Karl Barth*, edited by John Webster, 57–71. Cambridge: Cambridge University Press, 2000.

Weatherhead, Leslie. *The Transforming Friendship*. Nashville: Abingdon, 1977.

Weber, Otto. *Foundations of Dogmatics*. Translated by Darrell L. Guder. Vol. 2. Grand Rapids, MI: Eerdmans, 1983.

Webster, John. "Introducing Barth." In *The Cambridge Companion to Karl Barth*, edited by John Webster, 1–16. Cambridge: Cambridge University Press, 2000.

Whybray, R. N. *The Book of Proverbs*. Cambridge Bible Commentary. Cambridge: Cambridge University Press, 1972.

White, James R. *Scripture Alone*. Minneapolis: Bethany, 2004.

Wilkins, Michael J. *Matthew*. NIV Application Commentary. Grand Rapids, MI, Zondervan, 2004.

Wilson, Jim. *Future Church: Ministry in a Post-Seeker Age*. Nashville: Broadman & Holman, 2004.

Wogaman, J. Philip. *Speaking the Truth in Love: Prophetic Preaching in a Broken World*. Louisville, KY: Westminster John Knox, 1998.

Woodley, Matt. "Introduction." in *Prophetic Preaching*, edited by Craig Brian Larson, 1–7. Peabody, MA: Hendrickson, 2012.

Wuthnow, Robert. *After the Baby Boomers*. Princeton: Princeton University Press, 2007.

Yong, Amos. *Beyond the Impasse: Toward a Pneumatological Theology of Religions*. Grand Rapids, MI: Baker Academic, 2003.

———. "Christological Constraints in Shifting Contexts: Jesus Christ, Prophetic Dialogue and the *Missio Spiritus* in a Pluralistic World." In *Mission on the Road to Emmaus: Constants, Contexts, and Prophetic Dialogue*, edited by Cathy Ross and Stephen B. Bevans, 19–33. London: SCM, 2015.

———. *Discerning the Spirit(s): A Pentecostal-Charismatic Contribution to Christian Theology of Religions*. Sheffield, England: Sheffield Academic Press, 2000.

———. "On Divine Presence and Divine Agency: Toward a Foundational Pneumatology." *Asian Journal of Pentecostal Studies* 3 (2000) 167–88.

———. "Pluralism, Secularism and Pentecost: Newbigin-ings for *Missio Trinitatis* in a New Century." In *The Gospel and Pluralism Today: Reassessing Lesslie Newbigin in the 21st Century*, edited by Scott W. Sunquist and Amos Yong, 147–59. Downers Grove, IL: IVP Academic, 2015.

———. *The Spirit Poured Out on All Flesh: Pentecostalism and the Possibility of Global Theology*. Grand Rapids, MI: Baker Academic, 2005.

———. *Spirit-Word-Community: Theological Hermeneutics in Trinitarian Perspective*. Reprint, Eugene, OR: Wipf & Stock, 2006.

Author Index

Adler, Jerry, 10n11

Anderson, Allan, 114n30, 114n32

Bainton, Roland H., 39–40n11, 41n16, 41n19, 41n21, 41n23, 41n24, 42n28

Barna Group, 6, 6n6, 10n10

Barrett, C. K., 126n6, 128n12, 178n106

Barrett, Matthew, 147n21, 149, 149n26, 149n27, 149n28, 151, 151n34

Barth, Karl, 4–5, 5n5, 7, 7n7, 7n8, 10–11n12, 11–12n13, 16n3, 19n14, 23n21, 24n23, 28n21, 28–29n32, 30n34, 31n36, 31n37, 32–33n40, 34–35n44, 53n70, 53n71, 64n3, 73–74n17, 75n18, 82n1, 86–87n12, 104n10, 106–7n17, 136n29, 138, 138n2, 139, 139n3, 141, 147, 152, 152n36, 153–54, 154n40, 154n41, 154n42, 155, 155n46, 156, 156n47, 156n48, 156n49, 157, 157n53, 158, 158n54, 159, 159n58, 160, 160n60, 161, 161n61, 161n62, 162, 162n63, 162n65, 162n66, 163, 163n67, 163n68, 163n69, 163n70, 164, 164n71, 164n72, 164n73, 165n77, 166–67, 167n83, 167n84, 167–68n85, 168, 168n88, 168n89, 169, 169n90, 170–71, 171n92, 171n93, 172, 173, 173n97, 173–74n98, 174, 174n99, 179, 179n107, 180

Barth, Heinrich, 53n70

Bavinck, J. H., 100, 100n1

Bhaskar, Roy, 16n2

Biggar, Nigel, 5n5, 82n1, 86–87n12

Bilezikian, Gilbert, 56, 56n74

Bird, Michael F., 36n2

Block, Matthew, 150n30, 150n31, 150n32, 151n33, 151n35

Bloesch, Donald, 96n29, 179, 179n107

Boersma, Hans, 143, 143n10, 143n11, 143n12, 143n13, 143n14, 166, 166n79, 166n80, 166n81, 175–76n102, 176–77n103, 177n104

Bolich, Gregory G., 162n63

Boren, M. Scott, 103n6, 104, 104n7, 104n9, 105

Braaten, Carl E., 18n7

Bromiley, Geoffrey W., 161n61

Bruce, F. F., 93n21, 128n11, 128n12, 178n106

Brueggemann, Walter, 124, 124n4, 142n4

Bruner, Dale Frederick, 93n21

Burge, Gary M., 126n7

Busch, Eberhard, 5n5, 7n7, 10–11n12, 106–7n17, 156, 162n63

Cairns, Earle E., 38, 38n5 38n6, 38n7, 41n15, 41n17, 41n21, 41n22, 41n25, 42n26, 42n27, 42n28, 42n29

Chan, Simon, 20n16

Chantry, Walter J., 149n24

Chia, Roland, 161n61

Clark, Chap, 10n10, 51–52n64, 78n26

Codling, Don, 149n24, 149n25, 150n29

Coe, John, 17, 20–21, 21n18, 21n19

Colyer, Elmer, 27n28, 27n29, 27n30, 31n35

Cooper, John W., 19n15

Currie, Thomas Christian, 165n77, 167, 167n85, 168, 168n86, 169, 170n91, 172n94, 173n97, 173–74n98, 174n99, 179n107

Davis, John Jefferson, 24, 24n22, 24n23, 25n24, 25n25, 33, 140, 140n4

Dean, Kenda Creasy, 10n10, 44n37, 44n38, 47, 47n53, 47n54, 48n55, 52, 52n65, 52n66

Denton, Melinda Lundquist, 44

Douglass, Jane Dempsey, 146n20

Dunn, James D. G., 22n20

Dunn, Richard R., 6n6, 51n64

Dyck, Drew, 10n10

Fee, Gordon, 127–28n10, 128n12, 178n106

Foulkes, Francis, 126–27n8, 127n9, 131n18

Fowl, Stephen, 176–77n103

France, R. T., 96n27, 131n18

Franke, John R., 5n5, 104n10, 161n61

Frye, John. W., 144, 144n15, 144n16, 145n18

Fung, Ronald Y. K., 128n11, 132n20

Godfrey, W. Robert, 147n21

González, Justo L., 40, 40n12, 40n13, 40n14

Graves, Michael, 142–43n9

Grenz, Stanley, 19n13

Grigg, Ty, 136n28

Grossman, Cathy Lynn, 6n6, 10n10

Guder, Darrell, 103n6, 106n16, 107n18, 108n19,

Gunton, Colin, 5n5, 23n21

Gushee, David P., 95n25

Hart, Trevor, 161n61

Holmes, Arthur, 95n25, 96n28

Hunsinger, George, 5n5, 10–11n12, 23n21, 28n32, 54n72, 73n15, 154n40, 157n53

Jenson, Robert W., 18n7, 153, 153n38

Kärkkäinen, Veli-Matti, 20n16, 54n73, 146n19

Käsemann, Ernst, 128n12, 178n106

Keener, Craig S., 90n17, 142–43n9, 175–76n102, 176–77n103

Kimball, Dan, 10n10

Kinnaman, David, 10n10, 76, 76n24, 77n25

Lyons, Gabe, 76n24, 77n25

Larson, Craig Brian, 141n2, 141n3, 142n5

Latourette, Kenneth Scott, 39, 39–40n11, 41n18, 41n19, 41n20, 41n25, 42n26, 42n27, 42n29, 42n30

Lovin, Robin, 95n25, 96n27

Loyer, Kenneth, 54n73

Macchia, Frank, x, 5n5, 10–11n12, 16–17n4, 22n20, 61n1

Mangina, Joseph L., 5n5, 64n3

Maraniss, David, 137, 137n1

Marshall, I. Howard, 128–29n13, 129n14

Mathison, Keith A., 147n21, 151n35

Maston, T. B., 95n25

McClung, Grant, 114n33

McCormack, Bruce, 5n5, 28–29n32

McGrath, Alister E., 154n40, 154n41

Miles, Todd, 20n16

Moltmann, Jürgen, 54n73, 61, 61n1, 61n2, 146n19

Morris, Leon, 93n21, 125–26n5, 126n7

Murphy, Roland, 90n17

Newbigin, Lesslie, 31n38, 101n3, 103n6, 105–6, 106n12, 106n13, 106n14 106n15, 108

Nullens, Patrick, 95n25

Michener, Ronald T., 95n25

Olson, Roger, E., 18n8, 37, 38, 38n3, 38n4, 39, 39n8, 39n9, 39n10, 39–40n11, 40n13, 41n16,

41n17, 41n18, 41n19, 41n20,
41n21, 41n22, 41n23, 41n24,
41n25, 42, 42n26, 42n27,
42n28, 42n29, 42n30, 42n31,
42n32, 43, 43n33, 52, 52n67,
52n68, 54n73, 146n19
Ortberg, John, 142n5
Pannenberg, Wolfhart, 17, 17n5,
17n6, 18, 18n10, 18n11,
18n12, 19, 19n13, 19n14,
19n15, 20n16, 21, 24n23,
33–34n42
Patton, C. Michael, 20n17
Peterson, Derrick, 24n23
Pinnock, C. H., 20n16
Piper, John, 129n15
Powell, Kara, 10n10, 47n53, 51–
52n64, 78n26, 79–80n28
Pomerville, Paul A., 114n33
Rae, Scott, 96n29
Ramm, Bernard, 162, 162n64
Richardson, Kurt Anders, 5n5,
31n38, 138, 138n2, 152n36,
161, 161n62, 167n84
Ridderbos, Herman, 93n21
Robeck, Cecil M., 113n29
Rogers, Eugene, 153, 153n39
Rosato, Philip J., 5n5, 30n34, 31n37,
32–33n40, 53n70, 73–74n17,
75n18, 106–107n17, 157–58,
158n54, 158n55, 158n56, 159,
157n57, 159n58, 160, 160n59
Roxburgh, Alan J., 103n6, 104,
104n7, 104n9, 105
Schaeffer, Francis, 122, 122n1
Sexton, Jason S., 19n15
Shults, F. LeRon, 27n30
Smith, Aaron T., 5n5, 7n8, 11–12n13,
16n3, 31n36, 156, 156n49,
156n50, 157, 157n51, 157n52,
157n53, 164, 164n74, 164n75,
165, 165n76, 165n77, 166,
166n78, 167, 167n82, 167n83,
167n84, 168, 169, 169n90,
172, 172n94, 172n95, 172n96
Smith, Christian, 44, 44n39, 45,
45n40, 45n41, 45n42, 45n43,
45n44, 45n45, 46, 46n46,
46n47, 46n48, 46n49, 47,
47n50, 47n51, 47n52, 47n53,
48, 48n55, 48n56, 48n57, 50,
50n60, 50n61, 51n62n 51n63,
83, 83n2, 83n3, 83n4, 83n5,
84n6
Smith, Patricia, 48n55
Sonderegger, Sandra, 5n5, 28–29n32,
154n40
Stassen, Glen H., 95n25
Stephenson, Christopher A., 34n43
Stott, John R. W., 130, 130n17
Stronstad, Roger, 110n22
Synan, Vinson, 113n29
Tennent, Timothy C., 54, 54n73,
145–46, 146n19, 150, 152–53,
153n57, 180, 180n109
Tisdale, Leonora Tubbs, 142n6
Thompson, John, 5n5, 106–7n17
Torrance, Alan, 5n5, 29n33
Torrance, Thomas F., 24n23, 25–27,
27n28, 27n29, 27n30, 28,
28–29n32, 29, 29n33, 30,
31n35, 31n38, 32, 32n39, 33,
154, 154n41, 154n42, 155,
155n44, 157
Tyra, Gary, ix, x, 2n2, 9n9, 25n26,
26n27, 43n35, 52n69, 67n8,
72n12, 72n13, 75n20, 76n22,
76n23, 84n7, 85n8, 86n9,
86n11, 86n12, 87n14, 89n16,
92n19, 93n20, 94n22, 96n29,
97n30, 101n3, 102n4, 103n5,
104n8, 105n11, 111n23,
111n24, 112n26, 113n27,
113n28, 114n31, 114n34,
115n35, 115n36, 115n37,
126n7, 128n11, 129n14,
132n22, 132n23, 133n24,
134n25, 134n26, 141, 142n8,
148n23, 155n45, 164n71,
168n87, 175n101, 177n104,
177n105, 180n108
Vanhoozer, Kevin J., 27n30, 142–
43n9, 176–77n103

Ward, Graham, 5n5, 28–29n32, 154n40

Ware, Kallistos, 36n1

Watson, Francis, 152n36

Weatherhead, Leslie, 65–66, 66n5, 66n6, 66n7

Weber, Otto, 17, 17n5, 18, 19n14

Webster, John, 152n36, 154n40, 157n53, 161n61, 162n63

Whybray, R. N., 90n17

White, James R., 147n21

Wilkins, Michael J., 128–29n13

Wilson, Jim, 49n58, 50, 50n59

Wogaman, J. Philip, 142, 142n7

Woodley, Matt, 141n2

Wuthnow, Robert, 6, 6n6, 10n10

Yong, Amos, 16–17n4, 20n16, 34n43, 106n15, 113n29

Subject Index

accountability, moral, 84
activity, prophetic, 108–13, 115–16,
    129n14, 134, 148
    See also speech and action,
      prophetic
adultery, woman caught in the act
    of, 93
adults, emerging, 6, 10, 44, 50, 62, 76,
    83–84, 92, 96–98, 98n31, 181
antinomians, ethical (anarchists,
    moral), 95
antithesis, false, 93
apparatus, perceptual, 31n36
    See also framework, cognitive;
      processes, cognitive
arrabōn (pledge and foretaste), 106
autonomy, moral, 51, 83–84, 97

call to continue (or abide), the, 63,
    65, 75
canon, closed, 149
capacity, prophetic, 108, 110, 112,
    132–35, 148
Cape Town Commitment, 100,
    100n2, 175n100
carefulness, moral, 84–85
certainty and control, craving for,
    133–34, 134n25
Christ
    buried but also raised with, 70
    circumcised by, 70
    incarnation of, 10–11n12, 28, 30,
      32n39, 33, 42, 74n17, 102,
      154–55, 164–65

intimate, interactive relationship
    with, 37, 71–72, 173
mind of, 31, 71n11, 91
mystical-experiential communion
    with, 63–66, 70, 70n10,
    72–73, 73n17
mystical union between believers
    and, 71
ongoing, moment-by-moment
    mentoring relationship with,
    71, 71n11, 72, 75, 78, 80, 131,
    133, 166,
spiritually real relationship with,
    70
volitional-intellectual
    commitment to, 63, 70, 72
wholistic connection to, 70
Christianity
    almost, 84, 99, 123, 139
    evangelical, 1, 2, 4, 4n4, 5, 5n5, 7,
      10, 12, 20n16, 21–22, 24–25,
      28, 28n31, 29n33, 31n35,
      32n39, 35, 35n44, 36n2, 37,
      44, 49–51, 52n69, 53, 53n71,
      54, 54n73, 56–57, 62, 80–82,
      85, 90–92, 101, 107, 115–116,
      118, 121–122, 126n7, 128n12,
      129n15, 130–31, 134–36,
      139–40, 145–46, 146n19,
      147–50, 150n30, 151, 151n35,
      152, 153n38, 154, 154n41–42,
      155n44, 155n46, 156, 162n63,
      162n64, 175, 177, 178n106,
      180–81
    fundamentalist, 92, 162n64

Christianity (*continued*)
  non-Pentecostal-Charismatic,
    20n16, 115, 130, 132, 135,
    140, 148, 149
  orthodox (orthodoxy), 2n2, 8,
    23–25, 26n27, 29, 33, 34n43,
    36–37, 42–43, 47, 52, 63, 69–
    70, 76, 76n22, 89n16, 101n3,
    102, 102n4, 104n8, 155,
    155n45, 164n71, 175n101,
    177n104
  Orthodox (Eastern), 19n14, 36
  Pentevangelical, 4n4, 5, 7, 10, 25,
    35, 50, 81, 104n10, 122, 124,
    131, 134, 139–40, 145
  Pentecostal-Charismatic, x,
    20n16, 22n20, 25n, 34n43,
    75n21, 101, 113, 113n29, 114,
    114n30, 114n32, 115, 135,
    140, 148–49, 175n102
  Roman Catholic, 20n16, 47, 116,
    153n38, 162, 167
  unorthodox, 151
Christocentrism, 5n5, 10–11n12,
    11–12n13, 106, 154, 156–57,
    166
  See also Christomonism
Christomonism, 10–11n12
  See also Christocentrism
Christology, 7n8, 10–11n12, 23n21,
    54, 145, 152, 156–57
  pneumatocentric, 11n13, 166
churches,
  progressive/emerging, 101
  traditional, 54, 101, 145
"churchianity," 76
"Colossians 3 Kind of Life," the, 67,
    69–71, 73
communion
  with Christ, see Christ, mystical-
    experiential communion with
  with God, 10–11n12, 32–33n40,
    54n72, 73n15, 157n53, 159,
    159n58, 176n103
compromise, moral, 83–84
consistency, moral, 84

context, post-Christian, 6, 8, 10, 24,
    57, 62, 76–80, 83–84, 92–94,
    96–98, 98n31, 99, 106, 118,
    139–41, 181
contextualization, gospel. *See*
    contextualization, ministry
contextualization, ministry, 2n2, 56,
    98n31, 102–4, 175n101, 177,
    177n104
  incarnational approach to, 2, 102
  pneumatological question at the
    heart of, 104, 175
  imaginative process of, 105
conversation, missional, 103
culture, emerging, see adults,
    emerging

deficit
  discipleship, 4n4, 10, 35, 52,
    52n69, 53–54, 139
  pneumatological, 4, 4n4, 5, 10,
    22, 35, 53–55, 90, 146–47,
    150, 180
definition, Chalcedonian, 102
deism
  classical, 37–42, 46
  functional (de facto), 21, 23,
    34–37, 43–44
  moralistic therapeutic (MTD), ix,
    37, 43, 43n5, 44–53
  See also nominalism, Christian
demonic, the, 129–30n15
diakonia (service), 106, 106n17
dialectic, pneumatocentric, 11–
    12n13, 157
dialogue, imaginative, 103, 105
discipleship (responsible Christian),
    ethic of, 85, 92, 94n24, 95–97,
    99
disciple making, 8, 35, 46, 76, 80,
    180n108
doctrine of the Spirit
  comprehensive, 19, 20n16, 125
  full throated, 37, 136, 139
  fully Trinitarian, ix, 4, 57, 140,
    145, 181
  robust, 4, 11, 20, 57, 125, 145

unmitigated, 61, 139
See also pneumatology
docetism, 18
dynamic
   kingdom representing, 105–6,
      113, 118
   post-Christian (*see* context, post-
      Christian)
   Spirit-devaluing, 147
dysfunction, missional, 134n25

edification, prophetic. *See* ministry,
   prophetic
empowerment, spiritual, ix, 4n4,
      6, 9, 24–25, 35, 53, 56, 80,
      85, 87n13, 92, 103, 106,
      110n22, 111–12, 118, 121–23,
      125, 127n10, 128, 128n12,
      128–29n13, 136, 140,
      145n17, 147–48, 152–53, 171,
      178n106, 181
encounter(s)
   existentially impactful (life-story
      shaping), 1, 16, 21–23, 31–32,
      55, 57, 128n11, 142, 143n14,
      152, 158–59, 169–70, 172–73
   history shaping, 33n42
   sacramental, 143n14, 145n17,
      147, 161, 166, 168, 180
   environment (ethos), ecclesial, 2,
      3, 5, 7, 15, 22, 33, 55, 85, 108,
      121–22, 130, 135–36, 138–39,
      180
epistemology
   foundationalism, 26–27
   realist, 25, 28–29n32
   non-foundationalism, 26–27,
      28n32
   post-foundationalism, 27, 27n30
equipping, prophetic, see ministry,
   prophetic
evil (the evil one), 67–68, 114,
      129n15
exegesis
   biblical, 175–76n102
   God's, 167
   patristic, 176–77n103

spiritual/theological, 142n9,
   143n14
sacramental, 143n11, 143n14,
   166, 175–76n102
expectancy
   pneumatological, 3, 53, 55–57,
      77, 118, 122, 124–25, 128n11,
      130, 131n19, 145, 147, 150,
      152, 160
   posture of (*see* expectancy,
      pneumatological)
expectation, holy, 169, 171–72
experience, phenomenal, 16, 16n3,
      22, 33n42, 126n8, 129n15,
      139, 145, 148, 152
evangelicalism. *See* Christianity,
   evangelical
evangelism, prophetic. *See* ministry,
   prophetic

faithfulness
   before God, 1–3, 6, 10, 62, 73, 75,
      85, 94, 96, 118, 124–25, 133
   Christ-honoring, 69, 132
   missional, 2, 3, 6, 9, 23, 57, 62, 99,
      100–120
   moral, 2, 3, 6, 9, 23, 57, 62, 81–99
   multifaceted, 2, 10, 136
   spiritual, 2, 3, 6, 8, 9, 23, 57,
      61–80
   threefold, 2, 3, 4n4, 6, 10, 57, 59,
      62, 118, 123
fathers, church, 18, 40, 43, 102, 142–
      43n9, 143n14, 175–76n102,
      176–77n103
fellowship (friendship), transforming,
   65–66
fix, religious, 49–50
formation
   ministry, 8, 23, 34, 37, 50,
      130n16, 136–37, 140
   moral, 8, 21n18, 23, 34, 37, 50,
      81, 85, 92, 130n16, 137
   spiritual, 8, 20, 20n17, 21, 23, 34,
      37, 50, 130n16, 137
framework, cognitive, 27, 31
   See also apparatus, perceptual;
      processes, cognitive

fruitfulness, ministry, 2, 3, 3n3, 37,
        56–57, 61–62, 76–77, 80,
        82–83, 92, 101, 116
fundamentals, commitment to,
        137–39
generation(s), emerging. *See* adults,
        emerging
glossolalia, 123n2, 128n12, 178,
        178n106

Gnosticism, 17–18, 19n14, 33n42
God
    character of (according to Micah
        6:8), 95
    Divine Butler (Cosmic Therapist),
        46
    incarnate in Christ, 18, 29, 29n33,
        46, 73, 155
    kingdom of, 19n15, 46, 103,
        105–6, 105–6n17, 108, 113,
        117–18, 125–26n5, 144
    sovereignty of, 46, 181
    Trinitarian, 3, 9, 16, 19n15, 24,
        24n23, 30, 30n34, 33, 46, 48,
        52, 123, 138, 140, 151–55,
        158, 177,
    See also doctrine of the Spirit,
        fully Trinitarian
graces
    of character, 128n11
    ethical, 128n11
guidance
    ministry, 105, 129, 170
    moral, 86–87n12, 87, 87n13,
        87n14, 88, 90–91, 91n18, 92,
        92n19
harbinger (preview community) of
        the coming reign of God,
        106–7n17, 107
heresy, 18, 42–43, 125
    See also pneumatological, heresy
hermeneutics
    pneumatologically grounded,
        16–17n4
    Spirit, 142–43n9, 175–76n102,
        176–77n103
holy expectation, 145, 171, 180

root of, 172–73
fruit of, 173
Holy Spirit
    agency of, 10–11n13, 21, 129n14,
        129–30n15, 157, 177n104
    depersonalized, overly-
        conceptualized depictions of,
        1, 22, 33, 139, 152–53
    divinity of, 16, 18, 19n15, 21, 29,
        31n37, 73–74n17, 91, 111,
        127n9, 131n18, 138–39, 145,
        148, 150–52, 154–55, 158,
        165n77, 166
    epistemological significance of,
        22, 32n40, 154, 157–58, 160,
        177
    existential significance of, 157–
        58, 160
    indwelling of, x, 21, 29–30, 61,
        132, 154–55
    marginalization of, 19, 146–47,
        153
    missionary nature of, 62, 100,
        108, 175
    prayerfully partnering with,
        122–23, 123n2
    prophetic working of, 134–35
    real dialogue with, 177
    realist understanding of, 3, 7,
        10, 15, 21–25, 54–55, 85, 87,
        99, 103, 106, 108, 118, 122,
        124–25, 128n11, 129–30n15,
        135–37, 139, 145, 158, 160–
        61, 172, 174, 178n106
    responsiveness to, 55, 86, 86n11,
        90–91, 94n22, 97, 129n14,
        136, 174
    source of communion, 32–33n40,
        159n18
hope (theological virtue), 9, 64n3,
        72n14, 74, 118, 130, 130n16,
        174, 179
horizon, hermeneutical, 176
hypostatic union, 102
humility (rather than arrogance or
        demagoguery), 67–68, 97
    homiletical, 163

ignorance, biblical and theological, 50
illumination, divine, 31–32, 34–
    35n44, 126n7, 142–43n9, 156,
    175–76n102, 176–77n103
immediacy, formational, 142–43n9
impact, existential, 1, 16, 21–22,
    22n20, 23, 31, 55, 57, 123,
    128n11, 142, 143n14, 152,
    158–59, 169–70, 172–73,
    See also encounters, existentially
    impactful (life-story shaping);
    encounters, history-shaping
impulse, religious, the, 133–34
incarnation, the, 10–11n12, 30,
    32–33, 42, 73–74n17, 154–55,
    165
indifference, posture of, 3, 53, 55–56,
    76, 118, 122–25, 131, 145, 147
    See also presumption, posture of
individualism, 52, 83, 98, 98n31
indwelling
    dynamic of, 27n29
    of the biblical narratives
    (Scriptures), 31, 38
    of the world, 27
    See also knowledge, personal;
    Holy Spirit, indwelling of
interpretation, aim of, 176–77n103
inverberation, 16n3, 164–166

Jesus, moral manner and message of,
    84, 94–96
justice (rather than exploitation),
    79–80n28, 96–97, 142
kerygma (proclamation), 106,
    106n17, 167
koinonia (community), 106, 106n17
knowledge
    personal, 27n30
    real, trustworthy, 27, 30–31,
    154–55
    spiritual, 28
    tacit, 26, 27n28, 31
    See also indwelling, dynamic of;
    Polanyi, Michael; Torrance,
    T. F.

Lady Wisdom, 90
leadership, of the Holy Spirit, 131
legalism, 77, 92, 94
Lombardi, Vince, 137–39
Lord Herbert of Cherbury, 40

members (congregants)
    church, 1, 3, 4, 4n4, 5n5, 6, 9,
    22–23, 30, 34, 37, 43, 50, 52–
    57, 66–67, 76–77, 80–81, 85,
    87, 92, 97n30, 99, 103, 105–6,
    114–16, 118, 121–25, 127n10,
    130–34, 134n25, 135, 139,
    145, 177, 177n105, 180
    of the body of Christ, 70n10, 73,
    104n10
    of the missional community,
    104–5
mercy, 77–78, 79–80n28, 95–97,
    97n30
    God's, 20n16, 104n10, 118
    rather than judgmentalism, 97
    saturated words and deeds, 115
ministries, formational, 3, 56, 122
ministry
    activities, 106, 113
    conversations, 115
    conversions, 115
    prophetic, 24, 68, 105, 110–118,
    129n14, 132–33, 135, 148
    promptings, 116, 132–33, 135
    Spirit-empowered engagement in,
    ix, 9, 24–25, 56, 121–22, 125,
    136, 140
missio Dei, 169, 180–81
missiology, Trinitarian, 106n15,
    146n19
mission, Spirit of, 78, 98, 103–5, 111–
    112, 114–18, 132, 148
moralism, Christian, 20–21

National Study of Youth and Religion
    (NSYR), The, 44, 47, 50–51,
    83, 92, 98n31
nihilism, ethical, 92

nominalism, Christian, 10, 21, 34–35, 62
  See also deism, functional

ontology, 18n9, 24, 24n31, 28–29n32
  sacramental, 143
orthodoxy, missional, 2n2, 8, 25, 26n27, 33, 34n43, 76, 76n22, 89n16, 101n3, 102, 102n4, 104n8, 155n45, 164n71, 175n101, 177n104

panentheism, 19n15
paraklētos (advocate, counselor, or mentor), 75
pastor(s), x, 2, 7, 9, 51, 100, 121–22, 124, 131, 134–35, 145n18, 162, 171, 179
pastoral,
  leadership, 3,
  objective 7,
  transitions/turnover, vacancy 9,
  thought and speech, 11–12n13, 157
  colleagues 51,
  rant/exhortations, 68–69,
  instruction, 132,
  burnout, 134n25,
  approach (to prophetic preaching), 142n6
Pentecost, day of, 110, 128–29n13,
Pentecostal-charismatic(s), 20n16, 22n20, 25, 34n43, 75n21, 101, 113n29, 115, 135, 140, 148–49, 175–76n102,
Pentecostalism(s), Global, 101, 113, 113n29, 113–114, 114n30, 114n32, 115, 149
Pentevangelicals, see Christianity, Pentevangelical
perseverance (in the faith), 129–30, 15
Pharisaism, Christian, 8, 52n69, 76, 76n23, 77, 79–80n28, 134, 134n25, 177n105, 180n108
  See also Pharisees
Pharisees, 77, 93
  See also Pharisaism, Christian

phenomenon, prophetic, the, 87n13, 109, 132, 142, 142n8, 150, 163, 175, 178
  See also prophecy, phenomenon of
pneumatological
  balance, 134
  drama (story), 109–10
  expectancy and experience, 56–57
  heresy (unorthodox perspectives), 150, 150n30, 151, 151n35
  nuance, 134–35
pneumatology, 1, 7, 11, 16, 19, 20–23, 25, 31–32, 34, 54–55, 64, 75, 101, 106–109, 111, 118, 125, 129, 135, 139, 145–46, 152–53, 156–58, 160
  cessationist, 148–50, 150n29
  Christocentric, 10–11n12, 11–12n13, 157
  continuationist, 148–49
  impoverished, 35, 153
  missional, 101, 108, 111
  realist/non-realist, 3, 7, 10, 15, 21–23, 55, 85, 99, 103, 106, 118, 129–30n15, 135, 139, 145, 160
  robust, 4, 11, 20, 57, 125, 145
  soteriological, 111
  Trinitarian, fully, see doctrine of the Spirit, fully Trinitarian
  "the turn to,"20n16
  vocational, 111
  See also doctrine of the Spirit
practice(s)
  devotional, 63–64, 131
  spiritual discernment, 86
prayer
  Barth and, 173–74, 174n99
  glossolalic, 123n2, 178
  Paul's, 73–74, 92, 130n16
  missionally discerning, 175
  and prophetic preaching, 173–80
  pneumatologically real, 173–74, 180
  theologically real, 174–75, 180

praying
        deferentially and enduringly in
                hope, 174, 179–80
        in the moment, 174, 179–80
        in the Spirit, 123n2, 129–30n15,
                130n16, 131n19, 174, 178
preachers
        evangelical, 170, 177
        proper attitude of (holy
                expectation, reverent
                submission), 171, 173, 180
preaching
        Barth's encounter-facilitating
                understanding of, 166–68
        Barth's high view of, 169–70
        pneumatologically real approach
                to, 147, 170–80
        prophetic, 8, 141–80
        sacramental, 143, 143n12,
                143n14, 144, 166, 166n81,
                176–77n103, 177n104
presence, real, 23, 25, 86n10, 143n11,
                143n12, 166, 166n79, 175–
                76n102, 176–77n103
presumption, pneumatological
                posture of, 3, 53, 55–57, 76,
                118, 122–25, 131, 139, 145,
                147
        See also indifference,
                pneumatological posture of
process(es)
        cognitive, 31n36
        culture-changing, 131
        See also apparatus, perceptual;
                framework, cognitive
proclamation, Barth's incarnational
                understanding of, 164–66
        See also word of God, proclaimed
profession, creedal, 3–4, 23, 37, 43,
                52, 63, 70
prompting, prophetic, 142–43n9,
                143n14,
prophecy, phenomenon of, 110
        See also phenomenon, prophetic,
                the

qualifier, therapeutic, 46
question, ministry-generating, 106

realism
        critical, 28–29n32, 34n43
        moral, 84, 87
        philosophical, 16
        theological, ix, x, 5n5, 24–25,
                28, 28–29n32, 30, 32–33, 36,
                53–54, 82n1, 87, 143, 154,
                154n41, 155
reality
        divine, 5n5, 28n32, 31n37, 138–
                39, 154, 158, 166, 172
        God's, 32–33n40, 159
        new, 106, 108
reason, human, 19n14, 37–38, 41–42
reflection questions, nine, the, 97,
                97n30, 98
Reformation,
        Protestant, the, 7, 19n14, 39, 54,
                145–146, 146n20, 147n21,
                149–150, 152–53, 166, 180
        sacramentology, 166
Reformers
        magisterial (Calvin, Luther,
                Zwingli), 146–47,
        radical, 149
regeneration, spiritual, 21, 125n5, 153
relationship,
        intimate, interactive, 37, 71–72,
                132n21, 134n26, 148, 170,
                173
        moment-by-moment mentoring,
                71, 75, 131, 133
relativism, moral, 83, 84, 92–95
religion,
        natural, 38–40
        of rules and rituals, 134, 134n26
religiosity, 70–71
research,
        Barna Group, 6, 6n6, 10n10
        Lifeway, 6, 150–51
revelation,
        as event, 161, 161n61
        encounter-oriented view of, 152,
                161
        new (additional, extra-biblical),
                149, 150

Scriptura, sola, 7, 141, 146–47,
    147n21, 148, 149n24, 150,
    150n29, 151, 151n35, 152,
    170, 180–81
Scriptura, solo (nuda), 151, 151n35
Scripture(s)
    authority of, 4, 54, 104, 129–
        30n15, 145, 147n21, 149
    canonical, 149, 151
    dual role of, 176–77n103
    inspired, 31, 129
    sufficiency of, 149
    See also word of God
self, sovereignty of, 46
    See also God, sovereignty of
sensual indulgence, restraining, 70
sermon, sacramental, 7, 141, 143,
    143n14, 144, 151, 168, 175–
    76n102, 177n104, 181
    Barth's transformational
        understanding of the, 168–70
speech and action, prophetic, 8, 108–
    9, 111, 113, 115, 142n8, 148
    See also activity, prophetic
spirituality
    Christ-centered, 131
    Spirit-sensitive, 131–32
supernaturalism, trinitarian, 24,
    24n23

tendencies, habitual sinful, 68, 128

theology
    Christocentric, 5n5, 10–11n12,
        11–12n13, 154, 156–57, 166
    deficient, 32–33n40, 52
    pneumatocentric, 11–12n13,
        156–57, 166,
    post-Reformation Protestant,
        19n14, 54, 145–46, 153, 180
    Spirit, 5n5, 106–7n17, 154
Third Article, theology of the, 156–57
tradition(s)
    human, 70
    interpretive, 175–76n102
training, moral, 80–81
    See also formation, moral
transformation, spiritual, 21, 144
Tyndale House, 7

verities, Christological, 102, 102n4
virtues, ethical, 128

wirkungsgeschichte (history of the
    influence of the text), 175–
    76n102
word of God, Barth's theologically
    real understanding of, 163–64
World, Majority, 113–15
worldview,
    naturalistic, 136
    supernaturalistic, 25

Scripture Index

OLD TESTAMENT

Genesis

3:1–7	133
3:4–5	133

Exodus

34:6–8	95n26

Numbers

11:25–28	109
11:25–29	148n22
11:29	109
24:2–3	109n20

Deuteronomy

7:9	2
34:10	109

Joshua

24:14	2

1 Samuel

10:6	109n20
10:6–11	148n22
10:9–10	109n20
19:19–20	109n20
19:23	109n20
19:19–24	148n22

1 Chronicles

12:18	109n20, 148n20

2 Chronicles

15:1–2	109n20
20:14–15	109n20
24:20	148n20

Psalms

5:8	91n18
16:7	91n18
23:3	91n18
25:4–5	91n18
25:8–9	91n18
25:8–10	62
27:11	91n18
32:8–9	90–91
34:8	79
36:5–6	95n26
43:3	91n18
51:6	91n18
51:12	91n18
73:24	91n18
78:32–37	62
86:11	91n18
89:8	2
89:14	95n26
119:18	91n18
119:19	91n18
119:26–27	91n18
119:33–37	91n18
119:64	91n18
119:66	91n18

Psalms (*continued*)

119:68	91n18
119:73	91n18
119:108	91n18
119:125	91n18
119:133	91n18
119:135	91n18
119:144	91n18
119:169	91n18
119:171	91n18
143:8	91n18
143:10	91

Proverbs

1:5	79n27
2	86
2:1–6	90
8–9	90
8:1–6	90
8:32–34	90
9:1–6	90
19:21	103–104
20:12	91n18

Ecclesiastes

7:18	101

Isaiah

61:1	109n20, 110
6:1–8	169

Ezekiel

2:2	16
11:5	109n20
36:24–27	91

Hosea

2:19–20	95n26
4:1	2

Joel

2:28–29	109, 148n22

Micah

6:8	95, 95n25, 96, 96n27, 97

৵৵

NEW TESTAMENT

Matthew

1:18	128–29n13
1:20	128–29n13
3:11	128–29n13
3:16	128–29n13
4:1	128–29n13
5:7	77–78
5:17–19	95
5:17–48	94n23
6:14–15	118n38
7:6	179
7:8–11	179
7:12	180
7:15–20	3n3
7:28–29	179
8	79
9:10–13	77
10:18–20	110, 128, 128–29n13
10:19–20	75n20, 179
12:7	77
12:18	128–29n13
12:28	128–29n13
16	29
18:21–35	77
21:43	3n3
22:34–40	95
23:1–36	77
23:23	77, 95
25:21	3n3, 8

Mark

3:1–6	94n23

Luke

1:41–45	148n22, 109
1:46–55	127n9
1:67	148n22
1:68–69	127n9
2:25–28	109, 148n22
2:29–32	127n9
3:21–22	110
4:1–13	110
4:14–30	110
4:31–44	110
6:36	78
7:29–35	77
7:36–39	77
12:1	77
12:11–12	110, 179
18:9–14	77
21:14–15	75n20
22:20	63
23:42	117
23:43	117
24:49	128–29n13

John

1:18	36
3:3–8	125, 125n5
3:8	134
4:24	127
5:1–18	94
5:19	132n21
5:30	132n21
5:39	77
6:44	125
7:14–24	94n23
7:45–46	179
8:1–11	93
8:11	94
8:28	132
9:16	77
9:24–34	77
10:37	132n21
12:49	132n21
14:10	132n21
14:15–18	75
14:15–26	126
14:23	64
14:24	132n21
14:24–25	127
14:25–26	71–72n11
14:26	75, 87, 126
14:31	132n21
15:1–8	63
15:5	3n3
15:15	132n21
16:7–8	179
16:7–11	125
16:12–15	71–72n11, 126, 166
16:13	75
16:14	126n7
20:30–31	64

Acts

1:8	100, 110n21, 128, 128–29n13
1:16	110n21
2:1–4	16n3
2:4	148n22
2:14–18	110
2:32–33	110
4:8	148n22
4:25	129n14
4:31	179
6:8–10	179
7:51	3, 124
8:4–19	148n22
8:17–19	16n3
9	133
9:10–22	112, 132, 148
9:17–18	148n22
10:17–20	129
10:19	87
10:44–46	148n22
13:1–3	129, 174
13:2	87, 129
13:9	148n22
13:9–12	111n25
14:21–22	64n4
16:6–10	129
16:7	1n1
16:25	127n9
17:6 (KJV)	112
17:28	139
19:1–2	34

Acts (*continued*)

19:2	15
19:3–4	34
19:6	16n3
20:28	129n14

Romans

1:1—11:36	130n16
4:18	130n16
5:1–5	130n16
6:1–14	69n9, 71
7:4	3n3
8:1–4	128
8:4	81, 91
8:5	71
8:5–13	131
8:9	1n1
8:15	16n3, 126
8:15–16	72n14, 111, 126
8:20	130n16
8:24–25	130n16
8:26	123n2, 128 n12, 131n19, 178n106
8:26–27	111, 128, 128n12, 178
8:28	178
10:9–10	102n4, 118n38
11:17–22	129–30n15
12:1—15:13	130n16
12:12	130n16
13:12–14	71
15:4	130n16
15:4–5	130n16
15:12–13	130n16
15:13	72n14, 130, 130n16

1 Corinthians

2:4–5	121
2:6–16	22, 71–72n11, 91
2:10–11	31
2:11–16	36
2:16	31
9:16	171n93
9:20–22	2n2, 101–2
9:24—10:12	129–30n15
11:25	63
12	127–28n10

12–14	111
12:4–8	127
13:12	31–32
14	127–28n10
14:3	127–28n10, 177, 180
14:13–15	123n2, 178
14:15	126n6
14:18	148n22
14:24–25	127, 127–28n10, 180
14:26	127n9
14:39	127–28n10
14:39–40	134
15:1–2	129–30n15
16:13	129–30n15

2 Corinthians

1:22	126
1:24	129–30n15
5:5	126
5:14–21	69n9
9:13	64n4
13:5	64n4

Galatians

3:3	36
4:6	1n1, 16n3, 72n14, 111, 126, 126–27n8
4:6–7	126
Gal 4:8–20	129–30n15
5:2–6	129–30n15
5:16–21	128
5:16–26	91
5:18	132n20
5:22–23	2, 22
5:22–25	128, 128n11
5:24–25	131
5:25	3, 6, 125

Ephesians

1:13–14	72n14, 106, 126, 126–27n8
1:15–23	74
1:17	22
2:18	125

2:22	125	3:8	68
3:14–19	74	3:9	68
3:16–17	125	3:11	68
3:16–19	22	3:12	68
4:1–6	74	3:13	68
4:11–13	121–22, 136	3:14	68
4:14–16	124n3	3:15	68
4:21–24	71	3:16	127n9
4:25–32	74	3:16a	68
4:30	3, 124, 126	3:16b	68
5:1–20	74	3:17	68
5:8–10	3n3, 87		

1 Thessalonians

5:15–20	111
5:18	131, 131n18
5:18–20	127, 148n22
5:19a	68
5:19b	68

1:4	145n17
3:5	129–30n15
4:8	3, 124
5:19	3, 124

5:20	68
6:10–18	129
6:18	123n2129–30n15, 131n19

2 Thessalonians

2:15	64n4

Philippians

1:9–11	87, 90
1:19	1n1
1:27	64n4

1 Timothy

1:18–19	64n4, 129–30n15
3:6–7	129–30n15
3:8–9	64n4
4:1	64n4
4:1–10	129–30n15
4:6	64n4
5:8	129–30n15
6:9–12	129–30n15
6:12	64n4
6:20–21	64n4, 129–30n15

Colossians

1:3–7	3n3
1:9	22, 92
1:9–10	69, 73, 87
1:10–12	22
1:21–23	63, 69, 129–30n15
2:1–7	69
2:6	63
2:8	70

2 Timothy

1:13–14	129
2:11–13	129–30n15
2:16–21	129–30n15
3:16	145n17, 176–77n103
4:7–8	129–30n15

2:9–10	70
2:9–15	70
2:11–15	70
2:16–19	70
2:19	70n10
2:20–23	70
3:1–4	65, 67, 69, 71, 73
3:5	68
3:5–10	70
3:5–17	67–69

Hebrews

1:1–3	36
2:1–4	129–30n15
3:1	71, 102n4

Hebrews (*continued*)

3:1–6	63
3:12–14	64n4
3:15	102n4
4:1–2	129–30n15
4:12	145n17
4:14	63, 64n4
6:4–12	129–30n15
8:6–13	63
9:15–28	63
10:19–39	63
10:26–39	129–30n15
10:29	124–25
12:1–3	71
12:15–17	129–30n15

James

1:5	105
1:22–25	177n105
5:13	127n9
5:19–20	129–30n15

1 Peter

4:12–14	75n19
5:8–9	64n4, 129–30n15

2 Peter

1:5–11	129–30n15
2:20–22	129–30n15

3:17	129–30n15
3:17–18	64n4

1 John

2:20	36
2:24–28	129–30n15
2:27	61
5	64
5:5	102n4
5:11–12	102n4

2 John

1:9	129–30n15

Jude

1:3	2n2, 64n4, 103
1:3–5	129–30n15
1:12	3n3
1:17–20	75n19
1:17–21	129
1:20	131n19, 123n2, 129–30n15
1:20–25	129–30n15

Revelation

3:20	64
13:10	2